ALEISTER CROWLEY
AND
THE PRACTICE OF THE
MAGICAL DIARY

OTHER BOOKS BY JAMES WASSERMAN

The Mystery Traditions: Secret Symbols & Sacred Art
The Templars and the Assassins: The Militia of Heaven
The Slaves Shall Serve: Meditations on Liberty

AS PRODUCER

The Egyptian Book of the Dead: The Book of Going Forth by Day

AS EDITOR

AHA! (Liber CCXLII), by Aleister Crowley
Booklet of Instructions for the Thoth Tarot Deck
The Weiser Concise Guide Series

WITH ESSAYS APPEARING IN

American Magus: Harry Smith
The Equinox, Volume 3, Number 10
Rebels & Devils: The Psychology of Liberation
Healing Energy, Prayer and Relaxation
Secret Societies of the Middle Ages
Secrets of Angels & Demons

ALEISTER CROWLEY
AND
THE PRACTICE OF THE MAGICAL DIARY

Including
John St. John
(Equinox I,1)

A Master of the Temple
(Equinox III,1)

And Other Material

Edited and Introduced by
JAMES WASSERMAN

With a Foreword by
J. DANIEL GUNTHER

WEISER BOOKS
San Francisco, CA / Newburyport, MA

First edition published 1993 by New Falcon Publication
Reprinted 2004 by Sekmet Books

This revised and expanded edition published 2006 by
REDWHEEL/WEISER, LLC
York Beach, ME
With offices at:
500 3rd Street, Suite 230
San Francisco, CA 94107
www.redwheelweiser.com

John St. John first appeared in
The Equinox, Volume I, Number 1, published in London, 1909.

A Master of the Temple first appeared in
The Equinox, Volume III, Number 1, published in Detroit, 1919.

The 28 Theorems of Magick first appeared in
Magick in Theory and Practice, Paris 1929.

Liber E vel Exercitiorum first appeared in
The Equinox, Volume I, Number 1, published in London, 1909.

Liber O vel Manus et Sagittae first appeared in
The Equinox, Volume I, Number 2, published in London, 1909.

The Method of Training first appeared in
Magick Without Tears, published in Hampton NJ, 1954.

The Book first appeared in *Book IV,* Part II, London 1913.

ISBN 1-5783-372-9

Cover llustration: The Silent Watcher, from *The Equinox,* I, 1.
Courtesy of Ordo Templi Orientis.
Cover design by MAIJA TOLLEFSON
Interior designed and produced by STUDIO 31
www.studio31.com

Printed in Canada TCP

10 9 8 7 6 5 4 3 2 1

CONTENTS

Illustrations

*Adonai is that thought which
informs and strengthens and purifies,
supreme sanity in supreme genius.
Anything that is not that
is not Adonai.*

The following abbreviations are used throughout the introduction to refer to the books designated below. Full information on these titles is provided in the selected bibliography.

[666]: *The Magical Record of the Beast 666*

[1923]: *The Magical Diaries of Aleister Crowley*

[Book IV]: *Book IV, Parts 1 & 2*

[Conf]: *The Confessions of Aleister Crowley*

[DDF]: *The Diary of a Drug Fiend*

[JSJ]: *John St. John*

[MT]: *A Master of the Temple*

[MTP]: *Magick in Theory and Practice*

[TSK]: *The Temple of Solomon the King*

PLEASE NOTE: In *John St. John* and *A Master of the Temple,* the abbreviation ED. refers to Aleister Crowley and/or the original editor. The editorial brackets [...] in the original text of *John St. John* have been replaced by braces {...}. Any translations or comments from the present editor are footnoted within editorial brackets in *John St. John*. In *A Master of the Temple,* my notes in editorial brackets are further identified with the initials JW. Page references in my introduction to *John St. John* and *A Master of the Temple* refer to the page numbers of this collection. Page references to *Book IV* are to the first edition, which are also cited in the margins of *Magick, Book IV* Parts I–IV.

Parties interested in contacting A∴A∴
may address their correspondence to:

Chancellor
BM ANKH
London WC1N 3XX ENGLAND

FOREWORD

Do what thou wilt shall be the whole of the Law.

When I was asked to write a few words as a foreword to a new edition of this book, I gladly accepted the task. The value of this little volume was apparent when it was first published. In addition to the classic diaries of Aleister Crowley and Charles Stansfeld Jones that form the core of this book, this collection is greatly enhanced with the introduction by James Wasserman. His deeply personal and genuine account of his own experience not only bears witness to the importance of the magical diary, it is a testament to the relevance and continuance of a living tradition.

Over three decades have passed since I first opened the pages of the initial installment of *Equinox*, Vol. 1 and found the remarkable diary Crowley titled *John St. John*. I was captivated by the photograph of Aleister Crowley in full regalia making the Sign of Blind Force. The photograph alone made me want to read the book. As I began to read, the photograph was forgotten, and the book itself held my attention. All these years later, I find myself returning to it again and again for inspiration and wisdom. I had much the same reaction when taking up the so-called "Blue Equinox" (*Equinox* III, 1) and discovering *Liber CLXV — A Master of the Temple,* prefaced with a photograph of Charles Stansfeld Jones in his Probationer robe, meditating in the Dragon Asana. The image spoke volumes about the seriousness of the work before me. Upon reading it, I was not disappointed.

It is highly appropriate that these two works are joined in this volume. While representing two completely different perspectives, that of a skilled Adept and that of a beginner, they are both wonderful examples of the practice of the magical diary.

Apart from the significant content of *John St. John,* which stirred my consciousness, I also became curious about why Crowley titled the work as he did. Since it is an account of the magical retirement of Frater O.M., why did he ascribe the pseudonym John St. John? Knowing Crowley's penchant for leaving magical clues like bread crumbs along the path, I pursued this line of inquiry. In the curriculum of A∴A∴ the book is Officially designated as *Liber DCCCLX*. The number 860 is simply the value of the word "John" in Greek. Crowley was steeped in the Bible as a youth, and that early influence permeated his work throughout his life. It should be no surprise that he chose the name of the apostle John, credited with writing not only the Gospel and Epistles by that name, but the Apocalypse as well. It is in the Gospel of John that we find the divine avatar described as *The Logos,* a term appropriated by Crowley and identified with the Magus. The influence of the Apocalypse of John on Crowley's personal mythopoeia should be self-evident to even the most casual reader of his works. In fact, within the text of *John St. John,* Crowley made a direct reference to the apostle John, calling him "my namesake." However, there is more here than simple identification with a religious figure for the purpose of being clever or creative. The key to the title of the Book lies in the double construction of the name — John the Man united with St. John the Divine: John St. John. In other words, it is a metaphor for the union of man and God, Microcosm and Macrocosm, which in the System of A∴A∴ is called the Knowledge and Conversation of the Holy Guardian Angel. By the time *John St. John* was composed, Crowley had already experienced this great Initiation. Yet, he sought to intensify this communion by undertaking a magical retreat solely dedicated to that purpose. The retreat was not to be a retreat of isolation from the world, but performed in the course of daily life. In taking this approach, he gave us the important lesson that the quest for the Spiritual Life need not be divorced from the mundane life. John, the average man, can become St. John, the Enlightened man, while living in this world and not apart from it. This is the great task undertaken by Frater O.M. and recorded in this priceless diary. While it is clear that this work was conceived as a literary form for the purpose of publication, and was written in that fashion, it was nevertheless described by Crowley as "A model of what a magical record should be, so far as accurate analysis and fullness of description are concerned." It is also replete with information pertaining to the aspirant and the quest for union with the Augoeides. For these reasons *John St. John (Liber*

DCCCLX) is required reading in the curriculum of the Dominis Liminis of A∴A∴

The portion of the magical record of Charles Stansfeld Jones (Frater Achad) presented under the title *A Master of the Temple* is another case entirely. The document contains only portions of Jones's actual record, with extensive commentary by Crowley under the aegis of Frater O.M. It has proved a practical tool for Instructors of A∴A∴ as an example of how the Teacher may analyze the results recorded in the Record and assist the Student in self-analysis by means of constructive comment. It also contains a good example of what a Teacher should never do.

It should be understood that the Record of Frater Achad is not typical of the average student of comparable experience. His was a unique case, and ultimately a tragic one that has served more as a warning than as an example to follow. The earliest entries in his diary show great promise and are a testament to his dedication and perseverance. However, even at the outset of his practices, there are subtle indications of a tendency toward grandiosity and inflation. This is a symptom not altogether foreign to beginners, especially those who have early experiences with trance states. One of the main tasks of the Instructor is to help the Student keep all things in perspective and not fall victim to ego-inflation. In all fairness to Frater Achad, it must be admitted that Crowley's overreaching desire for a resounding "success story" resulted in stupendous folly on Crowley's part, which played no small part in Achad's failure. In 1913, Frater Achad received notification that he had been advanced from Probationer to Neophyte. In the text of that letter there was the following note: "We wish our Body to be a Body of Servants of Humanity. A time will come when you will obtain the experience of the 14th Aethyr. You will become a Master of the Temple. That experience must be followed by that of the 13th Aethyr, in which the Master, wholly casting aside all ideas of personal attainment, busies himself exclusively with the care of others."

Crowley stated that this note written to Frater Achad "is important in the light of later events." Indeed it is. Crowley apparently had forgotten or chose to ignore the very instructions given to him in the 13th Aethyr, wherein he beheld the Vision of the Master of the Temple tending his garden of disciples. The Mystical Name of the Master of the Temple is Nemo, "No Man." The task of every person who becomes Nemo is to tend the garden, not knowing or caring which one shall become Nemo after him. In the words of the Angel of the 13th Aethyr, "He that tendeth the garden seeketh not to single out the flower that shall be NEMO. He doeth naught but tend the garden." Unfortunately, the care of others was not Crowley's strong suit. Frater Achad would come to take the Oath of the Abyss prematurely as a Zelator, and in a few short years would self-destruct, dashing a promising life of service upon the rocks of self-delusion and madness. The first indications of error, both by Frater Achad and his Instructor, are documented clearly in this Record. For all those who have followed in their footsteps, whether as Student or Instructor, it is an invaluable aid.

As James Wasserman indicates in his introduction, the confrontation of one's own error and folly, and recording them in a diary, is a disquieting and disturbing process. Keeping track of our success is easy; recording our weakness and failure is far more difficult, but usually proves to be the most helpful in the long run. We hope these magical Records, which contain honest examples of both success and failure, inspire and give hope to those who take up the Great Work.

"Thou dost faint, thou dost fail, thou scribe; cried the desolate Voice; but I have filled thee with a wine whose savour thou knowest not." (*Liber LXV*, IV:59)

Love is the law, love under will.

— J. Daniel Gunther
   April, 2005 e.v.

Preface to the Second Edition

Do what thou wilt shall be the whole of the Law.

The first edition of this book was published in 1993. I had been asked by Christopher Hyatt of New Falcon Publishing to suggest a book by or about Aleister Crowley that "needed to be published." What was missing from the growing body of Thelemic literature? I immediately proposed a book on the Magical Diary, composed of Crowley's two most important published sets of instructions. I also suggested that someone add his own experience with the practice. I then forgot about it until a few months later when he asked me to create the book I had described.

Over the years, many people have praised this work as a true missing ingredient. So many of us are uneasy about committing our personal thoughts to paper. And Crowley's repeated insistence on this practice might be dismissed as simply his personal preference as a writer. However, the diary practice came relatively naturally to me. Some 35 years after starting, I am happy I did.

In preparing this new edition for publication, many possibilities suggested themselves. Since the first edition of this book was published, Caliph Hymenaeus Beta of Ordo Templi Orientis has done some masterful work in putting out original editions of other Crowley diaries. He initiated a series of Crowley's collected diaries, beginning in 1998, with *Equinox* IV, 2, *The Vision and the Voice and Other Papers* (which includes the Paris Working diary mentioned here). Crowley's American diaries from 1914–1919 will appear as *Equinox* IV, 3, *The Diary of a Magus and Other Papers*. A volume of his earlier diaries from 1898–1908 is also in preparation.

There are numerous unpublished diaries of Crowley's students around, and they make for fascinating reading. Keith Richmond has released an excellent book of Frank Bennett's diaries. And Michael Kolson has labored well on a diary of Victor Neuberg, as well as other historical diary material. We also have some fascinating diaries in manuscript of Crowley's female students. Over time, I hope many other books will make their way to published form.

In fact, we are especially looking forward to the first publication of the second part of the diary presented here, Frater Achad's *A Master of the Temple, Liber CLXV,* as edited by Aleister Crowley and Hymenaeus Beta, in the long awaited reconstruction of the *Equinox,* Volume 3, Number 2, to be released by Thelema Media. (This book will also include the definitive publication of Achad's most important paper, *Liber XXXI,* which caused Crowley to proclaim him as the Magical Son promised in *The Book of the Law,* particularly verses I:55–56 and III:47.

Yet with all this wealth of new material — either now available, in production, or in manuscript — the two books included here, *John St. John* and *A Master of the Temple* (Part 1), are the only instructions on the proper use and form of the Magical Diary specifically published by Crowley during his lifetime. After some research and soul searching, I decided to keep this book what it has always been — the best introduction to the Magical Diary for either a beginning or more advanced practitioner, with the least amount of extraneous information.*

When it was reprinted in 2004, I reviewed my decade-old introduction to see how it needed be updated and improved. What I read were the very honest and revealing words of someone who had loved and practiced Thelema to the best of his ability his entire life. There was little to add, and a simple reprint seemed in order.

However, with the interest expressed by Redwheel/Weiser, I am delighted to have the opportunity to try to improve on this book, while being careful not to throw out the proverbial baby with the bath water. The most important improvement is the Foreword by my friend J. Daniel Gunther. The quality and extent of his service to Thelema is a largely untold story at this moment, and it is with much gratitude and delight that his work appears here. All those interested in Thelema will welcome the forthcoming publication of his most important book, *The Inward Journey,* to follow, we hope, before too much longer.

---

* The two volume edition of the full 10 volumes of *The Equinox* (published by Weiser in 1998) includes an appendix of Crowley's marginal annotations to *John St. John,* to which the interested reader is referred.

I have modified my introduction where I think it may help, while consciously avoiding removing some of the more personal parts that still cause me to wince. I have also taken the opportunity to translate foreign terms employed by Crowley, footnoting them in *John St. John* within editorial brackets. In *A Master of the Temple,* I have added very few footnotes, also in editorial brackets, and marked with my initials to clearly identify the speaker. Most of the footnotes in *A Master of the Temple* are Crowley's own. *Liber O vel Manus et Sagittae* has been added to the appendix. It is an excellent instruction and, like *Liber E vel Exercitiorum,* also included, highlights the importance of the diary in practice and gives some guidance as to what to include. O.T.O. Frater Superior Hymenaeus Beta provided a 1942 letter from Crowley to American disciple and Agapé Lodge member Roy Leffingwell that offers concise instruction in the Diary practice. He has also allowed me to include his Tree of Life design to help illustrate the relationship between concepts discussed in the text. The reader may refer to this glyph for unfamiliar references to follow the connections between number, planet, astrological sign, Tarot card, A∴A∴ Grade, part of the Soul, and the four Worlds of the Qabalah — all of which Crowley dances through so deftly. Photos of Crowley making the Sign of Blind Force and Jones in his Asana have been returned to *John St. John* and *A Master of the Temple,* while The Silent Watcher image from *Equinox* I, 1 has been included in the appendix. On a lighter note, an alphabetical glossary of the foods recorded in *John St. John* has been compiled to highlight the sophisticated fare enjoyed by this Adept during his Operation. Finally, I have updated the bibliographical data.

While the goal of this book has always been to let Crowley describe in his own words his thought on the practice of keeping the Magical Diary, I still believe it is important to offer the (perhaps unsolicited) experience of someone who took Crowley's teaching to heart. Thus far my apologia for including my own contribution.

I thank Dr. Christopher S. Hyatt, who tricked me into writing this; Michael Miller for his investment in the first printing; Genevieve Mikolajczak who typed the manuscript, helped with countless proofreading cycles, and contributed her insightful critique throughout its creation; and Nancy Wasserman for a great deal of both help and patience in bringing this book to the light of day. Thanks are also due to my Brothers Martin Starr and William Breeze for their invaluable support and assistance with this (and most of the other projects of my life). Michael Kolson has contributed valuable ideas in numerous discussions. I am indebted to J. Daniel Gunther for his friendship and guidance. Gwynneth Cheers has used her culinary skills to elucidate upon the sophisticated fare Crowley took such pains to record. I am also grateful for the encouragement so freely offered by Brenda Knight, Kat Sanborn, and Michael Conlon of Redwheel/Weiser.

While Hymenaeus Beta and Martin P. Starr have raised the editorial bar to just about where it belongs for the Crowley literary corpus, the first person to teach me proper respect for this material, especially the Class A writings, was my Instructor Marcelo Motta. Although we had a stormy relationship and a stormier parting, I am honor bound to pay my respects to him, and to express my gratitude for the insights and disciplines he shared with me.

Finally, my thanks to the readers of the first edition whose enthusiasm has been heartening.

Love is the law, love under will.

— James Wasserman
   2005 e.v.

Introduction

Do what thou wilt shall be the whole of the Law.

The Record is both chart and log to the bold Sea-Captains of The Voyage Marvelous. (MT, p. 131)

'Excuse the interruption,' she said, 'but the Magical Record is always the first consideration in the Abbey.' (Sister Athena to Unlimited Lou and Sir Peter in DDF, p. 320)

A LEISTER CROWLEY insisted on the importance of the Magical Diary in his particular system of attainment. Through the years, I have met many fellow students who have overlooked this instruction. On the other hand, I have enjoyed keeping my own magical diary along the lines Crowley suggested for well over three decades. This introduction is an attempt to communicate the value of the magical diary practice, primarily in Crowley's own words, as well as through my experience. The collection itself contains his two most important instructions and models of the magical diary, *John St. John* (1909) and *A Master of the Temple* (1919). These were both edited by Crowley for publication, and are officially designated as A∴A∴ *libri* (or books), *Liber DCCCLX* and *Liber CLXV* respectively. I have also added other relevant materials from Crowley's published writing, which are included in the appendix.

A Brief Biography of Aleister Crowley

Aleister Crowley (1875–1947) was the greatest magician of the twentieth century. His all-pervasive influence on modern magical thought is consistent with his position as the Prophet or Logos of the current Age. A controversial figure to say the least, Crowley has both devoted followers and ardent enemies.

His parents were fundamentalists, members of the Plymouth Brethren, a literalist Protestant sect in which his father was a preacher. Shortly after his father's death, Crowley rebelled against

the strictness of the group — which prompted his mother to identify him with the Beast 666 of Revelation. He suffered greatly in
childhood from her rabid orthodoxy and that of the other sect
members who surrounded him. Much of the poignancy of this
period of his life is captured in *The World's Tragedy.*

After attending Cambridge, he began his formal occult training in 1898 in the Hermetic Order of the Golden Dawn. Founded
ten years earlier, this magical order included some of the leading
lights of English occult and literary society, including two of its
founders, William Wynn Westcott and S. L. MacGregor Mathers,
the poet W. B. Yeats, novelist Arthur Machen, and occult writer
Arthur Edward Waite. Another notable member was the brilliant
engineer Allen Bennett, who was later to become a Buddhist monk.
Crowley rose rapidly through the ranks of the Golden Dawn, and
began to study on a personal basis with Bennett.

The Golden Dawn became beset with dissensions and the
assorted behavioral dramas familiar to members of magical societies. Crowley, never one to avoid a good fight, became a key
player in the shakeup. Ultimately wearied by the behavior of his
fellow aspirants and in need of a change of scenery, he began to
travel extensively in 1900. He went to the United States, Mexico,
Hawaii, Ceylon, Burma, India, the Himalayas, Egypt, France, and
back to England. In 1903, he met and married Rose Edith Kelly,
and they took off on a honeymoon to Paris, Cairo, and Ceylon.

On their return journey to England in 1904, they stopped in
Cairo again where an event occurred that changed Crowley's life,
and marked a profound nexus point in the evolution of the human
species. On March 20, 1904, directed by his wife's telepathic contact with a Higher Intelligence, he performed an invocation of
Horus, the Egyptian God of Force and Fire. Again directed by her
instructions, on April 8, 9, and 10, he received the three chapters
of *The Book of the Law* in three hour-long sessions of direct voice
communication.

The Book of the Law announces the planetary transition to
the Aeon of Horus (popularly called the Age of Aquarius). The
book provides the new formulas and the moral code appropriate
for this period. The revelation can be summarized simply in the
two phrases most often quoted from the book, "Do what thou wilt
shall be the whole of the Law," and "Love is the law, love under
will." Crowley's concept of the True Will has been blasphemed for

over a century by the now familiar ululations of yellow journalists and other media hysterics. Crowley's actual thought on the True Will was so exalted that he describes the moral code of *The Book of the Law* as the most austere ever proposed to mankind. The reader is referred to *The Equinox of the Gods* and *The Law Is for All* to begin an investigation of the subject.

The rest of Crowley's life was spent in relation to the *Book of the Law.* Initially he rebelled against it. Some five years later, he began his conscious surrender to the Forces responsible for the message — propagating, interpreting, and serving Them through his personal magical and mystical practices, his writings, his work with students, and his efforts in the magical societies of A∴A∴ and O.T.O.

Crowley formulated the A∴A∴ in 1907 with George Cecil Jones at the direction of the Spiritual Hierarchy responsible for the guidance of mankind. The best description of the event is "The History Lection" in *Liber LXI vel Causae,* published in *Equinox* Vol. III, No. 1; *The Holy Books of Thelema;* and *Gems from The Equinox.* The A∴A∴ consists of a series of Grades corresponding to the Sephiroth of the Tree of Life (see diagram on page liv). The Tree of Life system, descended from the Jewish Qabalists, became the basis of the workings of the Western esoteric tradition. The Tree is a diagram that graphically describes the Universe as composed of 10 spheres or Sephiroth, which correspond to the numbers 1 to 10, connected by 22 Paths, which correspond to the 22 letters of the Hebrew alphabet. The Tree of Life model forms the basis of all occult practice from Tarot to Path working, ritual magic to astrology. An excellent introduction to the system is *The Mystical Qabalah* by Dion Fortune, where she essentially analyzes Crowley's masterpiece 777 in prose form.

The Grades of A∴A∴ are arranged in three sections on the Tree of Life. These consist of the Outer Order of G.D. or Golden Dawn, Inner Order of R.C. or Rose Cross, and Higher Order of S.S. or Silver Star. Its official organ is *The Equinox,* which began publishing in the Spring of 1909. The motto of A∴A∴, boldly included on the logo of *The Equinox,* is "The Method of Science, The Aim of Religion." The magical system it teaches is called Scientific Illuminism.

Crowley insisted on all students keeping a magical diary. The diary is a formal requirement of the Outer College of A∴A∴ (see

Liber CLXXXV in *Equinox* IV, 1, *Commentaries on the Holy Books*), and a necessary part of most practices. "One Star in Sight," the manifesto of A∴A∴ first published in *Magick in Theory and Practice,* gives numerous instances in its descriptions of the Grades from Ipsissimus to Probationer of the relevance of the diary at all levels of attainment. Crowley believed the diary accompanies the Magician through his entire career. In support of this statement, one could cite his description of the Magus and Master of the Temple Grades in "One Star in Sight," where he mentions both his own and Frater Achad's diaries.

The Equinox

Among the duties that Crowley accepted was the encapsulating of the ancient wisdom teachings in "a sort of Rosetta stone" designed to survive the dark ages he saw looming before mankind. He called *The Equinox* the "Encyclopedia of Initiation." Volume I of the series contained 10 numbers, some 4000 pages, published twice annually for five years at the Spring and Fall Equinoxes. It includes a wealth of practical magical instruction as well as exalted and inspired texts, combined with poetry, short stories, book reviews and other accoutrements of a literary journal. Volume II of the series is designated a "Volume of Silence." Crowley commenced with Volume III, No. 1 in the United States in 1919. Volume III was published quite sporadically. No. 2 was never released in Crowley's lifetime although page proofs survived. (It is finally to be published under the editorship of Hymenaeus Beta of O.T.O.) *Equinox* III, Nos. 6–10 were also posthumously issued by the O.T.O.

In Number 1 of both Volume I and Volume III of *The Equinox,* Crowley devoted a considerable amount of space to his instructions on the magical diary. (Both are included in the present collection.) *Equinox* I, 1 included as a special supplement *Liber DCCCLX, John St. John, being The Record of the Magical Retirement of G.H. Frater O.M.* It served as "a perfect model of what a magical record should be, in respect of the form." (MTP, p. 207). It is Crowley's diary of a Greater Magical Retirement, lasting 13 days, whose purpose was the conscious invocation of the Holy Guardian Angel within the context of "normal" urban life in Paris. It was written with the ultimate intention of being published. It is also the record of his writing and using for the first time the Ritual Pyramidos.

The second diary instruction included here is *Liber CLXV, A Master of the Temple,* which first appeared in *Equinox* III, 1. It is an edited version of a portion of the magical diary of Frater Achad, Charles Stansfeld Jones, extending from 1907 to 1913. It includes an extensive commentary by Crowley on Jones's work. Jones's diary and Crowley's comments were used as an example of A∴A∴ in action. It became the basis for an analysis of Scientific Illuminism and a direct endorsement of Crowley's instructions in the Magical Record. It also demonstrates the method a Teacher can use to comprehend and direct the Student to ferret through the complexes that bind him, as long as the student provides clear and honest evidence of himself in the Record. The second part of this diary is included in *Equinox* III, 2.

The Temple of Solomon the King

This massive text was published as a serial that ran throughout nine of the ten numbers of *The Equinox,* Volume I. It was a history and analysis of Crowley's magical career, taken from his magical diary. Captain (later Major-General) J. F. C. Fuller did the editing and writing for at least the first four installments. His motto in A∴A∴ was *Per Ardua* (By Labor) and he was the Neophyte Frater P.A. referred to in *A Master of the Temple.* He broke with Crowley in 1911 midway through *The Equinox* series.

The Temple of Solomon the King presented the basic metaphysical principles and intellectual components of the Western Magical Tradition, including an extensive review of the teachings of the Golden Dawn order. It also contained an analysis and overview of both the Buddhist and Yogic systems of attainment and their relevance to the work of A∴A∴, along with extensive records of Crowley's practices with these systems extracted from his magical diaries.

The section of *The Temple of Solomon the King* published in *Equinox* I, 4 includes detailed charts condensing Crowley's meditation and concentration exercises of the periods under examination, as well as numerous verbatim transcriptions from his scrupulously maintained journals. The journals describe magical practices, yoga, meditation and concentration exercises, dream records, and daily observations. The installment in *Equinox* I, 8 contains a deeply moving account of Crowley's Augoeides invocation of 1906. The Augoeides refers to the Higher Genius, Holy Guardian Angel, or Divine Self, the union with whom is the Great Work. Crowley's persistence in the face of illness, personal tragedy, and the frustrations of a very full life form an epic document. It was determined not to include that record in this collection only because it was not published specifically as a magical diary instruction. However the reader is encouraged to pursue it and will be rewarded with a real insight into the majesty of this man Aleister Crowley.

A Brief Biography of Frater Achad

Charles Stansfeld Jones, Frater Achad, (1886–1950) was, at one time, the most promising pupil of Aleister Crowley, who considered him to be the child prophesied in *The Book of the Law*. See, among other verses, chapter 3, verse 47: "but one cometh after him, whence I say not, who shall discover the Key of it all.... It shall be his child & that strangely." Jones did in fact discover the Qabalistic key to *The Book of the Law* in the word AL whose number is 31, which he discusses in a brilliant essay extracted from his diary and known as *Liber XXXI*.

Crowley felt Frater Achad was his magical son when he learned that on June 21, 1916, Jones took the Oath of the Abyss and claimed to be reborn into the Third Order of A∴A∴ as a Master of the Temple. Jones's announcement coincided with a period when Crowley was acutely concerned with producing a magical heir. Nine months earlier, he had performed a magical operation to beget a child, which he had interpreted as a physical child. But Jones's announcement of a magical birth fit perfectly into Crowley's world view.

In addition, Crowley felt Jones's attainment validated the method of training he had taught mankind through A∴A∴ Jones was also deeply involved with the O.T.O., becoming the X° Grand Master of North America some years after founding the continent's first O.T.O. group in Canada.

In 1918, Crowley wrote *Liber Aleph*. Although he was still convinced Jones was his magical son, chapter 166 of the book contains evidence of Crowley's fears for him even at this early date. Shortly after delivering the manuscript of *Liber XXXI* to Crowley in 1919, Jones began to exhibit ever-increasing symptoms of mental imbalance and megalomania. He and Crowley became progressively estranged. In *Q.B.L.*, *The Egyptian Revival*, and *The Anatomy of the Body of God*, published between 1922 and 1925, Jones turned the paths of the Tree of Life upside down in conjunction with new revelations he was experiencing. In 1928 he traveled to England where he joined the Roman Catholic Church. He was finally expelled from O.T.O. by Crowley in 1936. In 1948, soon after Crowley's death, Achad announced that the Age of Aquarius, which he named Ma-Ion, had superseded the Aeon of Horus after a mere 44 years.

In addition to his Qabalistic books, Achad wrote several smaller monographs on various subjects, and an exquisite collection of poetry, *XXXI Hymns to the Star Goddess*. Whatever may have been the psychological imbalances that ultimately destroyed him, his discovery of the key to *The Book of the Law* was never in dispute. Nor can one doubt the sincerity and intensity of his efforts to perform the Great Work, particularly after reading his magical record in *A Master of the Temple*.

A Brief Autobiography

I was born in 1948 and first encountered the teachings of Aleister Crowley in college toward the end of 1967. I began at that time to keep scattered notes of my Qabalistic studies, but it was a fledgling effort, with no systematic form. My journal begins in earnest in 1970, when I had read a number of Crowley's books and began to practice some of the exercises he described. Since then, my record is unbroken, numbering over 20 volumes. There is a fair degree of "periodicity" in my diaries, some phases being documented on a moment-to-moment basis, in others there are gaps of weeks and some of months. What is true is that the practice has continued unabated. I can say unequivocally that the more I have written in my diary, the better I understand the period in question. I can also say that, for the most part, the more spiritually active I have been, the more my diary reflects it.

WHY THE DIARY

The first question that needs to be asked before beginning a diary practice is obvious. "Why keep a Magical Diary?"

Scientific Illuminism

To begin with, what is "The Method of Science, the Aim of Religion"? A scientific system of mystical attainment must include a recorded, measurable, repeatable series of actions, that tend toward union with Higher Consciousness. Mary d'Este Sturges, whose motto was *Virakam* (I Construct, or I Perform), was the co-author of *Book IV* and editor of *The Equinox* Vol. I, Nos. 7–10 after Fuller's departure. Describing *John St. John* in *The Temple of Solomon the King,* she wrote:

> The ostensible object of this Retirement was to discover for certain whether by the use of the plain straightforward methods accessible to the normal man he could definitely attain Samadhi within a reasonable time. In other words, whether the methods themselves were valuable.... He was sufficiently satisfied with the efficacy of the methods to determine upon a course for which he had hitherto found no excuse — that of undertaking the gigantic task of the publication of all these methods on the basis of pure scepticism. (TSK, No. 9, p. 10)

This "gigantic task" began with the publication of *The Equinox* and literally continued to the end of Crowley's life.

The diary is the fundamental tool whereby the individual magician can keep a scientific record of his own perceptions of himself, the first matter of the Great Work.

> In a hospital a chart is usually kept of each patient, upon which may be seen the exact progress, from its very commencement, of the case in question. By it the doctor can daily judge the growth or decline of the disease he is fighting.
>
> ...
>
> Thus if he be a worthy physician, he will study his patient, never overlooking the seemingly most unimportant details

which can help him realise his object, namely, recovery and health.

Not only does this system of minute tabulation apply to cases of disease and sickness, but to every branch of healthy life as well, under the name of 'business'; the best business man being he who reduces his special occupation in life from 'muddle' to 'science.'

In the West religion alone has never issued from chaos; and the hour, late though it be, has struck when without fear or trembling adepts have arisen to do for Faith what Copernicus, Kepler and Newton did for what is vulgarly known as 'Science.' (TSK, No. 1, pp. 146–147)

The effect of an Adept keeping a record will be to place mysticism on a firmer basis. In *The Confessions of Aleister Crowley,* Crowley discusses the "hand of the Gods" arranging the conditions of his life in an elaborately programmed manner, particularly in regard to *The Book of the Law.* He is led to muse on an incident of divine intervention, experienced in 1919. He quotes from his diary as follows:

But what nobody before me has done is to prove the existence of extra-human intelligence, and my Magical Record does this. I err in the interpretation of course; but it is impossible to doubt that there is somebody there, a somebody capable of combining events as Napoleon forms his plans of campaign, and possessed of powers unthinkably vast. (Conf, p. 601)

The work of attainment begins with the individual. It is, by nature, threatening to the forces in society, such as religion and politics, that cower in fear of the individual and bleat in the name of the herd.

The Universe of Magic is in the mind of a man . . . (JSJ, p. 5)

Therefore we set out diligently to explore and map these untrodden regions of the mind. (JSJ, p. 6)

The peculiar nature of the data used in the scientific process of the Great Work, and the need for a dedicated laboratory record in its performance is well demonstrated in this quotation from *The Temple of Solomon the King.*

> Indeed, it must have been discouraging to him to think that on the 6th of May 1901 he, in a meditation of thirty-two minutes had only experienced ten breaks, whilst during a meditation of similar length, on the 13th of July 1903, the number of breaks had been three times as many. But like most statistics, such a comparison is misleading: for the beginner, almost invariably, so clumsy is his will, catches quickly enough the gross breaks, but lets the minor ones dart away from his grasp, like the small fry which with ease swim in and out of the fisherman's net. Further, though in twelve meditations the number of breaks may be identical, yet the class of the breaks, much more so than the actual number, will tell the meditator more certainly than any-thing else, whether he has progressed or retrograded. (TSK, No. 4, p. 184)

In discussing his experimentation with the magical methods of the O.T.O. in what later became known as the Paris Working, Crowley again invokes the scientific aspect of the record.

> To me, however, as a student of nature, the one important result of this work was the proof of the efficacy of the magical method employed. Henceforth, I made it my principal study, kept a detailed record of my researches, and began to discover the rational explanation of its operation and the conditions of suc-cess. (Conf, p. 723)

The following quotations from various instructions in *Magick in Theory and Practice,* demonstrate that Crowley insisted stu-dents keep an active Magical Diary.

> The only way to test clairvoyance is to keep a careful record of every experiment made. (MTP, p. 145)

> ... invoke Mercury, for example, and examine carefully your record of the resulting vision — discover whether the symbols which you have seen correspond with the conventional symbols of Mercury.

This testing of the spirits is the most important branch of the whole tree of Magick. Without it, one is lost in the jungle of delusion. [boldface type in original] (MTP, p. 147)

Apart from the regular tests — made at the time — of the integrity of any spirit, the Magician must make a careful record of every vision, omitting no detail; he must then make sure that it tallies in every point with the correspondences in *Book 777* and in *Liber D.* (MTP, p. 254, Appendix 3 "Notes on the Astral Plane")

In Section V of *Liber O vel Manus et Sagittae* (see appendix 3, pp. 184–186), which discusses rising on the planes, after the vision is exited and the return to the body has been duly performed through the Sign of Silence, Crowley thus commands the student:

Then let him 'awake' by a well-defined act of will, and soberly and accurately record his experiences. (See p. 186.)

And in Section VI of *Liber O,* he writes:

... on coming to himself, let him write down soberly and accurately a record of all that hath occurred, yea a record of all that hath occurred. (See p. 187.)

Magick in Theory and Practice contains other examples of the practical importance he placed on the Magical Record:

3. Let him investigate the following statements and prepare a careful record of research. a) Certain actions induce the flow of the breath through the right nostril (Pingala); and conversely, the flow of the breath through Pingala induces certain actions.... (MTP, p. 405, *Liber RU vel Spiritus*)

Thine arm then serveth thee both for a warning and for a record. Thou shalt write down thy daily progress in these practices, until thou art perfectly vigilant at all times ... (MTP, p. 428, *Liber III vel Jugorum*)

In *Book IV,* while discussing the work of the Probationer, he again stipulates the use of the diary.

> He may select any practices that he prefers, but in any case must keep an exact record, so that he may discover the relation of cause and effect in his working ... (Book IV, Part 2, p. 93)

In the chapter of *Book IV,* Part 2 devoted to the Wand, Crowley discusses the nature of, and the need for, training the magical will, and makes an important statement about the Magical Record.

> The Magical Will is in its essence twofold, for it presupposes a beginning and an end; to will to be a thing is to admit that you are not that thing.
>
> Hence to will anything but the supreme thing, is to wander still further from it — any will but that to give up the self to the Beloved is Black Magick — yet this surrender is so simple an act that to our complex minds it is the most difficult of all acts; and hence training is necessary. . . .
>
> How then is the will to be trained? All these wishes, whims, caprices, inclinations, tendencies, appetites, must be detected, examined, judged by the standard of whether they help or hinder the main purpose, and treated accordingly.
>
> Vigilance and courage are obviously required. . . . [as well as] denial of those things which hamper the self. It is not suicide to kill the germs of malaria in one's blood.
>
> Now there are very great difficulties to be overcome in the training of the mind. Perhaps the greatest is forgetfulness, which is probably the worst form of what the Buddhists call ignorance. Special practices for training the memory may be of some use as a preliminary for persons whose memory is naturally poor. *In any case the Magical Record prescribed for Probationers by the A∴A∴ is useful and necessary.* [italics added] (Book IV, Part 2, pp. 39–41)

Again using the laboratory model, Crowley elaborates on a diary technique designed to improve the student's objective powers of observation.

> Only in the absolute calm of the laboratory, where the observer is perfectly indifferent to what may happen, only concerned to

observe exactly what that happening is, to measure and to weigh it by means of instruments incapable of emotion, can one even begin to hope for a truthful record of events. . . .

Let then the Student practice observation of those things which normally would cause him emotion; and let him, having written a careful description of what he sees, check it by the aid of some person familiar with such sights. (Book IV, Part 2, p. 107–108)

Spiritual Honesty

The practice of the Magical Diary is invaluable as a tool of self-reflection. The theme of spiritual integrity will reappear throughout this essay, but here are a couple of interesting examples from *John St. John.* The diary can be a real help to the person honest enough to both record his true thoughts and feelings and courageous enough to review them in the light of later experience, when initial assumptions may be proven wrong.

That is the great usefulness of this record; one will be able to see afterwards whether there is any trace of poetic or other influence. (JSJ, p. 52)

. . . and so, even in religion, when we are dealing with our own souls, we try to cheat. (JSJ, p. 57)

The Key fits the Door perfectly; but he who is drunk on the bad wine of Sense and Thought fumbles thereat. (JSJ, p. 71)

This, by the way, is the supreme use of a record like this. It makes it impossible to cheat oneself. (JSJ, p. 78)

When discussing the Magical Memory in *Magick in Theory and Practice,* Crowley coincidentally provides another excellent argument for a carefully maintained Magical Record.

The great obstacle is the phenomenon called Freudian forgetfulness; that is to say, that, though an unpleasant event may be recorded faithfully enough by the mechanism of the brain, we fail to recall it, or recall it wrong, because it is painful. (MTP, p. 51)

The States of Mind in Magick

Another key reason in favor of keeping a magical diary is the actual nature of the mental states with which one deals on the magical path. The familiar reference points of normal life simply do not exist in magick. Here is a tenuous realm, a shadow zone, between objective rational consciousness and the world of unconscious dream time, the well-spring of archetypal creativity. This state is essentially the opposite of the scientific. It therefore demands great concentration to "bring it back" and make it accessible to the rational mind. This tenuous nature adds extra weight to Crowley's advice to record the experience in "real time." Here is Achad speaking in *A Master of the Temple*.

> I should really have to read my diary if I wanted to know any details in succession right now. (MT, p. 135)

> I find more and more difficulty in remembering any details of these practices the next day. (MT, p. 141)

In *The Confessions*, Crowley notes the inherent uncertainties of these states of mind, when unexamined by the rational consciousness.

> Not once nor twice in my fair island story have I found myself in honest doubt which, believe me, is worth half the creeds, as to whether any given incident took place in sleeping or waking. It may be thought that my accounts of various magical incidents are under suspicion; but being aware of my peculiarities, I have naturally been at great pains to eliminate any such source of error. (Conf, p. 353)

Listen here to the vagueness Crowley describes in *Book IV* when attempting to discuss a stage of meditation. Because the nature of the phenomena so defies standard labeling, the need for evidence becomes paramount.

> It should be remembered that at present there are no data for determining the duration of Dhyana. One can only say that, since it certainly occurred between such and such hours, it must

have lasted less than that time. Thus we see, from Frater P.'s record, that it can certainly occur in less than an hour and five minutes. (Book IV, Part 1, footnote pp. 74–75)

In a succinct entry in his *1923 Diary*, Crowley sums up one of the main reasons for his insistence on the diary practice.

4 June 7:15 pm. Incidentally I have quite serious doubts as to whether I shall continue to understand myself as I do now in an hour's time, but I have a certain confidence that I have succeeded in explaining myself fairly well in the course of the above paragraph. This state of mind should be especially interesting, for it is very familiar to me. It has in fact been my established method to try to write down what I may call my illuminated thoughts at the time of thinking, well aware that their significance will, to a great extent, escape me on my return to normal consciousness, but also imbued with a conviction that the record will help me to remember what I have experienced and so to educate me; also that it will form the first childish attempts at a language which shall ultimately serve to enable superior thinkers to communicate with each other. (1923 Diary, p. 47)

The Clarification Writing Brings to an Issue

Achad calls attention to another excellent reason for the diary when he mentions writing in his record to clarify his thought. "… I am entering it so as to try and formulate the proposition clearly." (MT, p. 128)

Where else in our society (other than in "psychotherapy") are we encouraged to take our own minds as seriously as school children do tests, job-seekers do résumé changes, or homemakers do shopping lists?

In *Equinox* I, 3, in *The Temple of Solomon the King,* Golden Dawn material is presented. In a document discussing divination, it is clear that the Golden Dawn also recognized the value of writing in helping to organize thought.

Accurately define the term of the question: putting down clearly in writing what is already known , what is suspected or implied, and what is sought to be known. And see that thou verify in the

beginning of the judgment, that part which is already known.
(TSK, No. 3, p. 164)

Teacher and Student

The special area of the relationship between student and teacher is
a critical component of Scientific Illuminism. In some systems of
attainment, the student is encouraged to follow the party line
uncritically. Individual thought is thoroughly discouraged. Guide-
lines are provided for all areas of behavior: what to eat, what to
wear, what to read, and what to do about sex. At the other
extreme of the spiritual path are people who can be so isolated
from critical contact with their fellows, they become capable of the
most shamelessly deluded thinking. How many times have you met
Aleister Crowley's reincarnation?

Crowley steered a middle path through this labyrinth by having a seeker assigned to a spiritual guide. Someone perhaps only
just beyond him in experience, but capable of providing a relatively objective viewpoint. The mentor will review the student's
diary at intervals and comment. *A Master of the Temple* provides
an excellent example of how this process works.

In his novel *Diary of a Drug Fiend*, Crowley gives some of his
most practical teachings on the use of the Magical Diary. The diary
functions as the central pillar in the cure of two drug addicts who
fall under the enlightened guidance of a Master Adept, King
Lamus. Toward the end of the book, which describes the success of
the treatment, we see that the final clue is provided to Lamus after
he has read Sir Peter's diary, which of course, he has enjoined Sir
Peter to keep. This conversation spurs Peter to the crucial initiation
of the discovery of his True Will, and the subsequent mastery of his
drug addiction. We therefore reproduce it in full.

> But when the episode was over, I found the old despair of life as
> strong as ever. The will to live was really dead in me.
>
> But two evenings later King Lamus came to smoke a pipe
> with me on the terrace at sunset. In his hand was the Paradiso
> record which I had written. Sister Athena had typed it.
>
> 'My dear man,' he said, 'what I can't see is why you should
> be so blind about yourself. The meaning of all this ought to be

perfectly obvious. I'm afraid you haven't grasped the meaning of 'Do what thou wilt.' Do you see how the application of the Law has helped you so far?'

'Well, of course,' I said, 'it's pretty clear I didn't come to this planet to drug myself into my grave before my powers have had a chance to ripen. I've thought it necessary to keep off heroin in order to give myself a show. But I'm left flat. Life becomes more tedious every day, and the one way of escape is barred by flaming swords.'

'Exactly,' he replied. 'You've only discovered one thing that you don't will; you have still to find the one thing that you do will. And yet there are quite a number of clues in this manuscript of yours. I note you say that your squad commander, who didn't become that without some power of dealing with men, told you that you were not a great flyer. How was it exactly that you came to take up flying?'

That simple question induced a very surprising reaction. There was no reason why it should produce the intense irritation that it did.

Basil noticed it, rubbed his hands together gleefully, and began to hum 'Tipperary.' His meaning was evident. He had drawn a bow in a venture; and it had pierced the King of Israel between the joints of his harness. He got up with alacrity, and went off with a wave of the hand. (DDF, p. 339)

Diary of a Drug Fiend was a fictional account of Crowley's real life teaching methods. Here are some comments reproduced from *The Confessions* on the diaries of three different disciples at the Abbey of Thelema in Cefalu, Italy (where much of *Diary of a Drug Fiend* takes place).

[Ninette Shumway] I had, of course, insisted on her recording her experiences in a Magical Diary, and what of my amazement, on reading the first section, to find it an unsurpassed masterpiece. (Conf, p. 858)

[C. F. Russell] I wish I had a copy of his Magical Record of this Retirement. It was an incoherent scrawl of furious ravings ... (Conf, p. 873)

[Frank Bennett] The Spirit of the Lord descended upon him and opened his eyes to a series of visions of a class far more exalted and intense and intimate than anything he had hitherto experienced. He was inspired to write these down during their actual occurrence.... What, then, was my amazement to perceive in his style an originality and power of the first order. (Conf, p. 876)

In *The Magical Record of the Beast 666,* we see a rather startling reaction on Crowley's part to reading Ninette Shumway's diary. I have no idea what she wrote there; however, she was sent packing two days later. (Please do not be intimidated into not keeping your diary after reading the following extract — I must include it here, in the name of Science!)

3 November. Read through the Diary of Mrs. N.F. Shumway. I am utterly appalled at the horrors of the human heart. I never dreamed such things were possible. I am physically sick — it is the greatest shock of my life. I had this mess in my own circle. It poisoned my work; it murdered my children. It really does seem as if a magick circle were a sort of advantage. (666, p. 289)

Crowley proceeded to "direct magical action" against her and attached in his diary this "copy of the Exorcism."

5 November. Do what thou wilt shall be the whole of the Law. Initiation purges. There is excreted a stench and a pestilence. In your case two have been killed outright, and the rest made ill. There are signs that the process may lead to purification and make things safe within a short time. But we cannot risk further damage; if the hate is still in course, it had better coil back on its source. Keep your diary going carefully. Go and live in Cefalu alone; go to the hospital alone; the day before you come out send up your diary and I will reconsider things. I shall hope to see the ulcers healing. Do not answer this; simply do as I say. Love is the law, love under will. 666 (666, p. 290)

Getting Started

The journey of a thousand miles begins with the first step. Thus the diary begins by purchasing a suitable book. I prefer the kind you buy in art supply or stationary stores, $5^1/2$ x $8^1/2$ or 6 x 9 hardcovers, 200 pages or so. I personally don't like the kind that have the day and date for each page, because I find that some days I write little or nothing, and others I can write a great deal. I do know that other Thelemites have found the day/date system works best to keep them organized in a regular practice. Loose-leaf books tend to get fairly damaged. Your diary accompanies you on airplanes, camping trips, and so on, so it should be fairly compact and sturdy. I also keep a small pocket-sized notebook with me during the day for experiences that may demand immediate recording and later transcription into the major notebook. If you haven't kept a diary, you have no idea how valuable this can sometimes be.

I do not recommend using a computer for the diary because of the limitations of traveling with it, especially outdoors, and the changes in technology that will occur throughout your lifetime. Transcribing one's diary onto a computer may be useful if you archive and update the files as operating systems and software evolve.

Beginning some time around 2000 e.v., an Internet diary phenomenon developed called "Live Journal," essentially a series of shared Web logs (or blogs) used by a number of people in the magical community. I have not availed myself of this practice, nor do I understand its motivation or value, but like many things in life, different people are attracted to different behaviors. I'm sure someone will write a book explaining it all one day.

People often like to record the astrological aspects of the day in their diaries. Depending on the depth of one's interest in Astrology, this can be simple or elaborate. Here's another tip. Years ago I had determined on a daily course of practices. Experimenting with different ways of recording these, I arrived at a chart format set up for one-week periods, in addition to my normal essay format. The advantage of a chart was that it gave me instant graphic information on my success, or lack thereof, in self-discipline. For some of the practices, I just left space for check marks; for others, I also left room for comments.

Liber E vel Exercitiorum is included as appendix 2 of this book. If this is your first book about Aleister Crowley, you'll immediately be able to start some of the practices that demand a Magical Diary. As Crowley makes clear in *Book IV,* the method is simple.

> In order to test our progress, for we shall find that (as in all physiological matters) meditation cannot be gauged by the feelings, **we shall have a note-book and pencil,** and we shall also have a stop watch. We shall then endeavour to count how often, during the first quarter of an hour, the mind breaks away from the idea upon which it is determined to concentrate. [boldface in original] (Book IV, Part 1, p. 12)

> Please understand that in doing this practice you are to be seated in Asana, and to have a note-book and pencil by your side, and a watch in front of you. . . . The student is supposed to count the number of times his thought wanders; this he can do on his fingers or on a string of beads. If these breaks seem to become more frequent instead of less frequent, the student should not be discouraged; this is partially caused by his increased powers of observation. . . . Soon, however, the control will improve faster than the observation. When this occurs the improvement will become apparent in the record. (Book IV, Part 1, p. 57–58)

And in *Diary of a Drug Fiend,* he again makes it quite clear in the following dialogue that the object is a careful, scientific, no-nonsense recording of the facts.

> Lamus: '. . . You're keeping your magical diary of course.'
> Lou: 'Oh, yes,' I cried gladly, I knew how important he thought the record was.
> He shook his head comically.
> 'Oh, no, Miss Unlimited Lou, not what I call a magical diary. You ought to be ashamed of yourself for not knowing the hours, minutes, and seconds since the last dose.' (DDF, p. 190)

In *Magick in Theory and Practice,* Crowley gives a brilliant instruction on the diary that outlines in a nutshell the assertions of this introduction, and, in fact, of this entire book. Please note that use of bold type for emphasis was done in the original.

Immediately after the License to Depart, and the general closing up of the work, it is necessary that the Magician should sit down and write up his magical record. However much he may have been tired by the ceremony, he ought to force himself to do this until it becomes a habit. **Verily, it is better to fail in the magical ceremony than to fail in writing down an accurate record of it.** One need not doubt the propriety of this remark. Even if one is eaten alive by Malkah be-Tarshishim ve-Ruachoth ha-Schehalim, it does not matter very much, for it is over so very quickly. But the record of the transaction is otherwise important. Nobody cares about Duncan having been murdered by Macbeth. It is only one of a number of similar murders. But Shakespeare's account of the incident is a unique treasure of mankind. And, apart from the question of the value to others, there is that of the value to the magician himself. **The record of the magician is his best asset.**

It is as foolish to do Magick without method, as if it were anything else. To do Magick without keeping a record is like trying to run a business without book-keeping. There are a great many people who quite misunderstand the nature of Magick. They have an idea that it is something vague and unreal, instead of being, as it is, a direct means of coming into contact with reality. It is these people who pay themselves with phrases, who are always using long words with no definite connotation, who plaster themselves with pompous titles and decorations which mean nothing whatever. With such people we have nothing to do. But to those who seek reality the Key of Magick is offered, and they are hereby warned that the key to the treasure-house is no good without the combination; and the combination is the magical record.

From one point of view, magical progress actually consists in deciphering one's own record. For this reason it is the most important thing to do, on strictly magical grounds. But apart from this, it is absolutely essential that the record should be clear, full and concise, because it is only by such a record that your teacher can judge how it is best to help you. Your magical teacher has something else to do besides running around after you all the time, and the most important of all his functions is that of auditor. Now if you call in an auditor to investigate a business, and when he asks for the books you tell him that you have not thought it worth while to keep any, you need not be surprised if he thinks you every kind of an ass.

It is — at least, it was — perfectly incredible to THE MASTER THERION that people who exhibit ordinary common sense in the other affairs of life should lose it completely when they tackle Magick. It goes far to justify the belief of the semi-educated that Magick is a rather crazy affair after all. However, there are none of these half-baked lunatics connected with A∴A∴, because the necessity for hard work, for passing examinations at stated intervals, and for keeping an intelligible account of what they are doing, frightens away the unintelligent, idle and hysterical.

There are numerous models of magical and mystical records to be found in the various numbers of the Equinox, and the student will have no difficulty in acquiring the necessary technique, if he be diligent in practice. (MTP, p. 140–142)

A WORD ON CONTENT

Undoubtedly, the beginner is daunted by an innumerable series of questions: What is right to put in the diary? Can I add my feelings? What about ... and then what about ... ?

It's really pretty easy. I think anything that you find interesting and germane to your understanding of yourself and the Great Work is useful to record. The structure can be as loose and free as desired, as long as you do it. The two diary examples given in this collection should give some guidance.

What is difficult is acquiring the habit. Once you have done that — once you have overcome the laziness and nay-saying, the sense of meaninglessness and exposure, of vulnerability and shame — once you can acquire the zeal for the practice, you can certainly be trusted to know what makes sense to record.

Also, note the instructions in Libers *E* and *O*, and the extract of Crowley's letter to Roy Leffingwell in the appendix. In *Liber E*, for example, the guideline for content is strict but inclusive.

9. The more scientific the record is, the better. Yet the emotions should be noted, as being some of the conditions. Let then the record be written with sincerity and care; thus with practice it will be found more and more to approximate to the ideal. (See p. 163.)

In *The Magical Record of the Beast 666,* we get a sense of Crowley the diarist talking to himself about the practice. The method he describes here is fairly open-ended.

25 May. And so I come to the end of a quite fat MS book within thirty-four days. (666, p. 132)

25 May. (Digression: I've been regretting the Form of this Diary; but it's quite right that these speculations should alternate with the record of the purchase of a pair of socks!) (666, p. 133)

31 May. Seventeen pages of drivel about this question ... (666, p. 140)

18 June. I accuse myself of not keeping my Diary properly. There ought to be a discoverable relation between my health, my worldly affairs, and the tone of my thoughts. For even the Absolute Ego in eruption makes the relation between its modes of illusion a 'true', or harmonious one; for all moods are alike to It, despair a theme of pastime equally with exaltation. (666, p. 175)

I begin a new MS book. My Magical Diary has been very voluminous in these last weeks; I seem to find that it is the sole mode of my initiated expression. I don't write regular essays on a definite subject, or issue regularly planned instructions. This is presumably normal to my tense and exalted state, to the violent Motion proper to my resolution of all symbols. (666, p. 175)

In *John St. John,* Crowley muses on the proper content of the diary as follows.

(Odd memoranda during lunch. Insist on pupils writing down their whole day; the play as well as the work. 'By this means

they will become ashamed and prate no longer of beasts.')
(JSJ, p. 11)

And as you go on with the diary practice, you'll probably recognize this line of thinking.

It is true, by the way. I was — and am — in some danger of
looking on this Record as a Book; i.e., of emphasizing things for
their literary effect, and diminishing the importance of others
which lend themselves less obviously.
But the answer to this, friend Satan! is that the Canon of
Art is Truth, and the Canon of Magic is Truth; my true record
will make a good book, and my true book will make a good
record. (JSJ, p. 67)

A WORD ON SECRECY

First Amendment Story

I had an odd experience with the Magical Diary that may be of
value to the magical community. I was involved with Marcelo
Motta in the mid 1970s, a Brazilian A∴A∴ representative, who
published his first American book with Weiser Publishing Com-
pany in 1975, where I was employed. We had a falling out that is
somewhat documented in *The Equinox* III, 10. Some years later,
in 1982, he sued Weiser for the control of Crowley copyrights.
I offered to help Weiser, because in my opinion, Motta had become
psychologically disturbed and would endanger any responsible
Crowley publishing in the future.
    Because we had been in a student-teacher relationship, Motta
knew I kept a Magical Diary and had it subpoenaed for the trial!
    I was alarmed, to say the least, but told Weiser's lawyer that I
absolutely refused to turn over the diary because it was, in my
opinion, protected by the First Amendment as a part of my religious practice. He communicated my objection to the judge and
Motta's lawyer and then came back with this request for a compromise. Since I was trying to help Weiser win the suit, he asked
me not to press the issue any further. Motta's lawyer and the judge
had agreed that he, Weiser's lawyer, as an officer of the court,

could read the diary for the court, to determine if there was evidence of a conspiracy or other behavior, which the paranoid Mr. Motta was certain would be found in my diary.

Since I was committed to advancing the case, I did not push the First Amendment issue any further. The net effect of my raising it, however, was that I was able to sit with the lawyer as he read the diary, determine no copies were made, and thereby emerge with my privacy less violated than it might otherwise have been. I have told this story because, although I am not a lawyer, I believe a Magical Record is protected by the U.S. Constitution. (Those who are unfamiliar with that document will find it presented in full in my book *The Slaves Shall Serve*. It is worth studying.)

CODE WRITING AND PRIVACY

How many times have I heard people say they can't keep a Magical Diary because their [choose one] (a.) lover (b.) wife (c.) husband (d.) roommate (e.) other — might find it and read it! At the risk of sounding pedantic, a Thelemite who lives with someone who does not respect his or her privacy should move. This applies equally both ways. Attempting to violate the magical privacy of another human being is simply vile.

Of course, there is also the technique of code writing. The Qabalah is filled with nifty little correspondences that should allow most things to be "hidden from the profane" rather easily. And the less-than-profane can also be guarded against by more personalized and creative secret codes. On the other hand, there are numerous instances in my diary of coded writing that has become completely incomprehensible. The funny part is that I can clearly remember my thoughts as I made those cryptic entries, months, years, or decades ago — that, as concealed and circuitous as the message was going to be, I would never forget the key. Guess What!

Crowley makes reference to code writing in *The Confessions*, referring to an ill-fated mountain climbing expedition on Chogo Ri. "Foreseeing trouble, I kept part of my diary in magical cipher." (p. 279)

A Word on Discipline

Discipline is a fundamental issue with the Diary practice, especially in the beginning. After a while, it becomes fairly habitual, mainly because you will have the experience of NOT recording your experiences often enough to realize the mistake. Nothing encourages success quite like failure. This happens to Achad in *A Master of the Temple,* and Crowley is quick to jump on it in a footnote.

Commenting on an A∴A∴ document he just read, Achad says,

> ... this serves as a confirmation that I was on the right track. I should have no doubt mentioned these meditations more fully at the time. (MT, p. 131)

A.C. footnotes this entry and comments as follows:

> Observe how the least slackness in writing up the Record avenges itself. (MT, p. 131)

In *The Confessions,* Crowley writes poetically of the difficulty he experienced in properly recording an event of enormous spiritual impact. He undertook a Magical Retirement on Oesopus Island. The climax (part of his Magus initiation) was so profound that he was loathe to write at all. Yet he did, and he discusses the challenge in the following words.

> I feel I am more likely to be able to convey some hint of the colossal character of this revelation if I simply quote the broken staggering words in which I wrote it down at the time. As will be seen, I did not dare to write what it actually was, *but I remember at this moment how I had to invoke the deep-seated habit of years to get courage to drag myself to my diary.* I felt like a soldier wounded to death, scrawling in his own blood the horrifyingly disastrous information he has lost his life in seeking. [italics added] (Conf, p. 839)

Relationship with the Diary as "Other"

The keeping of a Record adds a sense of meaning and reality to the magical quest. The act of writing is a defining and creative act that further empowers the magical self.

Identifying one's seriousness and the extent of one's magical work with one's diary output is not without precedent in Crowley. In *The Confessions* he notes his lack of spiritual enthusiasm as reflected in his ignoring the diary.

> The condition of my soul is clearly indicated by my output.... I no longer aspired to become the redeemer of humanity. I doubt whether I should have been able to attach any meaning to any such words. After returning from Edinburgh, I do not seem even to have kept a record and I remember nothing about my doings. (Conf, p. 362)

> The love of my wife had made me the richest man on earth and developed my human soul to its full stature.... As my poetry had petered out, so had my Magick and my meditation.... I had not kept a diary. (Conf, p. 371)

Furthermore, the Record begins to assume the character of the "other," a projected super-ego, or eidolon of the Great Work itself. It functions as a visible barometer of one's magical state, and the seriousness and dedication you bring to the Work. One alternately develops affection, loathing, anticipation, boredom, and so on, as if the Record begins to live a life of its own — which in fact it does.

The following entry from *A Master of the Temple* serves as an excellent example of what I'm describing.

> I have not made an entry in this record for a whole week. I seem to be losing control and my diary, lying untouched in my drawer, is becoming like a horrible fiend. It worries me when I do not enter it ... Tonight I must write an entry. I MUST. (MT, p. 130)

Of course, as a symbol of one's adherence to the Great Work, the diary can easily become a symbol or object of rebellion as well.

In *Diary of a Drug Fiend,* Crowley brilliantly illustrates the stage of revulsion: to the practice, the Teacher, and the spiritual life in general. Note, however, the tenacious undercurrent of the Will, as Lou somehow insists on going on with her hated mentor's instructions, even in the face of her determination to commit suicide.

> To begin with, no more of this diary — why should I put myself out for King Lamus? 'Every step he treads is smeared with blood,' as Gretel once said. Yes, in some infernal way he has made me one of his victims. 'All right — you shall get enough magical diary to let you know that I'm out of your clutches — I'll put down just those things which will tell you how I hate you — how I have outwitted you — and you shall read them when my Dead Soul has got a Dead Body to match it.' (DDF, p. 210)

The vehemence of Lou's attitude was obviously not unfamiliar to Crowley in real life. For his rebellion at the time of the reception of *The Book of the Law,* and the paucity of his record during this period, were a never-ending source of disappointment and shame for him. He even claims to have deliberately defiled his diary just prior to the Cairo working (as his reception of *The Book of the Law* in 1904 is known). This is a source of frustration in trying to piece together the strands that ultimately resulted in the most important experience of his life. Here are two accounts of the period. The first is from *The Temple of Solomon the King, Equinox* I, 7, the second from his *Confessions.*

> Fra. P. never made a thorough record of this period. He seems to have wavered between absolute scepticism in the bad sense, a dislike of the revelation, on the one hand, and real enthusiasm on the other. And the first of these moods would induce him to do things to spoil the effect of the latter. Hence the "blinds" and stupid meaningless cyphers which deface the diary.
>
> And, as if the Gods themselves wished to darken the Pylon, we find that later, when P.'s proud will had been broken, and he wished to make straight the way of the historian, his memory (one of the finest memories in the world) was utterly incompetent to make everything certain. (TSK, No. 7, p. 364)

There was no tendency on my part to accept 'divine' interference in my affairs. There was, on the contrary, the bitterest opposition from me. I even went so far as to make unintelligible and false additions to my diary, with the deliberate intention of confusing the record, and perhaps even of making people think me untrustworthy in this stupendous circumstance. (Conf, p. 386)

Just after the Cairo working, he again fell into spiritual desolation and wrote, "I completely abandoned my diary" (Conf, p. 403).

Some 15 years later, he would suffer another lapse of faith in the Great Work, and again, the Magical Diary would become a symbol of both his rebellion and the eventual renewal of the battle.

Hope died in my heart. There was not a glimmer of light on the horizon anywhere. It seemed to me an obscene mockery to be called a Magus. I must have been afflicted by 'lust of result'; at least it came to this, that I felt that I could not go on with my work. On every side the wizened witches of religion and morality were shrill in celebration of their obscene sabbath. I felt that I had not only failed, but that it was little short of lunacy to imagine that I could ever make the slightest impression upon the monstrous mass of misery which was soaking through the very spine of mankind. *My faith failed me; I made a gesture of despair; I committed spiritual suicide, I closed my Magical Record and refused to write.* 'If the Masters want me to do their Work' said I, 'let them come forward and call me.'

This action is the only one of my life of which I am really ashamed. I should not have surrendered while there was a breath in my body....

The situation had not in any way changed; when I reopened my Magical Diary I did so entirely without hope of any kind ... [italics added] (Conf pp. 822–823)

Personal Anecdotes

Frustrations with the Practice

In my own diary practice, there are at least three frustrating issues that are never-ending sources of discomfort.

One is the fact of not having kept coherent diary records of the period from 1967 to 1969 when I really began to identify myself with the Spirit, and had some of the most important introductory experiences to the Great Work. Being able to examine those records now, written from the point of view of a 19-year-old seeker, would be invaluable.

Another disturbing experience was that during a move in 1974, I lost the diary volume on which I was working. It recorded one of the more philosophically important times of my life. I had packed it with some books in an unsealed carton and carelessly left the box unguarded for a moment in the New York City streets. Someone just walked by and carried a period of my life into oblivion. It is impossible to reconstruct the past from the point of view of the present, despite what anyone may say.

The third is more subtle — a tendency to miss recording certain major events. It is hard to describe (and even harder to admit), but I find some important incidents have been left out of my diary altogether. These failures in my practice are caused, I believe, by the all-consuming impact of these events. It is as if one is so involved with the new information, one neglects to chronicle it.

Reading Birth Entries to Satra

Surely the most tender incident of the Magical Diary practice for me took place in 1991. My then $11^1/2$ year old son was staying with me. During an intimate conversation together, I read aloud to him my diary entries describing his birth and earliest months.

Finding Notes Preserved in Diaries

On a practical level, the diary can be an excellent place to preserve certain material. I had developed a lecture for my O.T.O. Lodge around a Qabalistic analysis of some verses from *The Book of the Law*. In time I lost the notes. How delighted I was to realize they were taken from the initial work I had done in my diary and could be easily reconstructed from that more permanent record.

Similarly, on August 30, 1923, Crowley entered a commentary in his magical record on *The Book of the Law*, Chapter I, verses 1–20, which to my knowledge is otherwise unpublished and quite interesting. (1923, p. 136)

And Then the Diary Saved My Life

For what it is worth, I believe at one point my Magical Record helped stave off a potential suicide. It provided irrefutable data, during an intense psychological crisis, that negated the intensity of the emotional disturbance from which I was suffering. While this may sound a bit melodramatic, it is true and important enough as a personal experience with the diary practice to include here. Crowley, in fact, mentions something similar in the letter to Roy Leffingwell extracted in the appendix, "This acts as your conscience and your tutor; also, when you get fits of depression, it is immensely comforting." (See p. 193.)

OTHER EFFECTS OF THE PRACTICE

Stimulating Spiritual Growth

Some months prior to being asked to create this book, I experienced a psychological situation that heralded the need for a great deal of change, and for squarely facing some major life issues for perhaps the first time. Because of previous training and habit, I wrote about the process in elaborate detail in my diary for at least five months, filling a great many pages therein. I basically felt that I was able to write my way through the problem, and emerge out the other side. This might be called biblio-therapy. It worked extremely well.

Crowley also dealt with this aspect of the diary, where the practice of writing itself assists in the performance of the Great Work. For example, in *John St. John,* describing his recording of the "somewhat banal details" of his diet, he explains he has done it for reasons including the following.

In keeping the vow 'I will interpret every phenomenon as a particular dealing of God with my soul' the mere animal actions are
the most resistant. One cannot see the nature of the phenomenon; it seems so unimportant; one is inclined to despise it.
Hence I enter it into the record as a corrective. (JSJ, p. 60)

Thus the act of recording is seen as a spiritual discipline with
its own psychological component, in which the act itself creates
change in conformity with the Adept's Will.

In *Diary of a Drug Fiend,* the initial basis of the heroin treatment is simply the honest recording of the doses. In the early phase
of the treatment, King Lamus's Priestess, Lala, helps the very sick
couple arrange their affairs.

'I shall leave you children alone for an hour to get settled in ...
But of course you'll be needing heroin all the time, and I notice
that you have a plentiful supply, so there's nothing to worry
about there. It's not taking the drug that does the harm, it's the
not knowing what you take. So I brought you a couple of charts
marked off into hours; and what I want you to do is to promise
to make a cross in the proper space every time you take it.' (DDF,
p. 264)

When Lamus arrives and Peter feels the need for a dose,
Lamus interrupts his conversation.

'Go on,' I said feebly. 'I didn't mean to interrupt.'
'That's all right,' said Lamus. 'I'm only waiting for you to
put it down.'
Lala had pinned my chart to the wall. I looked at my watch
and went over and scrawled a cross in the proper section.
As I returned, I noticed that Lamus was watching with a
smile of singular amusement....
Lou and I fell to talking as soon as they were gone. We
were already better in this respect, that we had begun to take an
interest in ourselves once more.... we made a kind of little family joke of keeping each other up to the mark in the matter of
recording the facts.
I discovered what had amused King Lamus ... I was conscious of a distinct shade of annoyance at having to get up and

make a little cross. It had never occurred to me to break my word. There was a fascination in watching the record. (DDF, pp. 264–266)

As part of Lamus's plan to free them from their drug addiction, Peter and Lou were encouraged to write down their "reason" for taking each dose recorded on their charts. Despite the following statement being made in the context of a heroin cure, the principle enunciated has universal applicability.

It's a curious thing that once you've written down a reason you diminish its value. You can't go on using the same reason indefinitely. (DDF, p. 337)

Directly Accessing the Past

The ability to directly access earlier life periods is a major advantage of the diary in the quest for self-knowledge. I remember an incident in 1990 that was particularly helpful in understanding both the limitations of my subjective memory and the value of the diary as a corrective. I was to discuss an issue with a group of people that called for an analysis of my past. I had decided that a series of events had occurred and that my reaction to them had been of a certain nature. Quite convinced of all this, I prepared my talk. However as a check, I decided to read my diaries for the period in question (two decades earlier). What a surprise to find that the whole talk would have been based on self-mythologizing through faulty memory. Also that the reality was not only more accurate, but far more interesting.

The diary review can be an excellent thing, not only for the distant past, but as a particular process continues. The John St. John period lasted only 13 days, but several times we read Crowley searching through his record for illuminating clues otherwise easy to overlook by being caught up in the moment. These may either confirm or deny insights, or provide coherent patterns to otherwise discontinuous data. Crowley writes, "I think I will read through the whole Record to date and see if I can find an Ariadne-clue." (JSJ, p. 69). Approximately two hours later we find him ready to begin reading through the Record. After finishing he exclaims, "Before I was blind; now I see!" (JSJ, p. 69). There are numerous other examples within *John St. John* of his reviewing previous entries for further guidance. At last, filled with the ambrosial success of the operation, Crowley writes:

> I read through this volume of the Record; and I dissolve my being into quintessential laughter.
>
> The entries are some of them so funny! ... Previously, this had escaped me. (JSJ, p. 102)

In *Diary of a Drug Fiend,* when Lou and Peter were ready, King Lamus moved them to the Abbey of Thelema for the final stages of their cure. Sir Peter describes the writing of his memories in the magical record under the direction of King Lamus.

> It is only three months ago; but it seems a lifetime. My memory is now very good, and I remember more details of the past every day. I am writing this account of the past three months partly because my best friend tells me that it will strengthen it if I exercise it by putting down what has occurred in sequence. And you know, even a month ago, I couldn't have recalled anything at all with regard to certain periods.
>
> My friend tells me that memory fails me in part because nature mercifully wishes to hide from us things which are painful. The spider-web of protective forgetfulness is woven over the mouth of the cave which conceals the raw head and bloody bones of our misfortunes.
>
> 'But the greatest men,' says King Lamus, 'are those who refuse to be treated like squalling children, who insist on facing reality in every form, and tear off ruthlessly the bandages from their own wounds.' (DDF, p. 247)

Real life again provided Crowley with practical demonstrations of the utility of the Magical Record in allowing direct access to prior states of his life and magical career. In *The Confessions*, he gave diary extracts of magical workings that had taken place some 17 years before. He writes:

> I left Shanghai on the twenty-first of April. On the twenty-second I was sick and stayed in bed all day. I did no regular invocation, but thought over the recent crisis. I dismissed the

Shanghai experience as a morbid dream. Reading though the above record at this distance of time, after deliberately avoiding doing so for so long, I feel very uncertain about it; I feel that there was a great deal of genuine communication with the right people and that the Oracle is confused, contradictory and uneven because of the interference of our personalities. (Conf, p. 525)

One of the more interesting uses to which A.C. put his diaries, discussed at length in *The Confessions,* was in the analysis of his Magus Initiation. He charted the course of the "Chokmah Days" (73-day cycles) over some five years between 1914 and 1919, by studying his record and observing dates and corresponding events. Further discussion of this topic is completely out of context of this essay, except to note that for him to be able to break the events and experiences of five years into 73-day cycles would have required incredibly diligent use and analysis of his diary.

Increasing Self-Understanding

In my own diary, I have noticed that the level of honesty I am capable of using on myself grows in direct proportion to how much I exercise the muscles of fearless introspection. There is a definite horror attached to seeking one's darkest motivations and an extreme reticence in then exposing them to the light — even in the privacy of one's own journal. However it is an invaluable method of developing the psychological strength to take responsibility for your actions and become a real Thelemite.

If the reader will excuse a slight digression, I'd like to share Crowley's thoughts on the nature of a "real Thelemite," as recorded in his *1923 Diary.*

21 May, 10:15pm. There seems to be much misunderstanding about the True Will.... The fact of a person being a gentleman is as much an ineluctable factor as any possible spiritual experience; in fact, it is possible, even probable, that a man may be misled by the enthusiasm of an illumination, and if he should find apparent conflict between his spiritual duty and his duty to honour, it is almost sure evidence that a trap is being laid for him and he should unhesitatingly stick to the course which ordi-

nary decency indicates. Error on such point is precisely the 'folly' anticipated in *CCXX* 1, 36, and I wish to say definitely, once and for all, that people who do not understand and accept this position have utterly failed to grasp the fundamental principles of the Law of Thelema ... (1923, p. 21)

Helping Other Magicians

Here we at last come to the first principle of A∴A∴, and in fact, the entire thrust of Aleister Crowley's incarnation. I specifically refer to the Mahayana conception of the Bodhisattva Vow in which the Initiate pledges to devote the fruits of his attainment to the liberation of all sentient beings. In this regard, Crowley certainly viewed the Magical Record as a tool.

> I am taking all this trouble of the Record principally in hope that it will show exactly what mental and physical conditions precede, accompany and follow 'attainment' so that others may reproduce, through these conditions, that Result. (JSJ, p. 95)

> 21 July, 6:10 pm. I loathe the idea of writing the Comment so bitterly that I feel my 'troll' capable of deliberately wrecking the Work of Preparation — in such a way of course that the fault would appear to lie at the door of O.P.V. or of circumstances. I am of course on my guard against any such insane action: & note the facts for the benefit of future Magicians in similar conditions. (1923, p. 94)

> 8 August, 1:11 am. I have several times referred to morbidity of thought as afflicting me. I have not described the symptoms in proper detail & I am ashamed to say that the cause of this omission is that I have been too much ashamed of them to write them down. Yet it is important for mankind that I do so ... (1923, pp. 121)

Reading through Crowley's diaries, I am struck by his self-effacing honesty. He did not engage in hypocritical fictions and myth-making regarding either sanctimonious special holiness or chosen status conveyed on his person by virtue of his spiritual office as Prophet. In fact, he insisted on minutely describing his reveling, even wallowing, in his humanity. He openly and honestly shares his failings, weakness, poverty, confusion, despair, and cravings — as well as his brilliance and exaltation. His approach is completely unique among spiritual teachers. His promise seems to be that as a demonstrated, self-proclaimed, fellow human being, he attained. And our common humanity is the seal of the availability of attainment to us all.

> 23 September, 4:44 pm. I then recited mine Oath once more with all imaginable amplification. I demanded the Word of the Equinox on the ground that I was a Magus, pledged to the service of Mankind. I further swore to devote myself wholly to its welfare: and supported this oath by the affirmation that I was none other than mankind itself — as being the Beast 666. (1923, p. 171)

In closing, I pay my loving respects to this Master, who has so deeply influenced my life.

And best wishes to you as well, dear reader, in your journey through yourself.

A final quote from *Liber Aleph* eloquently describes the real Magical Diary.

> ... the Vellum of the Scroll is of Man's Skin, and its Ink of his Heart's Blood.

Love is the law, love under will

— JAMES WASSERMAN

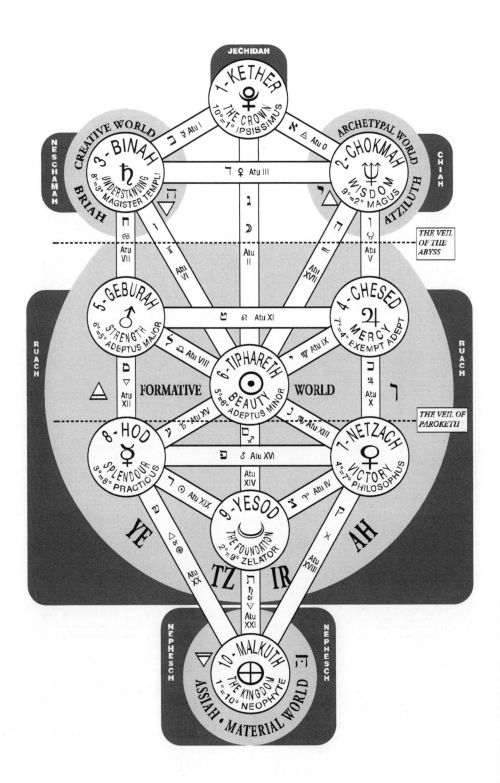

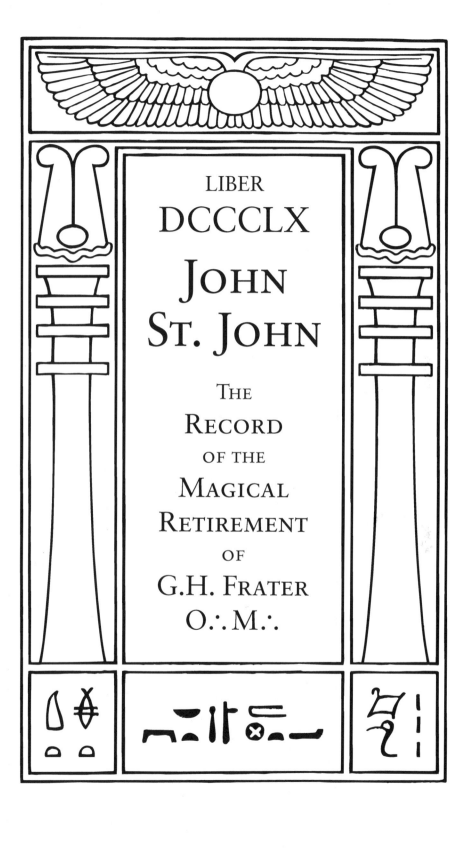

LIBER

DCCCLX

JOHN
ST. JOHN

THE

RECORD

OF THE

MAGICAL

RETIREMENT

OF

G.H. FRATER

O∴M∴

A∴A∴
Publication in Class C.

John St. John

Preface

NOBODY is better aware than myself that this account of my Retirement labours under most serious disadvantages.

The scene should have been laid in an inaccessible lamaserai in Tibet, perched on stupendous crags; and my familiarity with Central Asia would have enabled me to do it quite nicely.

One should really have had an attendant Sylph; and one's Guru, a man of incredible age and ferocity, should have frequently appeared at the dramatic moment.

A gigantic magician on a coal-black steed would have added to the effect: strange voices, uttering formidable things, should have issued from unfathomable caverns. A mountain shaped like a Svastika with a Pillar of Flame would have been rather taking; herds of impossible yaks, ghost-dogs, gryphons ...

But, my good friends, this is not the way things happen. Paris is as wonderful as Lhassa, and there are just as many miracles in London as in Luang Prabang.

I did not even think it necessary to go into the Bois de Boulogne and meet those Three Adepts who cause bleeding at the nose, familiar to us from the writings of Macgregor Mathers.

The Universe of Magic is in the mind of a man: the setting is but Illusion even to the thinker.

Humanity is progressing; formerly men dwelt habitually in the exterior world; nothing less than giants and Paynim and men-at-arms and distressed ladies, vampires and succubi, could amuse them. Their magicians brought demons from the smoke of blood, and made gold from baser metals.

In this they succeeded; the intelligent perceived that the gold and the lead were but shadows of thought. It became probable that the elements were but isomers of one element; matter was seen to be but a modification of mind, or (at least) that the two things matter and mind must be joined before either could be perceived. All knowledge comes through the senses, on the one hand; on the other, it is only through the senses that knowledge comes.

We then continue our conquest of matter; and we are getting pretty expert. It took much longer to perfect the telescope than the motor-car. And though, of course, there are limitations, we know enough to be able to predict them. We know in what progression the Power to Speed coefficient of a steamboat rises — and so on.

But in our conquest of Nature, which we are making principally by the use of the rational intelligence of the mind, we have become aware of that world itself, so much so that educated men spend nine-tenths of their waking lives in that world, only descending to feed and dress and so on at the imperative summons of their physical constitution.

Now to us who thus live the world of mind seems almost as savage and unexplored as the world of Nature seemed to the Greeks. There are countless worlds of wonder unpath'd and uncomprehended and even unguessed, we doubt not.

Therefore we set out diligently to explore and map these

untrodden regions of the mind.

Surely our adventures may be as exciting as those of Cortes or Cook!

It is for this reason that I invite with confidence the attention of humanity to this record of my journey.

But another set of people will find another disappointment. I am hardly an heroic figure. I am not The Good Young Man That Died. I do not remain in holy meditation, balanced on my left eyelash, for forty years, restoring exhausted nature by a single grain of rice at intervals of several months.

You will perceive in these pages a man with all his imperfections thick upon him trying blindly, yet with all his force, to control the thoughts of his mind, so that he shall be able to say "I will think this thought and not that thought" at any moment, as easily as (having conquered Nature) we are all able to say "I will drink this wine, and not that wine."

For, as we have now learnt, our happiness does not at all depend upon our possessions or our power. We would all rather be dead than be a millionaire who lives in daily dread of murder or blackmail.

Our happiness depends upon our state of mind. It is the mastery of these things that the Magicians of to-day have set out to obtain for humanity; they will not turn back, or turn aside.

It is with the object of giving the reins into the hands of others that I have written this record, not without pain.

Others, reading it, will see the sort of way one sets to work; they will imitate and improve upon it; they will attain to the Magistry; they will prepare the Red Tincture and the Elixir of Life — for they will discover what Life means.

PROLOGUE

It hath appeared unto me fitting to make a careful and even an elaborate record of this Great Magical Retirement, for that in the first place I am now certain of obtaining some Result therefrom, as I was never previously certain.

Previous records of mine have therefore seemed vague and obscure, even unto the wisest of the scribes; and I am myself afraid that even here all my skill of speech and study may avail me little, so that the most important part of the record will be blank.

Now I cannot tell whether it is a part of my personal Kamma, or whether the Influence of the Equinox of Autumn should be the exciting cause; but it has usually been at this part of the year that my best Results have occurred. It may be that the physical health induced by the summer in me, who dislike damp and chill, may bring forth as it were a flower the particular kind of Energy — Sammávayamo* — which gives alike the desire to perform more definitely and exclusively the Great Work, and the capacity to achieve success.

It is in any case remarkable that I was born in October (18—); suffered the terrible mystic trance which turned me toward the Path in October (18—); applied for admission to G∴D∴ in October(18—); opened my temple at B—e in October (18—); received the mysteries of L.I.L. in October (19—), and obtained the grade of 6°=5□; obtained the first true mystic results in October (19—); landed again in Egypt in October (19—); first parted from ... in October (19—); wrote the B.-i-M. in October (19—), and obtained the grade of 7°=4□; received the great Initiation in October 19—; and, continuing, received .... in October 19—.

[* Inherence: An intimate relation between inseparables.]

So then in the last days of September 19— do I begin to collect and direct my thoughts; gently, subtly, persistently turning them one and all to the question of retreat and communion with that which I have agreed to call the Holy Guardian Angel, whose Knowledge and Conversation I have willed, and in greater or less measure enjoyed, since Ten Years.

Terrible have been the ordeals of the Path; I have lost all that I possessed, and all that I loved, even as at the Beginning I offered All for Nothing, unwitting as I was of the meaning of those words. I have suffered many and grievous things at the hands of the elements, and of the planets; hunger, thirst, fatigue, disease, anxiety, bereavement, all these woes and others have laid heavy hand upon me, and behold! as I look back upon these years, I declare that all hath been very well. For so great is the Reward which I (unworthy) have attained that the Ordeals seem but incidents hardly worthy to mention, save in so far as they are the Levers by which I moved the World. Even those dreadful periods of "dryness" and of despair seem but the necessary lying fallow of the Earth. All those "false paths" of Magic and of Meditation and of Reason were not false paths, but steps upon the true Path; even as a tree must shoot downwards its roots into the Earth in order that it may flower, and bring forth fruit in its season.

So also now I know that even in my months of absorption in worldly pleasure and business, I am not really there, but stand behind, preparing the Event.

Imagine me, therefore, if you will, in Paris on the last day of September. How surprised was I — though, had I thought, I should have remembered that it was so — to find all my necessary magical apparatus to my hand! Months before, for quite other reasons, I had moved most of my portable property to Paris; now I go to Paris, not thinking of a Retirement, for I now know enough to trust my destiny to bring all things to pass without anxious forethought on my part and suddenly, therefore, here do I find myself and nothing is lacking.

I determined therefore to begin steadily and quietly, allowing the Magical Will to come slowly forth, daily stronger, in contrast to my old plan, desperation kindling a store of fuel dried by long neglect, despair inflaming a mad energy that would blaze with violence for a few hours and then go out — and nothing done. "Not hurling, according to the oracle, a transcendent foot towards Piety."

Quite slowly and simply therefore did I wash myself and robe myself as laid down in the Goetia, taking the Violet Robe of an Exempt Adept (being a single Garment), wearing the Ring of an Exempt Adept, and that Secret Ring which hath been entrusted to my keeping by the Masters. Also I took the Almond Wand of Abramelin and the Secret Tibetan Bell, made of Electrum Magicum with its striker of human bone. I took also the magical knife, and the holy Anointing Oil of Abramelin the Mage.

I began then quite casually by performing the Lesser Banishing Ritual of the Pentagram, finding to my great joy and some surprise that the Pentagrams instantly formulated themselves, visible to the material eye as it were bars of shining blackness deeper than the night.

I then consecrated myself to the Operation; cutting the Tonsure upon my head, a circle, as it were to admit the light of infinity: and cutting the cross of blood upon my breast, thus symbolising the equilibration of and the slaying of the body, while loosing the blood, the first projection in matter of the universal Fluid.

The whole formulating Ankh — the Key of Life!

I gave moreover the signs of the grades from 0°=0▯ to 7°=4▯.

Then did I take upon myself the Great Obligation as follows:

I. I, O.M. & c., a member of the Body of God hereby bind myself on behalf of the whole Universe, even as we are now physically bound unto the cross of suffering:

II. that I will lead a pure life, as a devoted servant of the Order:

III. that I will understand all things:

IV. that I will love all things:

V. that I will perform all things and endure all things:

VI. that I will continue in the Knowledge and Conversation of My Holy Guardian Angel:

VII. that I will work without attachment:

VIII. that I will work in truth:

IX. that I will rely only upon myself:

X. that I will interpret every phenomenon as a particular dealing of God with my soul.

And if I fail herein, may my pyramid be profaned, and the Eye be closed upon me!

All this did I swear and seal with a stroke upon the Bell.

Then I steadily sat down in my Asana (or sacred Posture), having my left heel beneath my body pressing into the anus, my right sole closely covering the phallus, the right leg vertical; my head, neck, and spine in one straight vertical line; my arms stretched out resting on their respective knees; my thumbs joined each to the fourth finger of the proper hand. All my muscles were tightly held; my breath came steady, slow and even through both nostrils; my eyes were turned back, in, up to the Third Eye; my tongue was rolled back in my mouth; and my thoughts, radiating from that Third Eye, I strove to shut in unto an ever narrowing sphere by concentrating my will upon the Knowledge and Conversation of the Holy Guardian Angel.

Then I struck Twelve times upon the Bell; with the new month the Operation was duly begun.

Oct. 1. The First Day

At Eight o'clock I rose from sleep and putting on my Robe, began a little to meditate. For several reasons — the journey and business of the day before, etc. etc., I did not feel fresh. But forcing myself a little I rose and went out to the Café du Dôme where I took coffee and a brioche, after buying an exercise book in which to write this record.

This was about 8.45; and now (10.10) I have written thus far. {Including the Prologue, but not the Preface. — ED.}

10.45. I have driven over to the Hammam through the beautiful sunshine, meditating upon the discipline of the Operation.

It seems only necessary to cut off definitely dispersive things, aimless chatter and such; for the Operation itself will guide one, leading to disgust for too much food and so on. If there be upon my limbs any chain that requires a definite effort to break it, perhaps sleep is that chain. But we shall see — *solvitur ambulando.* *

[* It will be resolved by practice.]

If any asceticism be desirable later on, true wariness will soon detect any danger, and devise a means to meet it and overcome it.

12.0. Have finished bath and massage, during which I continued steadily but quite gently, "not by a strain laborious and hurtful but with stability void of movement," willing the Presence of Adonai.*

12.5. I ordered a dozen oysters and a beefsteak, and now (12.10) find myself wishing for an apple chewed and swallowed by deglutition, as the Hatha Yogis do.
The distaste for food has already begun.

12.12. Impressions already *failing to connect.*
I was getting into Asana and thinking, "I will record this fact," when I saw a jockey being weighed.
I thought of recording *my own* weight which I had not taken. Good!

12.13–12.24. Pranayama {10 seconds to breathe in, 20 seconds to breath out, 30 seconds to hold in the breath.} Fairly good; made me sweat again thoroughly. Stopped not from fatigue but from lunch.
(Odd memoranda during lunch.
Insist on pupils writing down their whole day; the play as well as the work. "By this means they will become ashamed, and prate no longer of 'beasts.'")
I am now well away on the ascetic current, devising all sorts of privations and thoroughly enjoying the idea.

12.55. Having finished a most enjoyable lunch, will drink coffee and smoke, and try and get a little sleep. Thus to break up sleep into two shifts.

2.18. A nice sleep. Woke refreshed.

3.15. Am arrived home, having performed a little business and driven back.

[* The Holy Guardian Angel.]

Will sit down and do Asana, etc.

3.20. Have started. 3.28. 7 Pranayama cycles enough. Doubtless the big lunch is a nuisance.
I continue meditating simply.

3.36. Asana hurts badly, and I can no longer concentrate at all. Must take 5 minutes' rest and then persevere.

3.41. Began again. I shall take *Hua allalu alazi lailaha illa hua** for mantra {any sacred sentence, whose constant repetition produces many strange effects upon the mind. — ED.} if I want one, or: may Adonai reveal unto me a special mantra to invoke Him!

3.51. Broke down again, mantra and all.

3.52–4.14. Went on meditating in "Hanged Man posture" {Legs crossed, arms below head, like the figure of the Hanged Man in the Tarot Cards. — ED.} to formulate sacrifice and pain self-inflicted; for I feel such a worm, able only to remain a few minutes at a time in a position long since "conquered." For this reason too I cut again the Cross of Blood; and now a third time will I do it. And I will take out the Magical Knife and sharpen it yet more, so that this body may fear me; for that I am Horus the terrible, the Avenger, the Lord of the Gate of the West.

4.15–4.30. Read Ritual DCLXXI.† {The nature of this Ritual is explained later. — ED.}

5.10. I have returned from my shopping. Strange how solemn and dignified so trivial a thing becomes, once one has begun to concentrate!
I bought two pears, half a pound of Garibaldi biscuits, and a packet of Gaufrettes. I had a citron pressé, too, at the Dôme.
At the risk of violating the precepts of Zoroaster 170 and 144 I propose to do a Tarot divination for this Operation.‡

[* He is God, and there is no other God than He.]
[† This is the Ritual Pyramidos. The illuminated ritual manuscript mentioned throughout this diary is published in *The Equinox* IV, 1, pp. 59–72.]
[‡ See *Chaldean Oracles*.]

I should explain first that I write this record for other eyes than mine, since I am now sufficiently sure of myself to attain something or other; but I cannot foretell exactly what form the attainment may take. Just so, if one goes to call upon a friend, he may be walking or riding or sleeping.

Thus, then, is Adonai hidden from me. I know where He lives; I know I shall be welcome if I call; but I do not know whether He will invite me to a banquet or ask me to go out with Him for a long journey.

It may be that the Rota will give me some hint.

{We have omitted the details of this divination. — ED.}

I am never very content with such divinations; trustworthy enough in material concerns, in the things of the Spirit one rarely obtains good results.

The first operation was rather meaningless; but one must allow (a) that it was a new way of dealing those cards for the opening of an operation; (b) that I had had two false starts.

The final operation is certainly most favourable; we shall see if it comes true. I can hardly believe it possible.

6.10. Will now go for a stroll, get some milk, and settle down for the evening.

10.50. I regret to have to announce that on going across to the Dôme with this laudable intention, Nina brought up that red-headed bundle of mischief, Maryt Waska. This being in a way a "bandobast"* (and so inviolable), I took her to dinner, eating an omelette, and some bread and Camembert, and a little milk. Afterwards a cup of coffee, and then two hours of the Vajroli Mudra† badly performed.

All this I did with reluctance, as an act of self-denial or asceticism, lest my desire to concentrate on the mystic path should run away with me.

Therefore I think it may fairly be counted unto me for righteousness.

I now drink a final coffee and retire, to do I hope a more straightforward type of meditation.

[* An arrangement, tying, and binding (Root: Hindi).]
[† Yogic practice involving urethral suction. See ED. note p. 17.]

So mote it be.

Naked, Maryt looks like Corregio's Antiope. Her eyes are a strange grey, and her hair a very wonderful reddish gold a colour I have never seen before and cannot properly describe. She has Jewish blood in her, I fancy; this, and her method of illustrating the axiom *Post coitum animal triste** made me think of Baudelaire's *Une nuit que j'etais pres d'une affreuse Juive:*† and the last line

> *Obscurcir la splendeur des tes froides prunelles.*‡

and Barbey d'Aurevilly's *Rideau Cramoisi*§ suggested to me the following poem. {We omit this poem. — ED.}

11.30. Done! i'th'rough! i'th'rough! Now let me go back to my room, and Work!

(11.47.) Home — undressed — robed — attended to toilet — cut cross of Blood once more to affirm mastery of Body — sat down at 11.49 and ended the day with 10 Pranayamas, which caused me to perspire freely, but were not altogether easy or satisfactory.

THE SECOND DAY

The Stroke of Twelve found me duly in my Asana, practising Pranayama.

Let me continue this work; for it is written that unto the persevering mortal the Blessed Immortals are swift ...

What then should happen to a persevering Immortal like myself?

12.7. Trying meditation and mantra.

12.18. I find thoughts impossible to concentrate; and my

[* After sex every animal is sad.]
[† One night, as by a Jewess, like the dead I lay.]
[‡ Thou hast veiled the splendour of thine icy eyes.]
[§ "The Crimson Curtain," a short story published in 1874 in *Les Diaboliques*.]

Asana, despite various cowardly attempts to "fudge" it, is frightfully painful.

12.20. In Hanged Man posture, meditating and willing the Presence of Adonai by the Ritual "Thee I invoke, the Bornless One" and mental formulae.

12.28. I'm hopelessly sleepy! Invocation as bad as bad could be — attention all over the place. Irrational hallucinations, such as a vision of either Eliphaz Levi or my father (I can't swear which!) at the most solemn moment!

But the irrational character of said visions is not bad. They come from nowhere; it is much worse when your own controlled brain breaks loose.

12.33. I will therefore compose myself to sleep: is it not written that He giveth unto His beloved even in sleep? "Others, even in sleep, He makes fruitful from His own strength."

7.29. Woke and forced myself to rise. I had a number of rather pleasing dreams, as I seem to remember. But their content is gone from me; and, in the absence of the prophet Daniel, I shall let the matter slide.

7.44. Pranayama. 13 cycles. Very tiring; I began to sweat. A mediocre performance.

8.0–8.20. Breakfast. Hatha Yogi — a pear and two gaufrettes.

8.53. Have been meditating in Hanged Man position. Thought dull and wandering; yet once "the conception of the Glowing Fire" seen as a planet (perhaps Mars). Just enough to destroy the concentration; then it went out, dammit!

10.40. Have attended to correspondence and other business and drunk a citron pressé.

The Voice of the Nadi* began to resound.

[* The Nadi are the subtle energy channels in which Kundalini or the Life Force circulates through the body. This sound may be heard in meditation.]

10.50. Have done "Bornless One"* in Asana. Good; yet I am filled with utter despair at the hopelessness of the Task. Especially do I get the Buddhist feeling, not only that Asana is intensely painful, but that all conceivable positions of the body are so.

11.0. Still sitting; quite sceptical; sticking to it just because I am a man, and have decided to go through with it.

11.13. Have done 10 P.Y. cycles. A bit better, and a slight hint of the Bhuchari Siddhi† foreshadowed. Have been saying mantra; the question arises in my mind: Am I mixing my drinks unduly? I think not; if one didn't change to another mystic process, one would have to read the newspaper.

11.20. This completes my half-hour of Asana. Legs very painful; yet again I find myself wishing for Kandy (not sugar candy, but the place where I did my first Hindu practices and got my first Results) and a life devoted entirely to meditation. But not for me! I'm no Pratyeka-Buddha; a Dhamma-Buddha every inch of me! {A Pratyeka-Buddha attains the Supreme Reward for himself alone; a Dhamma-Buddha renounces it and returns to hell (earth) to teach others the Way. — ED.}
I now take a few minutes "off" to make "considerations."
I firmly believe that the minutest dose of the Elixir would operate as a "detonator." I seem to be perfectly ready for illumination, if only because I am so perfectly dark. Yet my power to create magical images is still with me.

11.40–12.0. Hanged Man posture. Will invoke Adonai once more by pure thought. Got into a very curious state indeed; part of me being quite perfectly asleep, and part quite perfectly awake.

2.10. Have slept, and that soundly, though with many dreams. Awaking with the utmost horror and loathing of the Path of the Wise — it seemed somehow like a vast dragon-demon with bronze green wings iridescent that rose up startled and angry. And I saw that the littlest courage is enough to rise and throw off sleep, like

[* Invocation of the Holy Guardian Angel. See the *Goetia*.
[† Hopping about like a frog in Pranayam. See *Shiva Sanhita*.]

a small soldier in complete armour of silver advancing with sword and shield — at whose sight that dragon, not daring to abide the shock, flees utterly away.

2.15. Lunch, 3 Garibaldis and 3 Gaufrettes. Wrote two letters.

2.50. Going out walk with mantra.

8.3. This walk was in a way rather a success. I got the good mantra effects, *e.g.*, the brain taking it up of its own accord; also the distaste for everything but Adonai became stronger and stronger.

But when I returned from a visit to B—e on an errand of comradeship — 1¹/₂ hours' talk to cut out of this mantra-yoga — I found all sorts of people at the Dôme, where I drank a citron pressé: they detained me in talk, and at 6.30 Maryt turned up and I had to chew a sandwich and drink coffee while she dined.

I feel a little headache; it will pass.

She is up here now with me, but I shall try to meditate. Charming as she is, I don't want to make love to her.

8.40. Mixed mantra and caresses rather a success. (At her request I gave M. a minimum dose of X.)

9.15. Asana and Meditation with mantra since 8.40. The blackness seems breaking. For a moment I got a vague glimpse of one's spine (or rather one's Sushumna*) as a galaxy of stars, thus suggesting the stars as the ganglia of the Universe.

9.18. To continue.

10.18. Not very satisfactory. Asana got painful; like a worm I gave up, and tried playing the fool; got amused by the New Monster, but did not perform the "Vajroli Mudra." {For this see the *Shiva Sanhita,* and other of the Holy Sanskrit Tantras. — ED.}

However, having got rid of her for the moment, one may continue.

[* Central Nadi or path of Kundalini within the spinal column.]

10.24–10.39. P.Y. {Prana Yama. — ED.} 14 cycles. Some effort required; sweating appears to have stopped and Bhuchari hardly begun.

My head really aches a good deal.

I must add one or two remarks. In my walk I discovered that my mantra Hua allahu, etc., really belongs to the Visuddhi Cakkrâm; so I allowed the thought to concentrate itself there. {The Visuddhi-Cakkrâm: the nerve centre, in Hindu mystic physiology, opposite the larynx. — ED.}

Also, since others are to read this, one must mention that almost from the beginning of this Working of Magick Art the changed aspect of the world whose culmination is the keeping of the oath "I will interpret every phenomenon as a particular dealing of God with my soul" was present with me. This aspect is difficult to describe; one is indifferent to everything and yet interested in it. The meaning of things is lost, pending the inception of their Spiritual Meaning; just as, on putting one's eye to the microscope, the drop of water on the slide is gone, and a world of life discovered, though the real import of that world is not apprehended, until one's knowledge becomes far greater than a single glance can make it.

10.55. Having written the above, I shall rest for a few moments to try and get rid of my headache.

A good simile (by the way) for the Yogi is to say that he watches his thought like a cat watching a mouse. The paw ready to strike the instant Mr. Mouse stirs. I have chewed a Gaufrette and drunk a little water, in case the headache is from hunger. (P.S. — It was so; the food cured it at once.)

11.2. I now lie down as Hanged Man and say mantra in Visuddhi.

11.10. I must really note the curious confusion in my mind between the Visuddhi Cakkrâm and that part of the Boulevard Edgar Quinet which opens on to the cemetery. It seems an identity.

In trying to look at the Cakkram, I saw that.

Query: What is the connection, which appeared absolute and essential? I had been specially impressed by that gate two days ago, with its knot of mourners. Could the scene have been recorded in a brain-cell adjoining that which records the Visuddhi-idea? Or did I at that time unconsciously think of my throat for some other reason? Bother! These things are all dog-faced demons! To work!

11.17. Work: Meditation and Mantra.

11.35. No good. Went off into a reverie about a castle and men-at-arms. This had all the qualities of a true dream, yet I was not in any other sense asleep. I soon will be, though. It seems foolish to persist.

And indeed, though I tried to continue the mantra with its high aspiration to know Adonai, I must have slept almost at once.

THE THIRD DAY

6.55. Now the day being gloriously broken, I awoke with some weariness, not feeling clean and happy, not burning with love unto my Lord Adonai, though ashamed indeed for that thrice or four times in the night I had been awakened by this loyal body, urging me to rise and meditate — and my weak will bade it be at ease and take its rest — oh, wretched man! slave of the hour and of the worm!

7.0–7.16. Fifteen cycles of Prana Yama put me right mentally and physically: otherwise they had little apparent success.

7.30. Have breakfasted — a pear and two Garibaldis. (These by the way are the small size, half the big squares.)

7.50. Have smoked a pipe to show that I'm not in a hurry.

8.5. Hanged Man with mantra in Visuddhi. Thought I had been much longer. At one point the Spirit began to move — how the devil else can I express it? The consciousness seemed to flow, instead of pattering. Is *that* clear?

One should here note that there may perhaps be some essential difference in the operation of the Moslem and Hindu mantrams. The latter boom; the former ripple. I have never tried the former at all seriously until now.

8.10–8.32. *Même jeu** — no good at all. Think I'll get up and have a Turker.

9.0. Am up, having read my letters. Continuing mantra all the time in a more or less conscious way.

9.25. Wrote my letters and started out.

10.38. Have reached the Café de la Paix, walking slowly with my mantra. I am beginning to forget it occasionally, mispronouncing some of the words. A good sign! Now and then I tried sending it up and down my spine, with good effect.

10.40. I will drink a cup of coffee and then proceed to the Hammam. This may ease my limbs, and afford an opportunity for a real go-for-the-gloves effort to concentrate.

It cannot be too clearly understood that nearly all the work hitherto has been preliminary; the intention is to get the Chittam (thought-stuff) flowing evenly in one direction. Also one practises detaching it from the Vrittis (impressions). One looks at everything without seeing it.

O coffee! By the mighty Name of Power do I invoke thee, consecrating thee to the Service of the Magic of Light. Let the pulsations of my heart be strong and regular and slow! Let my brain be wakeful and active in its supreme task of self-control! That my desired end may be effected through Thy strength, Adonai, unto Whom be the Glory for ever! Amen without lie, and Amen, and Amen of Amen.

11.0. I now proceed to the Hammam.

12.0. The Bath is over. I continued the mantra throughout, which much alleviated the torture of massage. But I could not get steady and easy in my Asana or even in the Hanged Man or Shavasana, the "corpse-positions." I think the heat is exciting, and makes me restless. I continue in the cooling-room lying down.

[* Same game.]

12.10. I have ordered 12 oysters and coffee and bread and butter.

O oysters! be ye unto me strength that I formulate the 12 rays of the Crown of *HVA!** I conjure ye, and very potently command.

Even by Him who ruleth Life from the Throne of Tahuti unto the Abyss of Amennti, even by Ptah the swathed one, that unwrappeth the mortal from the immortal, even by Amoun the giver of Life, and by Khem the mighty, whose Phallus is like the Pillar in Karnak! Even by myself and my male power do I conjure ye. Amen.

12.20. I was getting sleepy when the oysters came.
I now eat them in a Yogin and ceremonial manner.

12.45. I have eaten my oysters, chewing them every one; also some bread and butter in the same manner, giving praise to Priapus the Lord of the oyster, to Demeter the Lady of corn, and to Isis the Queen of the Cow. Further, I pray symbolically in this meal for Virtue, and Strength, and Gladness; as is appropriate to these symbols. But I find it very difficult to keep the mantra going, even in tune with jaws; perhaps it is that this peculiar method of eating (25 minutes for what could be done normally in 3) demands the whole attention.

1.30 Drifted into a nap. Well! we shall try what Brother Body really wants.

1.35. My attempt to go to sleep has made me supernaturally wakeful.

I am — as often before — in the state described by Paul (not my masseur; the other Paul!) in his Epistle to the Romans, cap. vii. v. 19.

I shall arise and go forth.

1.55. I have a good mind to try violent excitement of the Muladhara Cakkrâm;† for the whole Sushumna seems dead. This

[* "He." Divine name of the Supernal Triad of the Tree of Life. See p. 38.]
[† Nerve center of Kundalini located above the anus.]

at the risk of being labeled a Black Magician — by clergymen, Christian Scientists, and the "self-reliant" classes in general.

2.15. Arrived (partly by cab) at the Place. Certain curious phenomena which I have noticed at odd times *e.g.,* on Thursday night — but did not think proper to record must be investigated. It seems quite certain that meditation practices profoundly affect the sexual process: how and why I do not yet certainly know.

2.45. Rubbish! everything perfectly normal.
Difficult, though, to keep mantram going.

3.0. Am sitting on the brink of the big fountain in the Luxembourg. This deadness of the whole system continues.
To explain. Normally, if the thought be energetically directed to almost any point in the body, that point is felt to pulse and even to ache. Especially this is the case if one vibrates a mantra or Magical Name in a nerve-centre. At present I cannot do this at all. The Prana* seems equilibrated in the whole organism: I am very peaceful — just as a corpse is.
It is terribly annoying, in a sense, because this condition is just the opposite of Dharana;† yet one knows that it is a stage on the way to Samadhi.‡
So I rise and give confidently the Sign of Apophis and Typhon,§ and will then regard the reflection of the sweet October Sun in the kissing waters of the fountain. (P.S. — I now remember that I forgot to rise and give the Sign.)

3.15. In vain do I regard the Sun, broken up by the lips of the water into countless glittering stars — abounding, revolving, whirling forth, crying aloud — for He whom my soul seeketh is not in these. Nor is He in the fountain, eternally as it jets and falls in brilliance of dew; for I desire the Dew Supernal. Nor is He in the still depths of the water; their lips do not meet His. Nor — O my

[* Life force.]
[† Stage of meditation involving focusing the attention on a single point. See *Book IV,* Part I: Mysticism, chapter 5.]
[‡ The highest stage of meditation characterized by the union (and dissolution) of subject and object. See *Book IV,* Part I: Mysticism, chapter 7.]
[§ One of the LVX signs, illustrated in *Liber O,* see appendix 3, page 172.]

soul! — is He anywhere to be found in thy secret caverns, unlumi-nous, formless, and void, where I wander seeking Him — or seek-ing rest from that Search! O my soul! — lift thyself up; play the man, be strong; harden thyself against thy bitter Fate; for at the End thou shalt find Him; and ye shall enter in together into the Secret Palace of the King; even unto the Garden of Lilies; and ye shall be One for evermore. So mote it be!

Yet now — ah now! — I am but a dead man. Within me and without still stirs that life of sense that is not life, but is as the worms that feast upon my corpse.

... Adonai! Adonai! my Lord Adonai! indeed, Thou hast for-saken me. Nay! thou liest, O weak soul! Abide in the meditation; unite all thy symbols into the form of the Lion, and be lord of thy jungle, travelling through the servile Universe even as Mau the Lion very lordly, the Sun in His strength that travelleth over the heaven of Nu in His bark in the mid-career of Day.

For all these thoughts are vain; there is but One thought, though that thought be not yet born He only is God, and there is none other God than He!

3.30. Walking home with mantra; suddenly a spasm of weep-ing took me as I cried through the mantra — "My God, my God, why hast Thou forsaken me?" — and I have to stop and put it down!

A good thing; for it calms me.

3.45. At the Dôme, master of myself. The Mantra goes just 30 times a minute, 1800 times an hour, 43,200 times a day. To say it a million times would take longer than Mrs. Glyn's heroine did to conceive. Yet I will get the result if I have to say it a hundred and eleven million times. But oh! fertilise my Akasic egg to-day!

This remark, one should notice, is truly characteristic of the man John St. John. I see how funny it is; but I'm quite serious withal. Ye dull dogs!

{The Akasic Egg is the sphere of the personality of man. A theosophic term. — ED.}

3.55. N.B. — Mantras might with advantage be palindromes.

3.56. I try to construct a magic square from the mantra.

No good. But the mantra is going much better, quite mechanically and "without attachment" (*i.e.*, without conscious ulterior design. "Art for Art's sake" as it were.)

4.10. I drink a citron pressé.

4.25. Alas! here comes Maryt (with a sad tale of X. It appears that she fainted and spent some hours at the hospital. I should have insisted on her staying with me; the symptoms began immediately on her drinking some coffee. I have noticed with myself, that eating has started the action.)

5.30. An hour of mingled nap and mantra.
I now feel alive again. It was very strange how calm and balanced I was: yet now I am again energised; may it be to the point of Enthusiasm!
People will most assuredly smile at this exalted mystic; his life seems made up of sleep and love-making. Indeed, to-day I have been shockingly under the power of Tamas,* the dark sphere. But that is clearly a fatigue-effect from having worked so hard.
Oh Lord, how long?

5.50. The Mantra still ripples on. I am so far from the Path that I have a real good mind to get Maryt to let me perform the Black Mass on her at midnight. I would just love to bring up Typhon, and curse Osiris and burn his bones and his blood!
At least, I now solemnly express a pious wish that the Crocodile of the West may eat up the Sun once and for all, that Set may defile the Holy Place, that the supreme Blasphemy may be spoken by Python in the ears of Isis.
I want trouble. I want to say Indra's mantram till his throne gets red-hot and burns his lotus-buttocks; I want to pinch little Harpocrates till he fairly yells . . . and I will too! Somehow!

6.15. I have now got into a sort of smug content, grinning all over like some sleepy Chinese god. No reason for it, Lord knows!

[* One of the three *gunas* (qualities) of Hindu philosophy. *Sattva*: pure, illuminating; *Rajas*: active, energizing; *Tamas*: darkness, inertia. Compare to the three alchemical principles of Sulphur, Mercury, and Salt.]

I can't make up my mind whether to starve or sandwich or gorge the beast St. John. He's not the least bit hungry, though he's had nothing to call a Meal since Thursday lunch. The Hatha-Yoga feeding game is certainly marvellous.

I should like to work marching and breathing with this mantra as I did of old with Aum Tat Sat Aum.* Perhaps two steps to a mantra, and 4-8-16 steps to a breath-cycle? This would mean 28 seconds for a breath-cycle; quite enough for a marching man. We might try 4-8-8 to start; or even 8-8-8 (for the Chariot, wherein the Geburah of me rises to Binah — Strength winning the Wings of Understanding). {These symbols, allusions, and references will all be found in 777,† just published by *The Equinox** — see advt. — ED.}

6.55. I shall now ceremonially defile the *Beyt Allah* with Pig, to express in some small measure my utter disgust and indignation with Allah for not doing His job properly. I say in vain *Labbaik!* {I am here — ED.} He answers, "But I'm *not* here, old boy — another leg-pull!" He little knows His man, though, if He thinks he can insult me with impunity. André, un sandwich!

{*Beyt Allah,* the Mosque at Mecca, means "House of God" — ED.}

7.5. I shall stop mantra while I eat, so as to concentrate *(a)* on the chewing, *(b)* on defiling the House of God. Not so easy! the damned thing runs on like a prairie fire. Important then to stop it absolutely at will: even the Work itself may become an obsession.

11 hours with no real break — not bad.

The bad part of to-day seems the Asana, and the deadness. Or, perhaps worse, I fail to apprehend the true magical purport of my work: hence all sort of aimless formulae, leading — naturally enough — to no result.

It just strikes me — it may be this Isis Apophis Osiris IAO formula that I have preached so often. Certainly the first two days were Isis — natural, pleasant, easy events. Most certainly too to-day has been Apophis! Think of the wild cursing and black magic,

[* Hindu mantra whose syllables represent the three universal principles of Creation, Preservation, and Destruction.]
[† Both are available from Weiser Books. See also Tree of Life on p. liv.]

etc.... we must hope for the Osiris section to-morrow or next day. Birth, death, resurrection! IAO!

7.35. The Sandwich duly chewed, and two Coffees drunk, I resume the mystic Mantra. Why? Because I damn well choose to.

7.50. 'Tis a rash thing to say, and I burn incense to the Infernal Gods that the Omen may be averted; but I seem to have conquered the real Dweller of the Threshold once and for all. For nowadays my blackest despair is tempered by the certainty of coming through it sooner or later, and that with flying colours.

9.30. The last $^3/4$ hour I wasted talking to Dr. R——, that most interesting man. I don't mean talking; I mean listening. You are a bad, idle good-for-nothing fellow, O.M.! Why not stick to that mantra?

10.40. Have drunk two citrons pressés and gone to my room to work a mighty spell of magick Art.

11.0. Having got rid of Maryt (who, by the way, is Quite mad), and thereby (one might hope) of Apophis and Typhon, I perform the Great Ritual DCLXXI with good results magically; *i.e.*, I formulated things very easily and forcibly; even at one time I got a hint of the Glory of Adonai. But I made the absurd mistake of going through the Ritual as if I was rehearsing it, instead of staying at the Reception of the Candidate and insisting upon being *really* received.

I will therefore now (11.50) sit down again and invoke really hard on these same lines, while the Perfume and the Vision are yet formulated, though insensibly, about me. And thus shall end the Third day of my retirement.

THE FOURTH DAY

12.15. So therefore begins the fourth day of this my great magical retirement; I bleed from the slashes of the magick knife; I smart from the heat of the Holy Oil; I am bruised by the scourge of Osiris

JOHN ST. JOHN 27

that hath so cruelly smitten me; the perfume yet fills the chamber
of Art; — and I?

that hath so cruelly smitten me; the perfume yet fills the chamber
of Art; — and I?

Oh Adonai my Lord, surely I did invoke Thee with fervour;
yet Thou camest not utterly to the tryst. And yet I know that Thou
wast there; and it may be that the morning may bring remembrance of Thee which this consciousness does not now contain.

But I swear by Thine own glory that I will not be satisfied with
this, that I will go on even unto madness and death if it be Thy will
— but I will know Thee as Thou art.

It is strange how my cries died down; how I found myself quite
involuntarily swinging back to the old mantra that I worked all
yesterday.

However, I shall try a little longer in the Position of the
Hanged Man, although sleep is again attacking me. I am weary, yet
content, as if some great thing had indeed happened. But if I lost
consciousness — a thing no man can be positive about from the
nature of things — it must have happened so quietly that I never
knew. Certainly I should not have thought that I had gone on for
25 minutes, as I did.

But I do indeed ask for a Knowledge and Conversation of the
Holy Guardian Angel which is not left so much to be inferred from
the good results in my life and work; I want the Perfume and the
Vision. . . .

Why am I so materially wallowing in grossness? It matters little; the fact remains that I do wallow.

I want that definite experience in the very same sense as
Abramelin had it; and what's more, I mean to go on till I get it.

12.34. I begin, therefore, in Hanged Man posture, to invoke
the Angel, within the Pyramid already duly prepared by DCLXXI.

12.57. Alas, in vain have I tried even the supreme ritual of
Awaiting the Beloved, although once I thought — Ah! give unto
Thy beloved in sleep!

How ashamed I should be, though! For an earthly lover one
would be on tiptoe of excitement, trembling at every sound, eager,
afraid . . .

I will, however, rise and open (as for a symbol) the door and the window. Oh that the door of my heart were ever open! For He is always there, and always eager to come in.

1.0 I rise and open unto my Beloved.

... May it be granted unto me in the daylight of this day to construct from DCLXXI a perfect ritual of self-initiation, so as to avoid the constant difficulty of assuming various God-forms. Then let that ritual be a constant and perfect link between Us ... so that at all times I may be perfect in Thy Knowledge and Conversation, O mine Holy Guardian Angel! to whom I have aspired these ten years past.

1.5. And though as it may seem I now compose myself to sleep, I await Thee ... I await Thee!

7.35. I arise from sleep, mine eyes a little weary, my soul fresh, my heart restored.

8.0. Accordingly, I continue in gentle and easy meditation on my Lord Adonai, without fear or violence, quite directly and naturally.

One of the matters that came up last night with Dr. R—d was that of writing rubbish for magazines. He thought that one could do it in the intervals of serious work; but I do not think that one should take the risk. I have spent these many years training my mind to think cleanly and express beautifully. Am I to prostitute myself for a handful of bread?

I swear by Thyself, O Thou who art myself, that I will not write save to glorify Thee, that I will write only in beauty and melody, that I will give unto the world as Thou givest unto me, whether it be a consuming fire, or a cup of the wine of Iacchus, or a glittering dagger, or a disk brighter than the sun. I will starve in the street before I pander to the vileness of the men among whom I live — oh my Lord Adonai, be with me, give me the purest poesy, keep me to this vow! And if I turn aside, even for a moment, I pray Thee, warn me by some signal chastisement, that Thou art a jealous god, and that Thou wilt keep me veiled, cherished, guarded in Thine harem a pure and perfect spouse, like a slender fountain playing in Thy courts of marble and of malachite, of jasper, of topaz, and of lapis lazuli.

And by my magick power I summon all the inhabitants of the ten thousand worlds to witness this mine oath.

8.15. I will rise, and break my fast. I think it as well to go on with the mantra, as it started of its own accord.

9.0. Arrived at Panthéon, to breakfast on coffee and brioche and a peach.

I shall try and describe Ritual DCLXXI; since its nature is important to this great ceremony of initiation. Those who understand a little about the Path of the Wise may receive some hint of the method of operation of the L.V.X.*

And I think that a description will help me to collect myself for the proper adaptation of this Ritual to the purpose of Self-initiation.

Oh, how soft is the air, and how serene the sky, to one who has passed through the black rule of Apophis! How infinitely musical are the voices of Nature, those that are heard and those that are not heard! What Understanding of the Universe, what Love is the prize of him that hath performed all things and endured all things!

The first operation of Ritual DCLXXI is the preparation of the Place.

There are two forces; that of Death and that of Natural Life.

Death begins the Operation by a knock, to which Life answers.

Then Death, banishing all forces external to the operation, declares the Speech in the Silence.

Both officers go from their thrones and form the base of a triangle whose apex is the East. They invoke the Divine Word, and then Death slays with the knife, and embalms with the oil, his sister Life.

Life, thus prepared, invokes, at the summons of Death, the forces necessary to the Operation. The Word takes its station in the East and the officers salute it both by speech and silence in their signs; and they pronounce the secret Word of power that riseth from the Silence and returneth thereunto.

[* *Lux,* the Light of the Cross: Birth, Death, Resurrection. Identical to the formula of I.A.O., Isis, Apophis, Osiris: Nature, Destruction, Redemption. See *Book IV,* Part III, *Magick in Theory and Practice,* chapter 5.]

All this they affirm; and in affirming the triangular base of the Pyramid, find that they have mysteriously affirmed the Apex thereof whose name is Ecstasy.

This also is sealed by that secret Word; for that Word containeth All.

Into this prepared Pyramid of divine Light there cometh a certain darkling wight, who knoweth not either his own nature, or his origin or destiny, or even the name of that which he desireth. Before he can enter the Pyramid, therefore, four ordeals are required of him.

So, bound and blinded, he stumbles forward, and passes through the wrath of the Four Great Princes of the Evil of the World, whose Terror is about him on every side. Yet since he has followed the voice of the Officer who has prepared him, in this part of the Ritual no longer merely Nature, the great Mother, but Neschamah (his aspiration) and the representative of Adonai, he may pass through all. Yea, in spite of the menace of the Hiereus, whose function is now that of his fear and of his courage, he goes on and enters the Pyramid. But there he is seized and thrown down by both officers as one unworthy to enter. His aspiration purifies him with steel and fire; and there as he lies shattered by the force of the ritual, he hears — even as a corpse that hears the voice Israfel — the Hegemon that chants a solemn hymn of praise to that glory which is at the Apex, and who invisibly rules and governs the whole Pyramid.

Now then that darkling wight is lifted by the officers and brought to the altar in the centre; and there the Hiereus accuses him of the two and twenty Basenesses, while the Hegemon lifting up his chained arms cries again and again against his enemy that he is under the Shadow of the Eternal Wings of the Holy One. Yet at the end, at the supreme accusation, the Hiereus smites him into death. The same answer avails him, and in its strength he is uplifted by his aspiration — and now he stands upright.

Now then he makes a journey in his new house, and perceives at stated times, each time preceded by a new ordeal and equilibration, the forces that surround him. Death he sees, and the Life of Nature whose name is Sorrow, and the Word that quickeneth these, and his own self — and when he hath recognised these four in their true nature he passes to the altar once more and as the apex of a descending triangle is admitted to the lordship of the

Double Kingdom. Thus is he a member of the visible triad that is crossed with the invisible — behold the hexagram of Solomon the King! All this the Hiereus seals with a knock and at the Hegemon's new summons he — to his surprise — finds himself as the Hanged Man of the Tarot.

Each point of the figure thus formed they crown with light, until he glitters with the Flame of the Spirit.

Thus and not otherwise is he made a partaker of the Mysteries, and the Lightning Flash strikes him. The Lord hath descended from heaven with a shout and with the Voice of the Archangel, and the trump of God.

He is installed in the Throne of the Double Kingdom, and he wields the Wand of Double Power by the signs of the grade.

He is recognised an initiate, and the word of Secret Power, and the silent administration of the Sacrament of Sword and Flame, acknowledge him.

Then, the words being duly spoken and the deeds duly done, all is symbolically sealed by the Thirty Voices, and the Word that vibrateth from the Silence to the Speech, and from the Speech again unto the Silence. Then the Pyramid is sealed up, even as it was opened; yet in the sealing thereof the three men partake in a certain mystical manner of the Eucharist of the Four Elements that are consumed for the Perfection of the Oil.

Konx Om Pax. {With these mystic words the Mysteries Eleusinian were sealed. — ED.}

10.0. Having written out this explanation, I will read it through and meditate solemnly thereupon. All this I wrote in the Might of the Secret Ring committed unto me by the Masters; so that all might be absolutely correct.

One thing strikes me as worthy of mention. Last night when I went into the restaurant to speak to R—d, my distaste for food was so intense that the smell of it caused real nausea. To-day, I am perfectly balanced, neither hungry nor nauseated. This is indeed more important than it seems; it is a sure sign when one sees a person take up fads that he is under the black rule of Apophis. In the Kingdom of Osiris there is freedom and light. To-day I shall eat neither with the frank gluttony of Isis nor with the severe asceticism of Apophis. I shall eat as much and as little as I fancy; these violent means are no longer necessary. Like Count Fosco, I shall "go on my way sustained by my sublime confidence, self-balanced by my impenetrable calm."

10.50. I have spent half an hour wandering in the Musée du Luxembourg.

I now sit down to meditate on this new ritual.

The following, so it appears, should be the outlines — damn it, I've a good mind to write it straight off — no! I'll be patient and tease the Spirit a little. I will be coquettish as a Spanish catamite.

1. Death summons Life and clears away all other forces.
2. The Invocation of the Word. Death consecrates Life, who in her whirling dance invokes that Word.
3. They salute the Word. The Signs and M—M must be a Chorus, if anything.
4. The Miraculous appearance of Iacchus, uninvoked.

1. The 3 Questions.
2. The 4 ordeals. Warning and comfort as an appeal to the Officers.
3. The Threshold. The Chorus of Purification. The Hymn "My heart, my mother!" as already written, years ago.
4. At the altar. The accusation and defence as antiphonies.
5. The journey. Bar and pass, and the 4 visions even as a mighty music.
6. The Hanged Man — the descent of Adonai.
7. The installation — signs, etc.

Sealing as for opening; but insert Sacrament.

1.15. During a lunch of 12 oysters, Cêpes Bordelaise, Tarte aux Cérises, Café Noir, despatched without Yoga or ceremonial, I wrote the Ritual in verse, in the Egyptian Language. I don't think very well. Time must show: also experience. I'd recite Tennyson if I thought it would give Samadhi!

Now more mantra, though by the Lord I'm getting sick of it.

1.40. It occurs to me, now that I am seeing my way in the Operation a little more clearly, that one might consider the First Day as Osiris Slain ✠, the Second as that of the Mourning of Isis ʊ, the third as that of the Triumph of Apophis **V**, and to-day that of Osiris Risen **X**; these four days being perfect in themselves as a 5°=6° operation (or possibly with one or two more to recapitulate L.V.X. Lux, the Light of the Cross). Thence one might proceed to some symbolic passage through the 6°=5° grade — though of course that grade is really symbolic of this soul-journey, not *vice versâ* — and through 7°=4°; so perhaps — if one could only dare to hope it! — to the 8°=3° attainment. Certainly what little I have done so far pertains no higher than Minor adeptship, though I have used higher formulae in the course of my working.

1.55. My Prana is acting in a feverish manner; a mixture of fatigue and energy. This is not good: it probably comes from bolting that big lunch, and may mean that I must sleep to recover equilibrium. I will, however, use the Pentagram ritual on my Anahata Cakkrâm {the heart; a nerve-centre in Hindu mystical physiology. — ED.} and see if that steadies me. (P.S. — Yes: instantly.) Notice, please, how in this condition of intense magical strain the most trifling things have a great influence. Normally, I can eat anything in any quantity without the slightest effect of any sort; witness my expeditions and debauches; nothing upsets me.

P.S. — But notice, please! Normally half a bottle of Burgundy excites me notably; while doing this magic it is like so much water. A "transvaluation of all values!"

3.55. Over a citron pressé I have revised the new Ritual. Also I have bought suitable materials for copying it fair; and this I did without solemnity or ceremonial, but quite simply, just as anybody else might buy them. In short, I bought them in a truly Rosicrucian manner, according to the custom of the country.

I add a few considerations on the grade of Adeptus Major 6°=5°.

(P.S. — Distinction is to be made between attainment of this grade in the natural and in the spiritual world. The former I long since possessed.)

1. It may perhaps mean severe asceticism. In case I should be going out on that path I will try and get a real good dinner to fortify myself.
2. The paths leading to Geburah are from Hod, that of the

Hanged Man, and from Tiphereth, that of Justice, both equilibrated aspects of Severity,* the one implying Self-Sacrifice, the other involuntary suffering. One is Freewill, the other Karma; and that in a wider sense than that of Suffering.

The Ritual DCLXXI will still be applicable: indeed, it may be considered sufficient; but of course it must be lived as well as performed.

(I must here complain of serious trouble with fountain pens, and the waste of priceless time fixing them up. They have been wrong throughout the whole operation, a thing that has not happened to me for near eight years. I hope I've got a good one at last — yes, thank God! this one writes decently.)

4.15. Somehow or other I have got off the track; have been fooling about with too many odd things, necessary as they may have been. I had better take a solid hour willing the Tryst with Adonai.

5.40. Have done all this, and a Work of Kindness. I will again revise the new ritual, dine, return and copy it fair for use.

Let Adonai the Lord oversee the Work, that it be perfect, a sure link with Him, a certain and infallible Conjuration, and Spell, and Working of true Magick Art, that I may invoke Him with success whenever seemeth good unto Him.

Unto Him; not unto Me! Is it not written that Except Adonai build the House, they labour in vain that build it?

6.15. Chez Lavenue. Not feeling like revision, will read through this record.

My dinner is to be Bisque d'Ecrevisses, Tournedos Rossini, a Coupe Jack, half a bottle of Meursault, and Coffee. All should now acquit adepts of the charge of not knowing how to do themselves well.

[* Refers to the Paths and Spheres of the Tree of Life, the central symbol of the Western Esoteric Tradition. An illustration appears on page liv of this book. It will help the reader to follow references to Paths, Sephiroth, A∴A∴ Grades, and Parts of the Soul mentioned in this diary and the Jones diary to follow.]

7.20. Dinner over, I return to Mantra-Yoga. One may note that I expected the wine to have an excessive effect on me; on the contrary, it has much less effect than usual.

This is rather important. I have purposely abstained from anything that might be called a drug, until now, for fear of confusing the effects.

With my knowledge of hashish-effects, I could very likely have broken up the Apophis-kingdom of yesterday in a moment, and the truth of it would have been 5 per cent drug and 95 per cent magic; but nobody would have believed me. Remember that this record is for the British Public, "who may like me yet." God forbid! for I cannot echo Browning's hope. Their greasiness, hypocrisy, and meanness are such that their appreciation could only mean my vileness, not their redemption. Sorry if I seem pessimistic about them! A nasty one for me, by the way, if they suddenly started buying me! I should have, in mere consistency, to cut my throat!

Calm yourself, my friend! There is no danger.

7.40. At home again and robed. Am both tired and oppressed, even in my peace; for the day has been, and the evening is, close and hot, with a little fog; and, one may suspect, the air is overcharged with electricity. I will rest quietly with my mantra as Hanged Man, and perhaps sleep for a little.

8.10. No sleep — no rest for the wicked! 'Tis curious how totally independent is mantra-yoga of reverie. I can say my mantra vigorously while my thought wanders all over the world; yet I cannot write the simplest sentence without stopping it, unless with a very great effort, and then it is not satisfactory to either party!

Meditation — of the "rational sort" — on this leads me to suggest that active "radiant" thought may be incompatible with the mantra, itself being (?) active. One can read and understand quite easily with the mantra going; one can remember things.

For example, I see my watch chain; I think. "Gold. Au, 196 atomic weight. $AuCl_3$, £3 10s. 0d. an ounce and so on *ad infinitum;** but the act of writing down these things stops the mantra. This may be (partly) because I always say under my breath each

[* To Infinity.]

word as I write it. {P.S. — But I do so, though less possibly, as I read.}

8.22. As I am really awake, I may as well do a little Pranayama.

8.40. How little I know of magic and the conditions of success! My 17 cycles of breath were not absolutely easy; yet I did them. After a big dinner!!! The sweating was quite suppressed, in spite of the heat of the night and the exercise; and the first symptoms of the Bhuchari-Siddhi — the "jumping about like a frog" — were well marked. I am encouraged to spend a few minutes (still in Asana) reading the *Shiva Sanhita.*

9.0. Asana very painful again. True, I was doing it very strictly.
I notice they give a second stage — trembling of the body — as preliminary to the jumping about like a frog — I had omitted this, as one is so obviously the germ of the other.
The Hindus seem to lack a sense of proportion. When the Yogi, by turning his tongue back for one half-minute, has conquered old age, disease and death; then instead of having a good time he patiently (and rather pathetically, I think!) devotes his youthful immortality to trying to "drink the air through the crow-bill"* ...... in the hope of curing a consumption of the lungs which he probably never had and which was in any case cured by his former effort!

9.40. Have been practising a number of these mudras and asanas.
Concerning the Visuddi Cakkrâm which is 'of brilliant gold or smoke colour and has sixteen petals corresponding to the sixteen vowel sounds,' one might make a good mantra of the English vowel sounds, or the Hebrew.
"Curiouser and curiouser!" The Yogis identify the Varana (Ganges) with the Ida-Nadi,[†] the Asi(?) with the Pingala-Nadi,[†]

[* *Shiva Samhita,* chapter 3.]
[† The Ida and Pingala Nadis are the left and right (respectively) channels of the Kundalini, runing parallel on either side of the spinal cord or central Nadi of the Sushumna.]

and Benares with the space between them. Like my identification of my throat with the Gate of the cimetière du Montparnasse.

Well, it requires very considerable discrimination and a good sound foundation of knowledge, if one means to get any sense at all out of these Hindu books.

10.20. A little Pranayama, I think.

10.22. Can't get steady and easy at all! Will try Hanged Man again.

10.42. Not much good. The mantra goes on, but without getting hold of the Cakkrâm.

'Tis difficult to explain; the best simile I can get is that of a motor running with the clutch out; or of a man cycling on a suspended machine.

There's no grip to it.

The fact of the matter is, I am quite unconcentrated. Evidently the Osiris Risen stage is over; and I think it is a case for violent measures.

If one were to slack off now and hope for the morning, like a shipwrecked Paul, one would probably wake up a mere man of the world.

The Question then arises: What shall I do to be saved?

The only answer — and one which is quite unconnected with the question — is that a Ritual of Adeptus Major should display the Birth of Horus and Slaying of Typhon. Here again are Horus and Harpocrates — the twins of the twin signs of $0°=0°$ ritual — are the slayers of Typhon. So all the rituals get mixed: the symbols recur, though in a different aspect. Anyway, one wants something a deal better than the path of Pé in $4°=7°$ ritual.

I think the postulant should be actually scourged, tortured, branded by fire for his equilibrations at the various "Stations of the Cross" or points upon his mystic journey. He must assuredly drink blood for the sacrament — ah! now I see it all so well! The Initiator must kill him, Osiris; he must rise again as Horus and kill the Initiator, taking his place in the ceremony thence to the end. A bit awkward technically, but 'twill yield to science. They did it of old by a certain lake in Italy!

Well, all this is dog-faced demon, ever seducing me from the Sacred Mysteries. I can't go out and kill anybody at this time o'night! We might make a start, though, with a little scourging, torturing, and branding by fire ...

Anything for a quiet life!

11.0. But scourging oneself is not easy with a robe on; and though one could take it off, there is this point to be considered: that one can never (except by a regrettable accident) hurt oneself more than one wants to. In other words, it is impossible thus to inflict pain, and so flagellants have been rightly condemned as mere voluptuaries. The only way to do so would be to inflict some torture whose severity one could not gauge at the time: *eg.,* one might dip oneself in petroleum and set light to it, as the young lady mystic did — I suppose in Brittany! — the other day. It's not the act that hurts, but the consequences; so, although one knows only roughly what will happen, one can force oneself to the act.

This, then, is a possible form of self-martyrdom. Similarly, mutilations; though it is perhaps just to observe that all these people are mad when they do these things, and their standard of pleasure and pain consequently so different from the sane man's as to be incomprehensible.

Look at my Uncle Tom! who goes about the world bragging of his chastity. The maniac is probably happy — a peacock who is all tail! And squawk.

Look at the Vegetarians and Wallaceites and all that crew of lunatics. They are paid in the coin of self-conceit. I shall waste no pity on them!

11.3. Rather pity myself, who cannot even make sensible "considerations" for a Ritual of Adeptus Major.

The only thing to do in short is to go steadily on, with a little extra courage and energy — no harm in that! — on the same old lines. The Winding of the Way must necessarily lead me just where it may happen to go. Why deliberately go off to Geburah? Why not aspire direct by the Path of Moon-Ray unto the Ineffable Crown? Modesty is misplaced here!

Very good. Then how aspire? Who is it that standeth in the Moon-Ray? The Holy Guardian Angel. Aye! O my Lord Adonai, Thou art the Beginning and the End of the Path. For as Thou אתה thou art also 406 = ת Tau the material world, the Omega. And as He הוא Thou art 12, the rays of the Ineffable Crown.

(A disaster has occurred; viz., a sudden and violent attack of that which demands a tabloid of Pepsin, Bismuth, and Charcoal — and gets it. On my return, 11.34, I continue.)

And as אני Ani I thou art also אין the Negative, that is beyond these on either side!

But this illness is a nuisance. I must have got a little chill somehow. Its imminence would account for my lack of concentration. And I could doubtless go on gloriously, but that another disaster has occurred! Enter Maryt, sitting and clothed and in her right mind — or comparatively so!

11.38. I suppose, then, I must quit the game for a minute or two.

11.56. Got rid of her, thank God. I may say in self-defence that I would never have let her in but for the accident of my being outside the room and the door left open, so that she was inside on my return.

Let me get into Asana.

The Fifth Day

12.26. So beginneth the Fifth Day of this great Magical Retirement. With two and twenty breath-cycles did I begin. This practice was a little easier; but not much better. It ought to become quite simple and natural before one devotes the half-minute of Kambhakam (breath held-in), when one is rigid to a strong projection of Will toward Adonai, as has been my custom. I hope to-day will be more hard definite magical Work, less discourse, less beatific state of mind — which is the very devil! the real Calypso, none the less temptress because her name happens to be Penelope. Ah Lord Adonai, my Lord! Grant unto me the Perfume and the Vision; let me attain the desirable harbour; for my little ship is tossed by divers tempests, even by Euroclydon, in the Place where Four Winds meet.

12.35. Therefore I shall go to rest, letting my mind rest ever in the Will toward Adonai. Let my sleep be toward Him, or annihilation; let my waking be to the music of His name; let the day be full to the uttermost of Him only.

2.18. My good friend the body woke me at this hour by means of disturbed dreams about a quite imaginary relative of whom nobody for years had ever seen anything but his head, which he would poke out of a waterproof sheet. He was supposed to be an invalid. I am glad to say that I woke properly and got quite automatically on to the mantra.

My Prana, however, seems feverish and unbalanced. So I eat a biscuit or two and drink some water and will put it right with Pentagram Ritual.

Done, but oh! how hard. Sleep fights me as Apollyon fought Christian! but I will up and take him by the throat.

(See; 'tis 2.30. Twelve minutes to do that little in!) And look at the handwriting!

3.6. How excellent is Prana Yama, a comfort to the soul! I did thirty-two cycles, easy and pleasant; could have gone on indefinitely. The muscles went rigid, practically of their own accord; so light did I feel that I almost thought myself to be "that wise one" who can balance himself on this thumb. Sleep is conquered right away from the word "jump." Indeed, if

> Satan trembles when he sees
> The weakest saint upon his knees;

then surely:

> Satan flees, exclaiming "Damn!"
> When any saint starts Pranayam!

So happy, indeed, was I in the practice that I devoted myself by the Waiting formula to Adonai; and that I got to "neighbourhood-concentration" is shewn by the fact that I several times forgot altogether about Adonai, and found myself saying the silly old Mantram.

I despair of asking my readers to distinguish between the common phenomenon of wandering thought and this phenomenon which is at the very portal of true and perfect concentration; yet it is most important that the distinction should be seized. The further difficulty will occur — I hope! — of distinguishing between the vacancy of the idiot, and the destruction of thought which we call Shivadarshana, or Nirvikalpa-samadhi. {We must again refer the reader to the Hindu classics. — ED.}

The only diagnostic I can think of is this; that there is (I can't be sure about it) no rational connection between the thought one left behind one and the new thought. In a simple wandering during the practice of concentration one can very nearly always (especially with a little experience) trace the chain. With neighbourhood-concentration this is not so. Perhaps there is a chain, but so great already is the power of preventing the impressions from rising into consciousness that one has no knowledge of the links, each one having been automatically slaughtered on the threshold of the consciousness.

Of course, the honest and wary practitioner will have no difficulty in recognising the right kind of wandering; with this explanation there is no excuse for him if he does.

I have another theory, though. Perhaps this is not a wandering at all, but a complete annihilation of all thought. Affirming Adonai, I lop off the heads of all others; and Adonai's own head falls. But in the momentary pause which this causes, some old habitual thought (to-night my mantra) rises up. A case of the Closure followed by the Moving of the Previous Question.

Oh Lord! when wilt Thou carry a Motion to Adjourn, nay, to Prorogue, nay! to Dissolve this Parliament?

3.32. I am not sleepy; yet will I again compose myself, devoting myself to Adonai.

7.7. Again woke and continued mantra.

8.10. I ought to have made more of it at 7.7; I went off again to sleep; the result is that I am rather difficult to wake again.

However, let me be vigilant now.

8.45. I have dressed and from 8.35–8.45 performed the Ritual of the Bornless One.

Though I performed it none too well (failing, *e.g.*, to make use of the Geometric Progression on the Mahalingam formula in the

Ieou section {We cannot understand this passage. It presumably
refers to the "Preliminary Invocation" in the *Goetia* of King
Solomon, published S.P.R.T., Boleskine Foyers, N.B., 1904. —
ED.},* and not troubling even to formulate carefully the Elemental
Hosts, or to marshal them about the circle) I yet, by the favour of
IAO, obtained a really good effect, losing all sense of personality
and being exalted in the Pillar. Peace and ecstasy enfolded me. It is
well.

8.50. But as I was ill last night, and as the morning has broken
chill and damp, I will go to the Café du Dôme and break my fast
humbly with Coffee and Sandwich. May it strengthen me in my
search for the Quintessence, the Stone of the Wise, the Summum
Bonum, True Wisdom and Perfect Happiness!

9.0. I hope (by the way) that I have made it quite clear that all
this time even a momentary cessation of active thought has been
accompanied by the rising-up of the mantra. The rhythm, in short,
perpetually dominates the brain; and becomes active on every
opportunity. The liquid Moslem mantra is much easier to get on to
than is the usual Hindu type with its *m* and *n* sounds predominat-
ing: but it does not shake the brain up so forcibly. Perhaps 'tis none
the worse for that. I think the unconscious training of the brain to
an even rhythm better than startling it into the same by a series of
shocks.

I should like, too, to remark that the suggestions in the *Herb
Dangerous* {We hope to publish this essay in No. 2 of *The Equinox*
— ED.}† for a ritual seem the wrong way round. It seems to me that
the Eastern methods are very arid, and chiefly valuable as a training of the Will, while the Ceremonies of the Magic of Light tune up
the soul to that harmony when it is but one step to the Crown.

The real plan is, then, to train the Will into as formidable an
engine as possible, and then, at the moment in the Ritual when
real work should be done, to fling forth flying that concentrated
Will "whirling forth with re-echoing Roar, so that it may comprehend with invincible Will ideas omniform, which flying forth from

[* Currently available from Weiser Books.]
[† Published in two parts in *Equinox* I, 1 and 2.]

that one Fountain issued: whose Foundation is One, One and Alone."

As therefore Discipline of whatever kind is only one way of going into a wood at midnight on Easter Eve and cutting the magic wand with a single blow of the magic knife, etc. etc. etc., we can regard the Western system as the essential one. Yet of course Pranayama, for one thing, has its own definite magical effect, apart from teaching the practitioner that he must last out those three seconds — those deadly long last three seconds — even if he burst in the process.

All this I am writing during breakfast.

My devotees may note, by the way, how the desire to sleep is breaking up.

Night	I.	$7^1/2$ hours, unbroken from 12.30.
"	II.	7 hours nearly, with dreams.
"	III.	8 hours nearly; but woke three or four times, and if I had not been a worm would have scattered it like chaff!
"	IV.	$6^1/2$ hours; and I wake fresh.
"	V.	$1^3/4 + 4^1/2 + 1$ hour; and real good work done in the intervals.
{P.S "	VI.	Probably 4 hours.
"	VII.	$2 + 2^1/2 +$ hours.
"	VIII.	6 hours much broken.
"	IX.	$1^1/2 + 2 + 2$ hours.
"	X.	$4 + 1^1/4$ hours.
"	XI.	$1^3/4 + 4^1/2$ hours.
"	XII.	Back to the normal — 7 hours perfect sleep.}

11.30. Have been walks with the mantra arranging for and modelling a "saddle" whereby to get Asana really steady and easy; also for some photographs illustrating some of the more absurd positions, for the instruction of my devotees.

I must now copy out the new Ritual.

This, you will readily perceive, is all wrong. Theoretically, everything should be ready by the beginning of the Operation; and one should simply do it and be done with it.

But this is a very shallow view. One never knows what may be required; *i.e.,* a beginner like myself doesn't. Further, one cannot write an effective Ritual till one is already in a fairly exalted state ... and so on.

We must just do the best we can, now as always.

2.0. I have been concentrating solely on the Revision and copying of the Ritual. Therefore I now live just as I always live in order to get a definite piece of work done: concentrating as it were *off* the Work. As Levi also adjures us by the Holy Names.

Coming back from lunch (a dozen Marennes Vertes and an Andouillette aux Pommes) I met Zelina Visconti, more lovely-ugly than ever in her wild way. She says that she is favourably disposed towards me, on the recommendation of her concierge!!! "The tongue of good report hath already been heard in his favour. Advance, free and of good report!"

4.45. And only two pages done! But the decorations "marvelious"!

5.15. Another half-hour gone! in mere titivating the Opus! and now I'm too tired to as much as start Prana Yama. I will go to the Dôme and see what a citron pressé and a sandwich does for me, at the same time taking over the MS. of *Liber DCCCCLXIII,* which has been given me to correct, and doing it.

Please the pigs, the Visconti will cheer me up in the evening; and I shall get a good day in to-morrow.

6.35. Still at *Liber DCCCCLXIII.* {To be published shortly by *The Equinox* — ED.}* I should like to write mantrams for each chapter.

7.20. Still at *Liber DCCCCLXIII.* I need hardly say that I am perfectly aware that in one sense all this working and ritual making and copying and illuminating is but a crowd of dog-faced demons, since the One Thought of Unity with Adonai is absent.

But I do it on purpose, making each thing I do into that Magic Will.

[* The Treasure House of Images was published as a Special Supplement in *Equinox* I, 3.]

So if you ask me, "Are you correcting *Liber DCCCCLXIII?*"
I reply, "No! I am Adonai!"

7.50. Arrival of the Visconti.

8.50. Departure of the Visconti. Really a necessary rest: for
my head had begun to ache, and her kiss, half given and half taken,
much refreshed me.

9.50. Have done *Liber DCCCCLXIII.* 'Tis hardly thinkable
that one could have read it (merely) in the time. Say three and a
half hours! Well, if it doesn't count as Tapas, and Jap, and Yama,
and Niyama,* and all the rest of it, all I can say is that I think
They don't play fair. I will now go and get something to eat, and
(God willing) on my return settle down to real work, for I need
daylight to copy my Ritual.

11.30. A sandwich and two coffees at the Versailles and a
citron pressé at the Dôme, some little chatter with M—e, B—e,
H—s, and others. In fact, I'm a lazy unconcentrated hound. I
started Mantra again, though; of course it goes quite easily.

11.50. Undressed, and the mantra going, and the Will toward
Adonai less unapparent.
To-day I began ill, full of spiritual pride — look at the records
of my early hours! One might have thought me a great master of
magic loftily condescending to explain a few elementary truths
suited to the capacity of his disciples.
The fact is that I am a toad, ugly and venomous, and if I do
wear a precious jewel in my hand, that jewel is Adonai, and —
well, come to think of it, I am Adonai. But St. John is not Adonai;
and St. John had better do a little humiliation to-morrow.
Nothing being more humiliating than Prana Yama, I will begin
with that.

[* *Tapas:* Austerities; *Japa:* Recitation of mantra; *Yama:* Restraint of behavior;
Niyama: Observance of the ten rules of conduct.]

THE SIXTH DAY.

12.5. Thus then — oh ye great gods of Heaven! — begins the Sixth Day of the Great Magical Retirement of that Holy Illuminated Man of God our Greatly Honoured Frater, O.M., Adeptus Exemptus 7°=4▫ Brother-Elect of the Most Secret and Sublime Order A∴A∴

He does with great difficulty (and no interior performance) just four breath-cycles.

Somebody once remarked that it had taken a hundred million years to produce me; I may add that I hope it will be another hundred million before God makes another cur.

12.15. Have performed the Equilibrating Ritual of the Scourge, the Dagger, and the Chain; with the Holy Anointing Oil that bringeth the informing Fire into their Lustral Water.

12.35. I am so sleepy that I cannot concentrate at all. (I was trying the "Bornless One.") The magic goes well; good images and powerful, but I slack right off into sleep. It's the hour for heroic measures or else to say: A good night's rest, and start fresh in the morning! I suppose, as usual, I shall say the first and do the second.

12.45. Have risen, washed, performed the ritual "Thee I invoke, the Bornless One" physically.

The result fair. One gets better magical sight and feeling when one is performing a ritual in one's Astral Body, so called. For one is on the same plane as the things one's dealing with.

If, however, serious work is wanted, one must be all there. To get "materialized" "spirits" — pardon the absurd language! — one should (nay, must!) work inside one's body. So, too, I think, for the highest spiritual work; for that Work extends from Malkuth to Kether.*

Here is the great value of the rationalistic Eastern systems. {P.S. Of course scientifically worked with pencil, note-book, and

---

[* The reader is referred once again to the Tree of Life diagram on page liv. Malkuth, the Kingdom, is the bottom sphere, Number 10, corresponding to the Neophyte Grade 1°=10▫; while Kether, the Crown, is the top sphere, Number 1, corresponding to the Ipsissimus Grade 10°=1▫.]

stop-watch. The Yogi is usually in practice just as vague a dreamer as the mystic.} They keep one always balanced by common sense. One might go off on lines of pleasing illusion for years, until one was lost on the "Astral Plane."

All this, observe, is very meaningless, very vague at the best. What is the Astral Plane? Is there such a thing? How do its phantoms differ from those of absinthe, reverie, and love, and so on?

We may admit their unsubstantiality without denying their power; the phantoms of absinthe and love are potent enough to drive a man to death or marriage; while reverie may end in anti-vivisectionism or nut-food-madness.

On the whole, I prefer to explain the many terrible catastrophes I have seen caused by magic misunderstood by supposing that in magic one is working with some very subtle and essential function of the brain, whose disease may mean for one man paralysis, for another mania, for a third melancholia, for a fourth death. It is not *à priori* absurd to suggest that there may be some one particular thought that would cause death. In the man with heart disease, for instance, the thought "I will run quickly upstairs" might cause death quite as directly as "I will shoot myself." Yet of course this thought acts through the will and the apparatus of nerves and muscles. But might not a sudden fear cause the heart to stop? I think cases are on record.

But all this is unknown ground, or, as Frank Harris would say, Unpath'd Waters. We are getting dangerously near "mental arsenic" and "all — god — good — bones — truth — lights — liver — mind — blessing — heart — one and not of a series — ante and pass the buck."

The common sense of the practical man of the world is good enough for me!

1.10 Will G. R. S. Mead or somebody wise like that tell me why it is that if I get out of my body and face (say) East, I can turn (in the "astral body") as far as West-Sou'-West or thereabouts, but no further except with very great difficulty and after long practice? In making the circle, just as I got to West, I would swing right back to West-Nor'-West: turn easily enough, in short, to any point but due West, within perhaps 5°, but never pass that point. I have taught myself to do it, but always with an effort.

Is this a common experience?

I connect it with my faculty of knowing direction, which all mountaineers and travellers who have been with me admit to be quite exceptional.

If I leave my tent or hut by a door facing, say, South-West, throughout that whole day, over all kinds of ground, through any imaginable jungle, in all kinds of weather, fog, blizzard, blight, by night or day, I know within 5° (usually within 2°) the direction in which I faced when I left that tent or hut. And if I happen to have observed its compass bearing, of course I can deduce North by mere judgment of angle, at which I am very accurate.

Further, I keep a mental record, quite unconsciously, of the time occupied on a march; so that I can always tell the time within five minutes or so without consulting my watch.

Further, I have another automatic recorder which maps out distance plus direction. Suppose I were to start from Scott's and walk (or drive; it's all the same to me) to Haggerston Town Hall (wherever Haggerston may be; but say it's N.E.), thence to Maida Vale. From Maida Vale I could take a true line for Piccadilly again and not go five minutes walk out of my way, bar blind alleys, etc., and I should know when I got close to Scott's again before I recognised any of the surroundings.

It always seems to me that I get intuition of direction and length of line A (Scott's to Haggerston bee-line; in spite of any winding, it would make little odds if I went viâ Poplar), another intuition of line B (Haggerston to Maida Vale), and obtained my line C (back to Scott's) by "Subliminal trigonometry."

In this example I am assuming that I had never been in London before. I have done precisely similar work in dozens of strange cities, even a twisted warren like Tangier or Cairo. I am worse in Paris than anywhere else; I think because the main thoroughfares radiate from stars, and so the angles puzzle one. The power, too, suits ill with civilised life; it fades as I live in towns, revives as I get back to God's good earth. A seven-foot tent and the starlight — who wants more?

1.35. Well, I've woke myself writing this. The point that really struck me was this: what would happen if by severe training I forced my "astral body" — damn it! isn't there a term for it free from L ... -prostitution? (One speaks of *les deux prostitutions;*[*] so

[* The two prostitutions.]

it's all right.) My Scin-Laeca, then — what would happen if I forced my Scin-Laeca to become a Whirling Dervish? I couldn't get giddy, because my Semicircular canals would be at rest.

I must really try the experiment.

{Scin-Laeca. See Lord Lytton's *Strange Story* — ED.}

1.58. I will now devote myself to sleep, willing Adonai. Lord Adonai, give me deep rest like death, so that in very few hours I may be awake and active, full of lion-strength of purpose toward Thee!

7.35. My heroic conduct was nearly worth a *Nuit Blanche*. For, being so thoroughly awake, I had all my Prana irritated, a feeling like the onset of a malarial attack, twelve hours before the temperature rises. I dare say it was after 3 o'clock when I slept; I woke too, several times, and ought to have risen to have done Prana Yama: but I did not. O worm! the sleepiest bird can easily catch *thee!* ... I am not nicely awake, though it is to my credit that I woke saying my mantra with vigour. 'Tis a bitter chill and damp the morn; yet must I rise and toil at my fair Ritual.

7.55. Settling down to copy.

10.12. Have completed my two prescribed pages of illumination.

Will go and break my fast and do my business.

10.30. After writing letters went out and had coffee and two brioches.

11.50. At Louvre looking up some odd points in the lore of Khemi {Egypt — ED.} for my Ritual.

12.20. I cannot understand it; but I feel faint for lack of food; I must get back to strict Hatha-Yoga feeding.

1.00. Half-dozen oysters and an entrecôte aux pommes.

2.05. Back to work. I am in a very low physical condition; quite equilibrated, but exhausted. I can hardly walk upright!

Lord Adonai, how far I wander from the gardens of Thy beauty, where play the fountains of the Elixir!

2.55. Wrote two pages; the previous were not really dry; so I must wait a little before illuminating.

I will rest — if I can! In the Hanged Man posture.

4.30. I soon went to sleep and stayed there.

It is useless to persist. . . . Yet I persist.

5.40. I was so shockingly cold that I went to the Dôme and had milk, coffee, and sandwich, eaten in Yogin manner. But it has done no good as far as energy is concerned. I'm just as bad or worse than I was on the day which I have called the day of Apophis (third day). The only thing to my credit is the way I've kept the mantra going.

5.57 One thing at least is good; if anything does come of this great magical retirement — which I am beginning to doubt — it will not be mixed up with any other enthusiasm, poetic, venereal, or bacchanalian. It will be purely mystic. But as it has not happened yet — and just at present it seems incredible that it should happen — I think we may change the subject.

... What a fool I am, by the way! I say that "He is God, and that there is no other God than He" 1800 times an hour; but I don't *think* it even once a day.

6.30. All my energy has suddenly come back.

Was it that Hatha-Yoga sandwich?

I go on copying the Ritual.

7.10. Copying finished. I will go and dine, and learn it by heart, humbly and thoughtfully. The illumination of it can be finished, with a little luck, in two more days.

I am disinclined to use the Ritual until it is beautifully coloured. As Zoroaster saith: "God is never so much turned away from man, and never so much sendeth him new paths, as when he maketh ascent to divine speculations or works, in a confused or disordered manner, and (as the oracle adds) with unhallowed lips, or unwashed feet. For of those who are thus negligent the progress is imperfect, the impulses are vain, and the paths are dark."

7.40. Chez Lavenue. Bisque d'Ecrevisses, demi-perdreau à la Gelée, Cêpes Bordelaise, Coupe Jack. Demi Clos du Roi. I am sure I made a serious mistake in the beginning of the Operation of Magick Art. I ought to have performed a true Equilibration by an hour's Prana Yama in Asana (even if I had to do it without Kambhakham) at midnight, dawn, noon, and sunset, and I should have allowed nothing in heaven above, or in earth beneath, or in the waters under the earth, to have interfered with its due performance.

Instead I thought myself such a fine fellow that to get into Asana for a few minutes every midnight and the rest go-as-you-please would be enough. I am well punished.

8.30. This food, eaten in a Yogin and ceremonial manner, is doing me good. I shall end, God willing, with coffee, cognac, and cigar. It is a fatal error to knock the body to pieces and leave the consciousness intact, as has been the case with me all day. It is true that some people find that if they hurt the body, they make the mind unstable. True; they predispose it to hallucination.

One should use strictly corporeal methods to tame the body; strictly mental methods to control the mind. This latter restriction is not so vitally important. Any weapon is legitimate against a public enemy like the mind. No truce nor quarter!

On the contrary, to use the spiritual forces to secure health, as certain persons attempt to do to-day, is the vilest black magic. This is one of the numerous reasons for supposing that Jesus Christ was a Brother of the Left-Hand Path.

Now my body has been treating me well, waking nicely at convenient hours, sleeping at suitable times, keeping itself to itself . . . an admirable body. Then why shouldn't I take it out and give it the best dinner Lavenue can serve? . . . Provided that it doesn't stop saying that mantra!

It would be so easy to trick myself into the belief that I had attained! It would be so easy to starve myself until there was "visions about!" It would be so easy to write a sun-splendid tale of Adonai my Lord and my lover, so as to convince the world and myself that I had found Him! With my poetic genius, could I not outwrite St. John (my namesake) and Mrs. Dr. Anna Bonus Kingsford? Yea, I could deceive myself if I did not train and fortify my scepticism at every point. That is the great usefulness of this record; one will be able to see afterwards whether there is any trace of poetic or other influence. But this is my sheet-anchor: I cannot write a lie, either in poetry or about magic. These are the serious things that constitute my personality; and I could more easily blow out my brains than write a poem which I did not feel. The apparent exception is in case of irony.

{P.S. I wonder whether it would be possible to draw up a mathematical table, showing curves of food (and digestion), drink, other physical impulses, weather, and so on, and comparing them with the curve of mystic enthusiasm and attainment.

Though it is perhaps true that perfect health and *bien-être** are the bases of any true trance or rapture, it seems unlikely that mere exuberance of the former can excite the latter.

In other words there is probably some first matter of the work which is not anything we know of as bodily. On my return to London, I must certainly put the matter before more experienced mathematicians, and if possible, get a graphic analysis of the kind indicated.}

9.20. How difficult and expensive it is to get drunk, when one is doing magic! Nothing exhilarates or otherwise affects one. Oh, the pathos and tragedy of those lines:

> Come where the booze is cheaper!
> Come where the pots hold more!

How I wish I had written them!

10.08. Having drunk a citron pressé and watched the poker game at the Dôme for a little, I now return home. I thought to myself, "Let me chuck the whole thing overboard and be sensible, and get a good night's rest" — and perceived that it would be impossible. I am so far into this Operation that

> pausing to cast one last glance back
> O'er the safe road — 'twas gone!

[* Well-being.]

I must come out of it either an Adept or a maniac. Thank the Lord for that! It saves trouble.

10.20. Undressed and robed. Will do an Aspiration in the Hanged Man position, hoping to feel rested and fit by midnight.

The Incense has arrived from London; and I feel its magical effects most favourable.

O creature of Incense! I conjure thee by Him that sitteth upon the Holy Throne and liveth and reigneth for ever as the Balance of Righteousness and Truth, that thou comfort and exalt my soul with Thy sweet perfume, that I may be utterly devoted to this Work of the Invocation of my Lord Adonai, that I may fully attain thereto, beholding Him face to face — as it is written "Before there was Equilibrium, Countenance" beheld not Countenance — yea, being utterly absorbed in His ineffable Glory yea, being That of which there is no Image either in speech or thought.

10.55. What a weary world we live in! No sooner am I betrayed into making a few flattering remarks about my body that I find everything wrong with it, and two grains of Cascara Sagrada* necessary to its welfare!

... I wish I knew where I was! I don't at all recognise what Path I am on; it doesn't seem like a Path at all. As far as I can see, I am drifting rudderless and sailless on a sea of no shore — the False Sea of the Qliphoth.† For in my stupidity I began to try a certain ritual of the Evil Magic, so called.... Not evil in truth, because only that is evil (in one sense) which does not lead to Adonai. (In another sense, all is evil which is not Adonai.) And of course I had the insane idea that this ritual would serve to stimulate my devotion. For the information of the Z.A.M.,‡ I may explain that this ritual pertained to Saturn in Libra; and, though right enough in its own plane, is a dog-faced demon in this operation. Is it, though? I am so blind that I can no longer decide the simplest problems. Else, I see so well, and am so balanced, that I see both sides of every question.

[* An herbal laxative.]
[† Unbalanced world of the Shells of the Qabalah.]
[‡ Zelator Adeptus Minor: Golden Dawn term equivalent to A∴A∴ Grade of Adeptus Minor (without). See "One Star in Sight." Adeptus Minor (within) equates to Golden Dawn Grade of Theoricus Adeptus Minor.]

In chess-blindness one used to abjure the game. I never tried to stick it through; I wish I had. Anyhow, I have to stick this through!

O Lord of the Eye, let thine Eye be ever open upon me! For He that watcheth Israel doth not slumber nor sleep!

Lord Shiva, open Thou the Eye upon me, and consume me altogether in its brilliance!

Destroy this Universe! Eat up thine hermit in thy terrible jaws! Dance Thou upon this prostrate saint of Thine!

... I suffer from thirst ... it is a thirst of the body ... yet the thirst of the soul is deeper, and impossible to quench.

Lord Adonai! Let the Powers of Geburah plunge me again and again into the Fires of Pain, so that my steel may be tempered to that Sword of Magic that invoketh Thy Knowledge and Conversation.

Hoor! Elohim Gibor! Kamael! Seraphim! Graphiel! Bartzabel! Madim!* I conjure ye in the Number Five.

By the Flaming Star of my Will! By the Senses of my Body! By the Five Elements of my Being! Rise! Move! Appear! Come ye forth unto me and torture me with your fierce pangs ... for why? because I am the Servant of the Same your God, the True Worshipper of the Highest.

Ol sonuf vaoresaji, gono ladapiel. elonusaha clazod.

I rule above ye, said the Lord of Lords, exalted in power. {From Dr. Dee's MSS. — ED.}

11.17. Will now try the Hanged Man again.

11.30. Very vigorous and good, my willing of Adonai.... I should like to explain the difficulty. It would be easy enough to form a magical Image of Adonai; and He would doubtless inform it. But it would only be an Image. This may be the meaning of the commandment "Thou shalt not make any graven image," etc., just as "Thou shalt not have any other Gods but me" implies single-minded devotion (Ekâgrata) to Adonai. So any mental or magical Image must necessarily fall short of the Truth. Consequently one

[* All these are Names pertaining to the planet Mars and the fifth Sephira Geburah. See Tree of Life diagram p. liv.]

has to will that which is formless; and this is very difficult. To concentrate the mind upon a definite thing is hard enough; yet at least there is something to grasp, and some means of checking one's result. But in this case, the moment one's will takes a magical shape — and the will simply revels in creating shapes — at that moment one knows that one has gone off the track.

This is of course (nearly enough) another way of expressing the Hindu Meditation whose method is to kill all thoughts as they arise in the mind. The difference is that I am aiming at a target, while they are preventing arrows from striking one. In my aspiration to know Adonai, I resemble their Yogis who concentrate on their "personal Lord"; but at the same time it must be remembered that I am not going to be content with what would content them. In other words, I am going to *define* "the Knowledge and Conversation of my holy Guardian Angel" as equal to Neroda-Samapatti, the trance of Nibbana.*

I hope I shall be able to live up to this!

11.55. Have been practising Asana, etc. I forgot one thing in the last entry: I had been reproaching Adonai that for six days I had evoked Him in vain. . . . I got the reply, "The Seventh Day shall be the Sabbath of the Lord thy God."

So mote it be!

THE SEVENTH DAY.

12.17. I began this great day with Eight breath-cycles; was stopped by the indigestion trouble in its other form. (P.S. — Evidently the introduction of the Cascara into my sensitive aura made its action instantaneous.) My breathing passages were none too clear, either; I have evidently taken a chill.

[* *Nirodha Samapatti:* The highest level of Buddhist meditation, the total cessation of all feeling and perception. The technical name of the exalted state of Samadhi achieved by the Buddha under the famous tree in Bodha Gaya. It is the experience of Nirvana while incarnate. (Nibbana, or Nirvana, is the highest goal of the Buddha's teaching, the Liberation from Suffering. The final stage of Nirvana is achieved at death.) Crowley compares *Nirodha Samapatti* to *Shivadarshana* in *Magick Without Tears,* letter 5.]

Now, O my Lord Adonai, thou Self-Glittering One, wilt Thou not manifest unto Thy chosen one? For see me! I am as a little white dove trembling upon Thine altar, its throat stretched out to the knife. I am as a young child bought in the slave-market ... and night is fallen! I await Thee, O my Lord, with a great longing, stronger than Life; yet am I as patient as Death.

There was a certain Darwesh whose turban a thief stole. But when they said to him, "See! he hath taken the road to Damascus!" that holy man answered, as he went quietly to the cemetery, "I will await him here!"

So, therefore, there is one place, O thou thief of my heart's love, Adonai, to which Thou must come at last; and that place is the tomb in which lie buried all my thoughts and emotions, all that which is "I, and Me, and Mine." There will I lay myself and await thee, even as our Father Christian Rosenkreutz that laid himself in the Pastos in the Vault of the Mountain of the Caverns, Abiegnus, on whose portal did he cause to be written the words, "Post Lux Crucis Annos Patebo."* So Thou wilt enter in (as did Frater N.N. and his companions) and open the Pastos; and with thy Winged Globe thou wilt touch the Rosy Cross upon my breast, and I shall wake into life the true life — that is Union with Thee.

So therefore — *perinde ac cadaver*† — I await Thee.

12.43. I wrote, by the way, on some previous day (IV. 12.57 A.M.) that I used the Supreme formula of Awaiting.... Ridiculous mouse! is it not written in the Book of the Heart that is girt about with the Serpent‡ that "To await Thee is the End, not the Beginning?"

It is as silly as rising at midnight, and saying, "I will go out and sleep in the sun."

But I am an Irishman, and if you offer me a donkey-ride at a shilling the first hour and sixpence the second, you must not be surprised at the shrewd silliness of my replying that I will take the second hour first.

[* Slight misquote of G.D. Adeptus Minor ritual — *"Post annos Lux Crucis Patebo"* ("At the end of the years, I, the Light of the Cross, will disclose myself.") *Equinox* I, 3, p. 217. See also *Fama Fraternitatis.* "Post CXX Annos Patebo" ("After 120 years I will open") was engraved on the tomb of Rosenkreutz.]
[† Just like a corpse. (As the Jesuits are supposed to obey.)]
[‡ *Liber LXV,* see *The Holy Books of Thelema.*]

But that is always the way; the love of besting our dearest friends in a bargain is native to us: and so, even in religion, when we are dealing with our own souls, we try to cheat. I go out to cut an almond rod at midnight, and, finding it inconvenient, I "magically affirm" that ash is almond and that seven o'clock is twelve. It seems a pity to have become a magician, capable of forcing Nature to accommodate herself to your statements, for no better use to be made of the power than this!

Miracles are only legitimate when there is no other issue possible. It is waste of power (the most expensive kind of power) to "make the spirits bring us all kinds of food" when we live next door to the Savoy; that Yogi was a fool who spent forty years learning to walk across the Ganges when all his friends did it daily for two pice; and that man does ill when he invokes Tahuti to cure a cold in the head while Mr. Lowe's shop is so handy in Stafford Street.

But miracles may be performed in an extremity; and are.

This brings us round in a circle; the miracle of the Knowledge and Conversation of the Holy Guardian Angel is only to be performed when the Magus has rowed himself completely out; in the language of the Tarot, when the Magus has become the Fool.

But for my faith in the Ritual DCLXXI. I should be at the end of my spells.

Well? We shall see in the upshot.

1.25. I really almost begin to believe IT will happen.

For I lay down quite free of worry or anxiety (hugging myself, as it were), perfectly sure of Him in the simple non-assertive way that a child is sure of its mother, in a state of pleased expectancy, my thoughts quite suppressed in an intent listening, as it were for the noise of the wind of His chariot, as it were for the rustle of His wings.

For lo! through the heaven of Nu He rideth in His chariot soon, soon He will be here!

Into this state of listening come certain curious things formless flittings, I know not what. Also, what I used to call "telephone-cross" voices — voices of strange people saying quite absurd commonplace things — "Here, let's feel it!" "What about lunch?" "So I said to him: Did you ..." and so on; just as if one were overhearing a conversation in a railway carriage. I beheld also

Khephra, the Beetle God, the Glory of Midnight. But let me compose myself again to sleep, as did the child Samuel.

If He should choose to come, He can easily awaken me.

3.35. I have been asleep a good deal — one long dream in which P—t, Lord M—y of B—n and my wife are all staying with me in my mother's house. My room the old room, with one page torn out — for I conceived it as part of a book, somehow! Oh such a lot of this dream! Most of it clearly due to obvious sources — I don't see where Lord M—y comes in. Very likely he is dead. I have had that happen now and again. {P.S. — this was not the case.}

The dream changed, too, to a liner; where Japanese stole my pipe in a series of adventures of an annoying type — every one acted as badly as he knew how, and as unexpectedly.

Waking just now, and instantly concentrating on Adonai, I found my body seized with a little quivering, very curious and pleasant, like

trembling leaves in a continuous air.

I think I have heard this state of Interior Trembling described in some mystic books. I think the Shakers and Quakers had violent shudderings. Abdullah Haji of Shiraz* writes: —

Just as the body shudders when the Soul
Gives up to Allah in its quick career
Itself . . .

It is the tiniest, most intimate trembling, not unlike that of Kambhakham or "Vindu-siddhi" {see the *Shiva Sanhita*. — ED.} properly performed; but of a female quality. I feel as if I were being shaken; in the other cases I recognise my own ardour as the cause. It is very gentle and sweet.

So now I may turn back to wait for Him.

3.50. The Voice of the Nadi has changed to a music faint yet

[* Author of the *Bagh-i-Muattar, The Scented Garden of Abdullah the Satirist of Shiraz* (and pseudonym of Aleister Crowley).]

very full and very sweet, with a bell-like tone more insistent than the other notes at intervals.

5.45. Again awake, and patient-eager. The dreams flow through me ceaselessly.

This time a house where I, like a new Bluebeard, have got to conceal my wives from each other. But my foolish omission to knife them brings it about that I have thirty-nine secret chambers, and only one open one in each case.

Oh, yards of it! And all sorts of people come in to supper — which there isn't any, and we have to do all sorts of shifts — and all the wives think themselves neglected — as they are bound to do, if one is insane enough to have forty — and I loathed them all so! it was terrible having to fly round and comfort and explain; the difficulty increases (I should judge) as about the fifth power of the number of wives ...

I'm glad I'm awake!

Yea, and how glad when I am indeed awake from this glamour life, awake to the love of my Lord Adonai! It is bitter chill at dawn. A consecrating cold it seems to me — yet I will not confront it and rejoice in it — I am already content, having ceased to strive.

7.15. Again awake, deliciously rested and refreshed.

9.45. Again awake, ditto.

11.35. I will now break my fast with a sandwich and coffee, eaten Yogin-wise.

I seem like one convalescent after a fever; very calm, very clean, rather weak, too weak, indeed, to be actually happy: but content.

I spent the morning posing for Michael Brenner, a sculptor who will one day be heard of. Very young yet, but I think the best man of his generation — of those whose work I have seen.

By the way, I am suffering from a swollen finger, since yesterday morning or possibly earlier. I have given it little attention, but it is painful.

I want to explain why I have so carefully recorded the somewhat banal details of all I have eaten and drunk.

1. All food is a species of intoxicant; hence a fruitful source of error. Should I obtain any good result, I might say "You were starved" or "You were drunk." It is very easy to get visions of sorts by either process, and to delude oneself into the idea that one has attained, mistaking the Qliphoth for Kether.

2. In keeping the vow "I will interpret every phenomenon as a particular dealing of God with my soul" the mere animal actions are the most resistant. One cannot see the nature of the phenomenon; it seems so unimportant; one is inclined to despise it. Hence I enter it in the record as a corrective.

3. If others are to read this, I should like them to see that elaborate codes of morality have nothing to do with my system. No question of sin and grace ever enters it.

If a chemist wants to prepare copper sulphate from its oxide, he does not hesitate on the ground that sulphuric acid, thrown in the eyes, hurts people. So I use the moral drug which will produce the desired result, whether that drug be what people commonly call poison or no. In short, I act like a sensible man; and I think I deserve every credit for introducing this completely new idea into religion.

12.25. That function of my brain which says "You ought to be willing Adonai" sometimes acts. But I am willing Him! It is so active because all this week it has been working hard, and doesn't realise that its work is done. Just as a retired grocer wakes up and thinks "I must go and open the shop."

In Hindu phrase, the thought-stuff, painfully forced all these days into one channel, has acquired the habit {*i.e.*, of flowing naturally in it. — ED.} I am Ekâgrata — one-pointed.

Just as if one arranges a siphon, one has to suck and suck for a while, and then when the balance in the two arms of the tube is attained, the fluid goes on softly and silently of its own act. Gravitation which was against us is now for us.

So now the whole destiny of the Universe is by me overcome; I am impelled, with ever-gathering and irresistible force, toward Adonai.

Vi Veri Vniversvm Vivvs Vici!*

12.57. Back home to illuminate my beautiful Ritual.

3.30. Two pages done and set aside to dry. I think I will go for a little walk and enjoy the beautiful sun.
Also to the chemist's to have my finger attended to.

4.05. The chemist refused to do anything; and so I did it myself. It is the romantic malady of ingrowing nail; a little abscess had formed. Devilish painful after the clean-up. Will go the walk aforesaid.

4.17. I ought to note how on this day there is a complete absence of all one's magical apparatus. The mantra has slowed down to (at a guess) a quarter of its old pace. The rest in unison. This is because the feeling of great power, etc. etc., is the mere evidence of conflict — the thunder of the guns. Now all is at peace; the power of the river, no more a torrent.
The Concourse of the Forces has become the Harmony of the Forces; the word Tetragrammaton is spoken and ended; the holy letter Shin is descended into it. For the roaring God of Sinai we have the sleeping Babe of Bethlehem. A fulfilment, not a destroying, of the Law.

4.45. Am at home again. I will lie down in the Position of the Hanged Man, and await the coming of my Lord.

6.00. Arisen again to go out to dinner. I was half-asleep some of the time.

6.15. Dinner — Hors d'Oeuvre — Tripes à la Mode de Caen — Filet de Porc — Glace — 1/2 Graves. Oh, how the world hath inflexible intellectual rulers! I eat it in a semi-Yogin manner.

6.20. I am wondering whether I have not made a mistake in allowing myself to sleep.

[* "By the force of Truth I have conquered the Universe while living." Crowley's motto as Master of the Temple, V.V.V.V.V.]

It would be just like me, if there were only one possible mistake to make, to make it! I was perfect, had I only watched. But I let my faith run away with me.... I wonder.

6.45. Dinner over, I go on as I am in calm faith and love. Why should I expect a catastrophic effect? Why should not the circumstances of Union with God be compatible with the normal consciousness? Interpenetrating and illuminating it, if you like; but not destroying it. Well, I don't know why it shouldn't be; but I bet it isn't! All the spiritual experience I have had argues against such a theory.

On the contrary, it will leave the reason quite intact, supreme Lord of its own plane. Mixing up the planes is the sad fate of many a mystic. How many do I know in my own experience who tell me that, obedient to the Heavenly Vision, they will shoot no more rabbits! Thus they found a system on trifles, and their Lord and God is some trumpery little elemental masquerading as the Almighty.

I remember my Uncle Tom telling me that he was sure God would be displeased to see me in a blue coat on Sunday. And today he is surprised and grieved that I do not worship his God — or even my own tailor, as would be surely more reasonable!

7.32. How is it that I expect the reward at once? Surely I am presuming on my magical power, which is an active thing, and therefore my passivity is not perfect. Of course, when IT happens, it happens out of time and space — now or ten years hence it is all the same. All the same to IT; not all the same to me, O.M. So O.M. (the dog!) persists irrationally in wanting IT, here and now. Surely, indeed, it is a lack of faith, a pandering to the time-illusion ... and so forth. Yes, no doubt it is all magically wrong, even magically absurd; yet, though I see the snare, I deliberately walk into it. I suppose I shall be punished somehow ... Good! there's the excuse I wanted. Fear is failure: I must dare to do wrong. Good!

7.50. It has just occurred to me that this Waiting and Watching is the supreme Magical strain. Every slight sound or other impression shocks one tremendously. It is easy enough to shut out sounds and such when one is concentrating in active magic: I did all my early evocations in Chancery Lane. But now one is deliberately opening all the avenues of sense to admit Adonai! One has destroyed one's own Magic Circle. The whole of that great Building is thrown down.... Therefore I am in a worse hole than I ever was before — and I've only just realised it. A footfall on the pavement is most acute agony — because it is not Adonai. My hearing, normally rather dull, is intensely sharpened; and I am thirty yards from the electric trams of the Boulevard Montparnasse at the busiest hour of the evening ...

And the Visconti may turn up! ...

Eli, Eli, lama sabacthani!*

8.45. I went out to the Dôme to drink my final citron pressé and to avoid the Visconti. Am returned, and in bed. I shall try and sleep now, waking in time for midnight and the quiet hours.

8.53. I have endured the supreme temptation and assault of the Enemy. In this wise. First, I found that I did not want sleep — I couldn't stop "Waiting." Next, I said "Since last night that Black Ritual (see entry 10.55) did at least serve to turn all my thoughts to the One Thought, I will try it again ..."

Then I said: "No; to do so is not pure 'waiting.' And then — as by a flash of lightning — the Abyss of the Pit opened, and my whole position was turned. I saw my life from the dawn of consciousness till now as a gigantic "pose"; my very love of truth assumed for the benefit of my biographer! All these strange things suffered and enjoyed for no better purpose than to seem a great man. One cannot express the horror of this thought; it is The thought that murders the soul — and there is no answer to it. So universal is it that it is impossible to prove the contrary. So one must play the man, and master it and kill it utterly, burying it in that putrid hell from which it sprang. Luckily I have dealt with it before. Once when I lived at Paddington J—s and F—r were with me talking, and, when they went, thoughtfully left this devil-thought behind — the agony is with me yet. That, though, was only a young mild devil, though of the same bad brood. It said: "Is there any Path or Attainment? Have you been fooled all along?"

But to-night's thought struck at my own integrity, at the inmost truth of the soul and of Adonai.

[* "My God, My God, Why hast thou forsaken me?" (The cry uttered by Jesus Christ during the Crucifixion).]

As I said, there is no answer to it; and as these seven days have left me fairly master of the fortress, I caught him young, and assigned him promptly to the oubliette.

I put down this — not as a "pose" — but because the business is so gigantic. It encourages me immensely; for if my Dweller on the Threshold be that most formidable devil, how vast must be the Pylon that shelters him, and how glorious must be the Temple just beyond!

9.30. It seems that there was one more mistake to make; for I've made it!

I started to attempt to awaken the Kundalini — the magical serpent that sleeps at the base of the spine; coiled in three coils and a half around the Sushumna; and instead of pumping the Prana up and down the Sushumna until Siva was united with Sakti in the Sahasrara-Cakkrâm,* I tried — God knows why; I'm stupider than an ass or H ... C ... — to work the whole operation in Mula-dhara — with the obvious result.

There are only two more idiocies to perform — one, to take a big dose of Hashish and record the ravings as if they were Samadhi; and two, to go to church. I may as well give up.

Yet here answers me the everlasting Yea and Amen: Thou canst not give up, for I will bring thee through. Yet here I lie, stripped of all magic force, doubting my own peace and faith, far-ther from Adonai than ever before and yet — and yet —

Do I not know that every error is a necessary step in the Path? The longest way round is the shortest way home. But it is disgust-ing! There's a grim humour in it, too. The real Devil of the Opera-tion must be sitting with sardonic grin upon his face, enjoying my perplexity —

For that Dweller-of-the-Threshold-thought was not as dead as I supposed; as I write he comes again and again, urging me to quit the Path, to abandon the unequal contest. Luckily, friend Dweller, you prove too much! Your anxiety shows me that I am not as far from attainment as my own feelings would have me think.

At least, though, I am thrown into the active again; I shall rise and chant the Enochian Calls and invoke the Bornless One, and clear a few of the devils away, and get an army of mighty angels

[* Nerve center of Kundalini located at the crown of the head.]

around me — in short, make another kind of fool of myself, I wonder?

Anyway, I'll do it. Not a bad idea to ask Thoth to send me Taphtatharath with a little information as to the route — I do not know where I am at all. This is a strange country, and I am very lonely.

This shall be my ritual.

1. Banishing Pentagram Ritual.
2. Invoking ditto. {These will appear in No. 2, *Liber O.* — ED.}*
3. "The Bornless One." {See the *Goetia.* — ED.}
4. The Calls I–VI with the Rituals of the five Grades. {From Dr. Dee's and the G∴D∴ MSS. — ED.}
5. Invocation of Thoth.
6. (No: I will *not* use the New Ritual, nor will I discuss the matter.) An impromptu invocation of Adonai.
7. Closing formulae.

To work, then!

11.15. The ceremony went well enough; the forces invoked came readily and visibly; Thoth in particular as friendly as ever — I fancy He takes this record as a compliment to Him — He's welcome to it, poor God!

The L.V.X. came, too; but not enough to pierce the awful shroud of darkness that by my folly I have woven for myself.

So at the end I found myself on the floor, so like Rodin's Cruche Cassée Danaide girl as never was ... As I ought to have been in the beginning! Well, one thing I got (again!), that is, that when all is said and done, I am that I am, and all these thoughts of mine, angels and devils both, are only fleeting moods of me. The one true self of me is Adonai. Simple! Yet I cannot remain in that simplicity.

I got this "revelation" through the Egyptian plane, a partial illumination of the reason. It has cleared up the mind; but alas! the mind is still there. This is the strength and weakness both of the Egyptian plane, that it is so lucid and spiritual and yet so practical.

[* See also appendix 3 this book.]

When I say weakness, I mean that it appeals to my weakness; I am easily content with the smaller results, so that they seduce me from going on to the really big ones. I am quite happy as a result of my little ceremony — whereas I ought to be taking new and terrible oaths! Yet why should Tahuti be so kind to me, and Asar Un-nefer so unkind?

The answer comes direct from Tahuti himself: Because you have learned to write perfectly, but have not yet taught yourself to suffer.

True enough, the last part!

Asar Un-nefer, thou perfected One, teach me Thy mysteries! Let my members be torn by Set and devoured by Sebek and Typhon! Let my blood be poured out upon Nile, and my flesh be given to Besz to devour! Let my Phallus be concealed in the maw of Mati, and my Crown be divided among my brethren! Let the jaws of Apep grind me into poison! Let the sea of poison swallow me wholly up!

Let Asi my mother rend her robes in anguish, and Nepti weep for me unavailing.

Then shall Asi bring forth Hoor, and Heru-pa-kraat shall leap glad from her womb. The Lord of Vengeance shall awaken; Sekhet shall roar, and Pasht cry aloud. Then shall my members be gathered together, and my bonds shall be unloosed; and my khu shall be mighty in Khem for ever and ever!

11.37. I return to the place of the Evil Triad, of Ommo Satan, that is before the altar. There to expiate my folly in attaching myself to all this great concourse of ideas that I have here recorded, instead of remaining fixed in the single stronghold of Unity with Myself.

11.54. And so this great day draws to its end.

These are indeed the Qliphoth, the Qliphoth of Kether, the Thaumiel, twin giant heads that hate and tear each other.

For the horror and darkness have been unbelievable; yet again, the light and brilliance have been almost insupportable.

I was never so far, and never so near ... But the hour approaches. Let me collect myself, and begin the new day in affirmation of my Unity with my Lord Adonai!

The Eighth Day

12.3. Thus the Eighth day, the Second Week, begins. I am in Asana.
For some reason or other, Pranayama is quite easy. Concentrating
on Adonai, I was in Kambhakham for a whole minute without
distress.

It *is* true, by the way. I was — and am — in some danger of
looking on this Record as a Book; *i.e.,* of emphasising things for
their literary effect, and diminishing the importance of others
which lend themselves less obviously.

But the answer to this, friend Satan! is that the Canon of Art
is Truth, and the Canon of Magic is Truth; my true record will
make a good book, and my true book will make a good record.

*Ekam evam advaitam!** friend Satan! One and not two. *Hua
allahu alazi lailaha illa Hua!*†

But what shall be my "consideration" for this week? I am so
absolutely become as a pantomorphous Iynx‡ that all things look
alike to me; there are just as many pros and cons to Pranayama as
to Ceremonial, etc. etc., — and the pros and cons are so numerous
and far-reaching that I simply dare not start discussing even one. I
can see an endless avenue in every case. In short, like the hashish-
drunkard in full blast, I am overwhelmed by the multitude of my
own magical Images. I have become the great Magician — Mayan,
the Maker of Illusion — the Lord of the Brethren of the Left-hand
Path.

I don't "wear my iniquity as an aureole, deathless in Spiritual
Evil," as Mr. Waite thinks; but it's nearly as bad as that. There
seems only one reply to this great question of the Hunchback (I
like to symbolise the spirit of Questioning by "?"— a little crooked
thing that asks questions) and that is to keep on affirming Adonai,
and refusing to be obsessed by any images of discipline or magic.

Of course! but this is just the difficulty — as it was in the
Beginning, is now, and ever shall be, world without end! My beautiful answer to the question, How will you become a millionaire?

[* He is the One without a second.]
[† He is God, and there is no other God than He.]
[‡ Daughter of Pan, she was a nymph who caused Zeus to fall in love with Io,
angering Hera, who turned her into a wryneck bird.]

is: I will possess a million pounds. The "answer" is not an answer; it is a begging of the question.

What a fool I am! and people think me clever. *Ergo,** perhaps!

Anyhow I will now (12.37) go quietly to sleep — as I am always saying, and never do when I say it! — in the hope that daylight may bring counsel.

7.40. Woke fresh and comfortable. Sleep filled with dreams and broken into short lengths. I ought to observe that this is a very striking result of forging this magic chain; for in my normal life I am one of the soundest sleepers imaginable. Nine solid hours without turning once is my irreducible minimum.

9.10. Having done an hour's illumination of the New Ritual, will go and break my fast with coffee and a brioche, and thence proceed to Michael Brenner's studio.

12.15. I have spent the morning in modelling Siddhasana† — a more difficult task than appeared. Rather like THE task!

But I went on with the mantra, and made some Reflections upon Kamma.

I will now have a Yogin coffee and sandwich, and return to my illumination of the Ritual.

In the desert of my soul, where no herb grows, there is yet one little spring. I am still one-pointed, at least in the lower sense that I have no desire or ambition but this of accomplishing the Great Work.

Barren is this soul of mine, in these 3½ years of drought (the 3½ coils of the Kundalini are implied by this) and this Ekâgrata is the little cloud like an hand (Yod, the Lingam of the great Shiva). And, though I catch up my robe and run before the chariot of the King into Jezreel,‡ it may be that before I reach those gates the whole sky may be one black flame of thundercloud, and the violet

[* Therefore.]
[† Yoga posture: sitting erect with legs crossed, feet over heels (rather than over thighs as in the full-lotus posture, or padmasana).]
[‡ Reference is to the incident between Elijah and Ahab as described in I Kings 18:46.]

swords of the lightning may split asunder its heavy womb, and the rain, laughing like a young child, may dance upon the desert!

12.58. The Light beginneth to dawn upon the Path, so that I see a little better where I stand. This whole journey seems under some other formula than IAO — perhaps a Pentagram formula with which I am not clearly acquainted. If I knew the Word of the Grade, I could foretell things: but I don't.

I think I will read through the whole Record to date and see if I can find an Ariadne-clue.

1.15. Back, and settled to Ritual-painting.

2.30. Finished: bar frontispiece and colophon, which I can design and execute to-morrow.

3.0 Took half an hour off, making a silly sketch of a sunset. Will now read through the Record, and Reflect upon it.

4.15. "Before I was blind; now I see!" Yesterday I was right up to the Threshold, right enough; but got turned back by the Dweller. I did not see the Dweller till afterwards (8.53 entry) for he was too subtle. I will look carefully back to try and spot him; for if I "knew his Name" I could pass by — *i.e.*, next time I climb up to the Threshold of the Pylon.

I think entries 1.25 and 3.35 A.M. explain it. "HUGGING MYSELF, AS IT WERE." How fatally accurate! I wrote it and never saw the hellish snare! I ought to have risen up and prepared myself ceremonially as a bride, and waited in the proper magical manner. Also I was too pleased with the Heralds of my Lord's coming — the vision of Khephra, etc. It was perhaps this subtle self-satisfaction that lost me . . . so I fell to the shocking abyss of last night!

The Dweller of the Threshold is never visible until after one has fallen; he is a Veiled God and smites like the Evil Knight in Malory, riding and slaying — and no man seeth him.

But when you are tumbled headlong into Hell, where he lives, then he unveils his Face, and blasts you with its horror!

Very good, John St. John, now you know! You are plain John St. John, and you have to climb right up again through the paths to the Threshold; and remember this time to mortify that self-satisfaction! Go at it more reverently and humbly — oh, you dog, how I loathe you for your Vileness! To have risen so high, and — now — to be thus fallen!

4.40. The question arises: how to mortify this self-satisfaction?

Asceticism notoriously fosters egoism; how good am I to go without dinner! How noble! What renunciation!

On the other hand, the good wine in one says: "A fine fellow I have made my coffin of!"

The answer is simple, the old answer: *Think not of St. John and his foolishness; think of Adonai!* Exactly: the one difficulty!

My best way out will be to concentrate on the New Ritual, learn it perfectly by heart, work it at the right moment....

I will go, with this idea, to have a Citron pressé; thence to my Secret Restaurant, and dine, always learning the Ritual.

I will leave off the mantra, though it is nearly as much part of me as my head by now; and instead repeat over and over again the words of the Ritual so that I can do it in the end with perfect fluency and comprehension. And this time may Adonai build the House!

6.10. Instead I met Dr. R—, who kindly offered to teach me how to obtain astral visions! (P.S. — The tone of this entry wrongs me. I sat patiently and reverently, like a *chela* with his *guru,* hoping to hear the Word I needed.) Thence I went my long and lonely walk to my Secret Restaurant, learning the Ritual as I went.

7.15. Arrived at the Secret Restaurant. Ordered 6 oysters, Râble de Lièvre poivrade purée de marrons, and Glace *Casserole* with a small bottle of Perrier Water.

I know the New Ritual down to the end of the Confession.

It was hard to stop the mantra — the moment my thought wandered, up it popped!

8.3. I shall add Café Cognac Cigare to this debauch.

I continue learning the Ritual.

8.40. I will return and humble myself before the Lord Adonai. It is near the night of the Full Moon; in my life the Full Moon hath ever been of great augury. But to-night I am too poor in spirit to hope.

Lo! I was travelling on the paths of Lamed and of Mem, of Justice and the Hanged Man, and I fell into both the pitfalls thereof. Instead of the Great Balance firmly held, I found only Libra, the house of Venus and of the exaltation of Saturn; and these evil planets, smiling and frowning, overcame me. And so for the sublime Path of Mem; instead of that symbol of the Adept, his foot set firmly upon heaven, his whole figure showing forth the Reconciler with the Invisible, I found but the stagnant and bitter water of selfishness, the Dead Sea of the Soul. For all is Illusion. Who saith "I" denieth Adonai, save only if he mean Adonai. And Daleth the Door of the Pylon, is that Tree whereon the Adept of Man hangeth; and Daleth is Love Supernal, that if it be inserted in the word *ANI*, "I," giveth *ADNI*, Adonai.

Subtle art thou and deadly, O Dweller of the Threshold (P.S. — This name is a bad one. *Dweller beside the Pylon* is a better term; for he is not in the straight path, which is simple and easy and open. He is never "overcome"; to meet him is the proof of having strayed. The Key fits the Door perfectly; but he who is drunken on the bad wine of Sense and Thought fumbles thereat. And of course there is a great deal of door, and very little key-hole), who dost use my very love of Adonai to destroy me!

Yet how shall I approach Him, if not with reverent joy, with a delicious awe? I must wash His feet with my tears; I must die at His gateway; I must ... I know not what ...

Adonai, be Thou tender unto me Thy slave, and keep my footsteps in the Way of Truth! ... I will return and humble myself before the Lord Adonai.

10.18. Home again; have done odd necessary things, and am ready to work. I feel slack; and I feel that I have been slack, though probably the Record shows a fair amount of work done. But I am terribly bruised by the Great Fall; these big things leave the body and mind no worse, apparently; but they hurt the Self, and later that is reflected into the lower parts of the man as insanity or death.

I must attain, or ... an end of John St. John.

An end of him, one way or the other, then!

Good-bye, John!

10.30. Ten minutes wasted in sheer mooning! I'm getting worse every minute.

10.40. Fooled away ten minutes more!

10.57. Humiliation enough! For though I made the cross with Blood and Flame, I cannot even remain concentrated in humiliation, which yet I feel so acutely. What a wormy worm I am! I tried the new strict Siddhasana, only to find that I had hurt myself so this morning with it that I cannot bear it at all, even with the pillow to support the instep.

I will just try and do a little Pranayama, to see if I can stay doing any one simple thing for ten minutes at a stretch!

11.30. Twenty-five Breath-Cycles ... But it nearly killed me. I was saying over the Ritual, and did so want to get to the Formulation of the Hexagram at least, if not to the Reception. As it was, I broke down during the Passage of the Pylons, luckily not till I had reached that of Tahuti.

But it is a good rule; when in doubt play Pranayama. For one can no longer worry about the Path: the Question is reduced to the simple problem: Am I, or am I not, going to burst?

I got all the sweating and trembling of the body that heart could desire; but no "jumping about like a frog" or levitation. A pity!

11.45. I shall read for a little in the Yoga-Shastra* as a rest. Then for the end of the day and the Beginning of the Ninth Day. Zoroaster (or Pythagoras?) informs us that the number Nine is sacred, and attains the summit of Philosophy. I'm sure I hope so!

11.56. I get into Asana ... and so endeth the Eighth Lesson.

[* Probabaly refers to the *Yoga Sutras of Patanjali*. Known as the Father of Yoga, Patanjali lived in India ca. 300 B.C.]

The Ninth Day

12.2. Thus I began this great day, being in my Asana firm and easy, and holding in my breath for a full minute while I threw my will with all my might towards Adonai.

12.19. Have settled myself for the night. Will continue a little, learning the Ritual.

12.37. Having learnt a few passages of a suitable nature to go to sleep upon, I will do so.
... Now I hope that I shall; surely the Reaction of Nature against the Magical Will must be wearing down at last!

2.12. I wake. It takes me a little while to shake off the dominion of sleep, very intense and bitter.

3.4. Thus John St. John — for it is not convenient further to speak as "I" — performed 45 Breath-cycles; for 20 minutes he had to struggle against the Root of the Powers of Sleep, and the obstruction of his left nostril.
During his Kambhakham he willed Adonai with all his might.
Let him sleep, invoking Adonai!

5.40. Well hath he slept, and well awakened.
The last entry should extend to 3.30 or thereabouts; probably later; for, invoking Adonai, he again got the beginnings of the Light, and the "telephone-cross" voices very strongly. But this time he was fortunately able to concentrate on Adonai with some fervour, and these things ceased to trouble. But the Perfume and the Vision came not, nor any full manifestation of the L.V.X., the Secret Light, the light that shineth in darkness.
John St. John is again very sleepy. He will try and concentrate on Adonai without doing Pranayama — much harder of course. It is a supreme effort to keep both eyes open together.
He must do his best. He does not wish to wake too thoroughly, either, lest afterward he oversleep himself, and miss his appointment with Michael Brenner to continue moulding Siddhasana.

7.45. Again I awake ... {O swine! thou hast felt in thyself "Good! Good! the night is broken up nicely; all goes very well" — and thou hast written "I!" O swine, John St. John! When wilt thou learn that the least stirring of thy smug content is the great Fall from the Path?}

It will be best to get up and do some kind of work; for the beast would sleep.

8.25. John St. John has arisen, after doing 20 breath-cycles, reciting internally the ritual, 70 per cent. of which he now knows by heart.

8.35. To the Dôme — a café-croissant. Some proofs to correct during the meal.

10.25. Having walked over to the studio reciting the Ritual (9.25–9.55 approximately), John St. John got into his pose, and began going for the gloves. The Interior Trembling began, and the room filled with the Subtle Light. He was within an ace of Concentration; the Violet Lotus of Ajna* appeared, flashing like some marvellous comet; the Dawn began to break, as he slew with the Lightning-Flash every thought that arose in him, especially this Vision of Ajna; but fear — dread fear! — gripped his heart. Annihilation stood before him, annihilation of John St. John that he had so long striven to obtain: yet he dared not. He had the loaded pistol to his head; he could not pull the trigger. This must have gone on for some time; his agony of failure was awful; for he knew that he was failing; but though he cried a thousand times unto Adonai with the Voice of Death, he could not — he could not. Again and again he stood at the gate, and could not enter. And the Violet Flames of Ajna triumphed over him.

Then Brenner said: "Let us take a little rest!" — oh irony! and he came down from his throne, staggering with fatigue....

If you can conceive of all his anger and despair! His pen, writing this, forms a letter badly, and through clenched teeth he utters a fierce curse.

Oh Lord Adonai, look with favour upon him!

[* Nerve center of Kundalini located above and between the eyes, the "Third Eye."]

11.30. After five minutes rest (to the body, that is), John St. John was too exhausted on resuming his pose, which, by the way, happens to be the Sign of the Grade 7°=4□, to strive consciously.

But his nature itself, forced through these days into the one channel of Will towards Adonai, went on struggling on its own account. Later, the conscious man took heart and strove, though not so fiercely as before. He passed through the Lightnings of Ajna, whose two petals now spread out like wings above his head, and the awful Corona of the Interior Sun with its flashing fires appeared, and declared itself to be his Self. This he rejected; and the Formless Ocean of White Brilliance absorbed him, overcame him; for he could not pass therethrough. This went on repeating itself, the man transformed (as it were) into a mighty Battering Ram hurling itself again and again against the Walls of the City of God to breach them. — And as yet he has failed. Failed. Failed. Physical and mental exhaustion are fairly complete.

Adonai, look with favour upon Thy slave!

12.20. He has walked, reciting the Ritual, to Dr. R— and H— for lunch. They have forgotten the appointment, so he continues and reaches Lavenue's at 12.4 after reading his letters and doing one or two necessary things. He orders Epinards, Tarte aux Fraises, Glace au Café and ½ Evian. The distaste for food is great; and for meat amounts to loathing. The weather is exceedingly hot; it may be arranged thus by Adonai to enable John St. John to meditate in comfort. For he is vowed solemnly "to interpret every phenomenon as a particular dealing of God with his soul."

12.50. During lunch he will go on correcting his proofs.

1.35. Lunch over, and the proofs read through.

1.45. He will make a few decorations further in his Ritual, and perhaps design the Frontispiece and Colophon. He is very weary, and may sleep.

2.25. He has done the illumination, as far as may be. He will now lie down as Hanged Man, and invoke Adonai.

4.45. He was too tired to reach nearer than the neighbourhood of that tremendous Threshold; wherefore he fell from meditation into sleep, and there his Lord gave him sweet rest thereof.

He will arise, and take a drink — a citron pressé — at the Dôme; for the day is yet exceeding hot, and he has had little.

4.53. One ought to remark that all this sleep is full of extravagant dreams; rarely irrational and never (of course) unpleasant, or one would be up and working with a circle every night. But O.M. thinks that they show an excited and unbalanced condition of John St. John's brain, though he is almost too cowed to express an opinion at all, even were the question, Is grass green?

Every small snatch of sleep, without exception, in the last three or four days, has these images.

The ideal condition seems likely to be perfect oblivion — or (in the Adept) is the Tamo-Guna, the Power of Elemental Darkness, broken once and for ever, so that His sleep is vivid and rational as another man's waking; His waking another man's Samadhi; His Samadhi — to which He ever strives —?????

At least this latter view is suggested by the Rosicrucian formula of Reception:

> May thy mind be open unto the Higher!
> May thy heart be the Centre of Light!
> May thy body be the Temple of the Rosy Cross!

and by the Hindu statement that in the attained Yogin the Kundalini sleeps in the Svadistthana,* no more in the Muladhara Cakkrâm.

See also the Rosicrucian lecture on the Microcosmos, where this view is certainly upheld, the Qliphoth of an Adept being balanced and trained to fill his Malkuth, vacated by the purified Nephesch† which has gone up to live in Tiphereth.‡

Or so O.M. read it.

The other idea of the Light descending and filling each principle with its glory is, it seems to him, less fertile, and less in accord with any idea of Evolution.

[* Nerve center of Kundalini located near the navel.]
[† Animal or emotional soul of man in the Qabalah.]
[‡ Beauty, central Sephira on Tree of Life, see illustration p. liv.]

(What would Judas McCabbage think?)

And one can so readily understand how tremendous a task is that of the postulant, since he has to glorify and initiate all his principles and train them to their new and superior tasks. This surely explains better the terrible dangers of the path....

Some years back, on the Red River in China, John St. John saw at every corner of that swift and dangerous stream a heap of wreckage.

... He, himself in danger, thought of his magical career. Alcoholism, insanity, disease, faddism, death, knavery, prison — every earthly hell, reflection of some spiritual blunder, had seized his companions. By dozens had that band been swept away, dashed to pieces on one rock or another. He, alone almost upon that angry stream, still held on, his life each moment the play-thing of giant forces, so enormous as to be (once they were loose) quite out of proportion to all human wit or courage or address — and he held on his course, humbly, not hopelessly, not fearfully, but with an abiding certainty that he would endure unto the end.

And now?

In this great Magical Retirement he has struck many rocks, sprung many leaks; the waters of the False Sea foam over the bow, ride and carry the quarter — is he perchance already wrecked, his hopeless plight concealed from him as yet by his own darkness? For, dazzled as he is by the blinding brilliance of the morning's Spiritual Sun, which yet he beheld but darkly, to him now even the light of earth seems dark. Reason the rudder was long since unshipped; the power of his personality has broken down, yet under the tiny storm-sail of his Will to Adonai, the crazy bark holds way, steered by the oar of Discipline — Yea, he holds his course. Adonai! Adonai! is not the harbour yet in sight?

6.7. He has returned home and burnt (as every night since its arrival) the holy incense of Abramelin the Mage. The atmosphere is full of vitality, sweetened and strengthened; the soul naturally and simply turns to the holy task with vigour and confidence; the black demons of doubt and despair flee away; one respires already a foretaste of the Perfume, and obtains almost a premonition of the Vision.

So, let the work go on.

6.23. 7 Breath-cycles, rather difficult. Clothes are a nuisance, and make all the difference.

6.31. John St. John is more broken up by this morning's failure than he was ready to admit. But the fact stands; he cannot concentrate his mind for three seconds together. How utterly hopeless it makes one feel! One thinks one is at least always good for a fair average performance — and one is undeceived.

This, by the way, is the supreme use of a record like this. It makes it impossible to cheat oneself.

Well, he has got to get up more steam somehow, though the boiler burst. Perhaps early dinner, with Ritual, may induce that Enthusiastic Energy of which the Gnostics write.

This morning the whole Sankhara-dhatu (the tendency of the being John St. John) was operating aright. Now by no effort of will can he flog his tired cattle along the trail.

So poor a thing is he that he will even seek an Oracle from the book of Zoroaster.

Done. Zoroaster respectfully wishes to point out that "The most mystic of discourses informs us — His wholeness is in the Supra-Mundane Order; for there a Solar World and Boundless Light subsist, as the Oracles of the Chaldeans affirm."

Not very helpful, is it?

As if divination could ever help on such exalted planes! As if the trumpery elementals that operate these things possessed the Secrets of the Destiny of an Adept, or could help him in his agony!

For this reason, divination should be discarded from the start: it is only a "mere toy, the basis of mercenary fraud" as Zoroaster more practically assures us.

Yet one can get the right stuff out of the Tarot (or other inconvenient method) by spiritualising away all the meaning, until the intuition pierces that blank wall of ignorance.

Let O.M. meditate upon this Oracle on his way to feed John St. John's body — and thus feed his own!

6.52. Out, out, to feed!

6.57. Trimming his beard in preparation for going out, he reflects that the deplorable tone (as one's Dean would say) of that last entry is not the cry of the famished beast, but that of the over-driven slave.

"Adonai, ply Thou thy scourge! Adonai, load Thou the chain!"

7.25. What the devil is the matter with the time? The hours flit just like butterflies — the moon, dead full, shines down the Boulevard. My moon — full moon of my desire! (Ha, ha, thou beast! are "I and Me and Mine" not dead yet?

Yea, Lord Adonai! but the full moon means much to John St. John; he fears (*fears*, O Lord of the Western Pylon!) lest, if once that full moon pass, he may not win through ...

"The harvest is over, the summer is ended, and we are not saved!"

Yet hath not Abramelin lashed the folly of limiting the spiritual paths by the motions of the planets? And Zoroaster, in that same oracle just quoted?

7.35. Hors d'Œuvres, Bouillabaisse, contrefilet rôti, Glace. 1/2 Graves.

The truth is that the Chittam is excited and racing, the control being impaired; and the Ego is springing up again.

7.50. This racing of the Chittam is simply shocking. John St. John must stop it somehow. Hours and hours seem to have passed since the last entry.

7.57. !!! He is in such a deuce of a hurry that (in a lucid moment) he finds himself trying to eat bread, radish, beef and potato at a mouthful.

Worse, the beast is pleased and excited at the novelty of the sensation, and takes delight in recording it. Beast! Beast!

8.3. !!!! After myriads of aeons. He has drunk only about one third of his half-bottle of light white wine; yet he's like a hashish-drunkard, only more so. The loss of the time-sense which occurs with hashish he got during his experiments with that drug in 1906, but in an unimportant way. (Damn him! he is so glad. He calls this a Result. A result! Damn him!) O.M. who writes this is so angry

with him that he wants to scrawl the page over with the most fear-
ful curses! and John St. John has nearly thrown a bottle at the
waiter for not bringing the next course. He will not be allowed to
finish his wine! He orders cold water.

8.12. Things a little better. But he tries 100 small muscular
movements, pressing on the table with his fingers in tune, and finds
the tendency to hurry almost irresistible. This record is here written at lightning speed.... Attempt to write slowly is painful.

8.20. The thought too, is wandering all over the world. Since
the last entry, very likely, the beast has not thought even once of
Adonai.

8.35. The Reading of the Ritual has done much service,
though things are still far from calm. Yet the mighty flood of the
Chittam is again rolling its tremendous tide toward the sea — the
Sea of annihilation. Amen.

9.0. Returning home, with his eyes fixed on the supreme glory
of the Moon, in his heart and brain invoking Adonai, he hath now
entered into his little chamber, and will prepare all things for the
due performance of the New Ritual which he hath got by heart.

9.35. Nearly ready. In a state of very intense magical strain —
anything might happen.

9.48. Washed, robed, temple in order. Will wait until 10
o'clock and begin upon the stroke. O.M. 7°=4$^\square$ will begin; and
then solemnly renounce all his robes, weapons, dignities, etc.,
renouncing his grades even by giving the Signs of them backwards
and downwards toward the outer. He will keep only one thing, the
Secret Ring that hath been committed unto him by the Masters; for
from that he cannot part, even if he would. That is his Password
into the Ritual itself; and on his finger it shall be put at the moment
when all else is gone.

11.5. Ceremony works admirably. Magical Images strong. At
Reception behold! the Sigil of the Supreme Order itself in a blaze

of glory not to be spoken of. And the half-seen symbol of my Lord Adonai therewith as a mighty angel glittering with infinite light.

According to the Ritual, O. M. withdrew himself from the Vision; the Vision of the Universe, a whirling abyss of coruscating suns in all the colours, yet informed and dominated by that supernal brilliance. Yet O.M. refused the Vision; and a conflict began and was waged through many ages — so it seemed. And now all the enemies of O.M. banded themselves against him. The petty affairs of the day; even the irritations of his body, the emotions of him, the plans of him, worry about the Record and the Ritual and — O! everything! — then, too, the thoughts which are closer yet to the great Enemy, the sense of separateness; that sense itself at last — so O.M. withdrew from the conflict for a moment so that the duty of this Record done might leave him free for the fight.

It may have been a snare — may the Lord Adonai keep him in the Path.

Adonai! Adonai!

(P.S. — Add that the "ultra-violet" or "astral light" in the room was such that it seemed bright as daylight. He hath never seen the like, even in the ceremony which he performed in the Great Pyramid of Gizeh.)

11.14–11.34. O. M. then passed from vision unto vision of unexampled splendour. The infinite abyss of space, a rayless orb of liquid and colourless brilliance fading beyond the edges into a flame of white and gold.... The Rosy Cross flashing with lustre ineffable.... and more, much more which ten scribes could hardly catalogue in a century.

The Vision of the Holy Guardian Angel itself; yet was He seen as from afar, not intimately....

Therefore is O.M. not content with all this wonder; but will now orderly close the temple, that at the Beginning of the Tenth Day — and Ten are the Holy Sephiroth, the Emanations of the Crown; Blessed be He! ... He may make new considerations of this Operation whereby he may discover through what error he is thus betrayed again and again into failure. Failure. Failure.

11.49. The Temple is closed.

Now then, O Lord Adonai! Let the Tenth Day be favourable unto O. M. For in the struggle he is as nothing worth. Nor valiant, nor fortunate, nor skilful — except Thou fight by his side, cover his breast with Thy shield, second his blows with Thy spear and with Thy sword.

Aye! let the Ninth Day close in silence and in darkness, and let O. M. be found watching and waiting and willing Thy Presence.

Adonai! Adonai! O Lord Adonai! Let Thy Light illumine the Path of that darkling wight John St. John, that being who, separate from Thee, is separate from all

Light, Life, Love.

Adonai! Adonai! let it be written of O.M. that "the Lord Adonai is about him like a thunderbolt and like a Pylon and like a Serpent and like a Phallus — and in the midst thereof like the Woman that jetteth the Milk of the Stars from Her paps; yea, the Milk of the Stars from Her paps."*

THE TENTH DAY

12.17. Now that the perfume of the incense is clearly away, one may most potently perceive the Invoked Perfume of the Ceremony Itself. And this mystical perfume of Adonai is like pure Musk, but infinitely subtilised — far stronger, and at the same time far more delicate. (P.S. — Doubt has arisen about this perfume, as to whether there was not a commonplace cause. On the balance of the evidence, carefully considered, one would pronounce for the mystic theory.)

One should add a curious omen. On sitting down for the great struggle (11.14) John St. John found a nail upon the floor, at his feet. Now a nail is Vau in Hebrew, and the Tarot Trump corresponding to Vau is the Hierophant or Initiator — whereby is O. M. greatly comforted.

So poor a thing hath he become!

Even as a little child groping feebly for the breast of its mother, so gropeth Thy little child after Thee, O Thou Self-Glittering One!

12.55. He hath read through Days VIII. and IX.

[* *Liber LXV*, V: 65.]

... He is too tired to understand what he reads. He will, despite of all, do a little Pranayama, and then sleep, ever willing Adonai.

For Pranayama with its intense physical strain is a great medicine for the mind. Even as the long trail of the desert and the life with the winds and the stars, the daily march and its strife with heat, thirst, fatigue, cure all the ills of the soul, so does Pranayama clear away the phantoms that Mayan, dread maker of Illusion, hath cumbered it withal.

1.13. 10 Breath-Cycles; calm, perfect, without the least effort; enough to go to sleep upon.

He will read through the Ritual once, and then sleep. (The Pranayama precipitated a short attack of diarrhea, started by the chill of the Ceremony.)

6.23. He slept from 1.45. (approximately) till now. The morn is cold and damp; rain has fallen.

John St. John is horribly tired; the "control" is worn to a thread. He takes five minutes to make up his mind to go through with it, five more to wash and write this up. And he has a million excuses for not doing Pranayama.

6.51. 15 Breath-cycles, steady and easy enough. The brain is cool and lucid; but no energy is in it. At least no Sammávayamo.* And at present the Superscription on John St. John's Cross is

FAILURE.

Marvellous and manifold as are his results, he hath renounced them and esteemeth them as dross.... This is right, John St. John! yet how is it that there is place for the great hunchbacked devil to whisper in thine ear the doubt: Is there in truth any mystic path at all? Is it all disappointment and illusion?

And the "Poor Thing" John St. John moves off shivering and sad, like a sot who has tried to get credit at a tavern and is turned away — and that on Christmas Eve!

[* See note page 7.]

There is no money in his purse, no steam in his boilers — that's what's the matter with John St. John.

It is clear enough, what happened yesterday. He failed at the Four Pylons in turn; in the morning Fear stopped him at that of Horus and so on; while in the evening he either failed at the Pylon of Thoth, *i.e.*, was obsessed by the necessity (alleged) of the recording his results, or failed to overcome the duality of Thoth. Otherwise, even if he comprehended the base, he certainly failed at the apex of the Pyramid.

In any case, he cannot blame the Ceremony, which is most potent; one or two small details may need correction, but no more.

Here then he is down at the bottom of the hill again, a Rosicrucian Sisyphus with the Stone of the Philosophers! An Ixion* bound to the Wheel of Destiny and of the Samsara,† unable to reach the centre, where is Rest.

He must add to the entry 1.13 that the "telephone-cross" voices came as he composed himself to sleep, in the Will to Adonai. This time he detached a body of cavalry to chase them to oblivion. Perhaps an unwise division of his forces; yet he was so justly indignant at the eternal illusions that he may be excused.

Excused! To whom? Thou must succeed or fail! O Batsman, with thy frail fortress of Three-in-One, the Umpire cries "Out;" and thou explainest to thy friends in the pavilion. But thy friends have heard that story before, and thy explanation will not appear in the score. *Mr. J. St. John, b. Maya,* o, they will read in the local newspaper. There is no getting away from that!

Failure! Failure! Failure!

Now then let me (7.35) take the position of the Hanged Man and invoke Adonai.

9.0. Probably sleep returned shortly. Not a good night, though dreamless, so far as memory serves.

The rain comes wearily down, not chasing the dryness, but soddening the streets. The rain of autumn, not the rain of spring!

So is it in this soul, Lord Adonai. The thought of Thee is heavy

[* In Greek mythology, the first man to shed the blood of a kinsman. Zeus later punished him for ingratitude by binding him to an ever-turning winged wheel.]
[† Literally "wandering on." In Hindu and Buddhist terminology refers to the impermanent and fragmentary nature of the material world.]

and uneasy, flabby and loose, like an old fat woman stupid-drunk in her slum; which was as a young maiden in a field of lilies, arrow-straight, sun-strong, moon-pure, dancing for her own excess of life.

Adonai! Adonai!

9.17. Rose, dressed, etc., reflecting on the Path. Blinder than ever! The brain is in revolt; it has been compressed too long. Yet it is impossible to rest. It is too late. The Irresistible God, whose name is Destiny, has been invoked, and He hath answered.

The matter is in His hands; He must end it, either with that mighty spiritual Experience which I have sought, or else with black madness, or with death. By the Body of God, swear thou that death would come — welcome, welcome, welcome!

And to Thee, and from Thee, O thou great god Destiny, there is no appeal. Thou turnest not one hair's breadth from Thy path appointed.

That which "John St. John" *means* (else is it a blank name) is that which he must be — and what is that? The issue is with Thee — cannot one wait with fortitude, whether it be for the King's Banqueting-House or for the Headsman and the Block?

9.45. Breakfast — croissant, sandwich, 2 coffees. Concentrating *off* the Work as well as possible.

10.10. Arrived at Brenner's studio. The rest has produced one luminous idea: why not end it all with destruction? Say a great ritual of Geburah, curses, curses, curses! John St. John ought not to have forgotten how to curse. In his early days at Wastdale Head people would travel miles to hear him!

Curse all the Gods and all the demons — all those things in short which go to make up John St. John. For *that* — as he now knows — is the Name of the great Enemy, the Dweller upon the Threshold. It was that mighty spirit whose formless horror beat him back, for it was he!

So now to return to concentration and the Will toward Adonai.

10.20. One thing is well; the vow of "interpreting every phenomenon as a particular dealing of God with my soul" is keeping itself. Whatever impression reaches the consciousness is turned by it into a symbol or a simile of the Work.

11.18. The pose over; recited Ritual, now known by heart; then willed Adonai; hopelessly unconcentrated.

... To interpret this Record aright, it must, however, be understood that the "Standard of Living" goes up at an incredible rate. The same achievement would, say five days ago, have been entered as "High degree of concentration; unhoped-for success."

The phenomena which to-day one dismisses with annoyed contempt are the same which John St. John worked four years continuously to attain, and when attained seemed almost to outstrip the possible of glory. The flood of the Chittam is again being heaped up by the dam of Discipline. There is less headache, and more sense of being on the Path — that is the only way one finds of expressing it.

11.45. Worse and worse; though pose even better held.

In despair returned to a simple practice, the holding of the mind to a single imagined object; in this case the Triangle surmounted by the Cross. It seems quite easy to do nowadays; why shouldn't it lead to The Result? It used to be supposed to do so.

Might be worth trying anyway; things can hardly be worse than they are.

Or, one might go over to the Hammam, and have a long bath and sleep — but who can tell whether it would refresh, or merely destroy the whole edifice built up so laboriously in these ten days?

12.15. At Pantheon. 1/2 dozen Marennes, Rognons Brochette, Lait chaud.

John St. John is aching all over, cannot get comfortable anyhow; is hungry, and has no appetite; thirsty, and loathes the thought of drinking!

He must do something — something pretty drastic, or he will find himself in serious trouble of body and mind, the shadows of his soul, that is sick unto death. For "where are now their gods?" Where is the Lord, the Lord Adonai?

12.35. The beast feels decidedly better; but whether he is more concentrated one may doubt. Honestly, he is now so blind that he cannot tell!

Perhaps a "café, cognac, et cigare" may tune him up to the point of either going back to work, or across Paris to the Hammam.

He will make the experiment, reading through his proofs the while.

One good thing; the Chittam is moving slowly. The waiters all hurry him — what a contrast to last night!

1.15. Proofs read through again. John St. John feels far from well.

2.15. A stroll down the Boul' Mich' and a visit to M—'s studio improve matters a good deal.

3.30. The cure continued. No worry about the Work, but an effort to put it altogether out of the mind.

A café crème, forty minutes at the Academie Marcelle — a gruelling bout without the gloves — and J.St.J. is at the Luxembourg to look at the pretty pictures.

3.40. The proof of the pudding, observes the most mystic of discourses (surely!), is in the Eating.

One might justly object to any Results of this Ten days' strain. But if abundant health and new capacity to do great work be the after-effect, who then will dare to cast a stone?

Not that it matters a turnip-top to the Adept himself. But others may be deterred from entering the Path by the foolish talk of the ignorant, and thus may flowers be lost that should go to make the fadeless wreath of Adonai. Ah, Lord, pluck *me* up utterly by the root, and set that which Thou pluckest as a flower upon Thy brow!

4.10. Walked back to the Dôme to drink a citron pressé through the lovely gardens, sad with their fallen leaves. Reflecting on what Dr. Henry Maudsley once wrote to him about mysticism "Like other bad habits (he might have said 'Like all living beings') it grows by what it feeds on." Most important, then, to use the constant critical check on all one's work. The devotion to Adonai might itself fall under suspicion, were it not for the definition of Adonai.

Adonai is that thought which informs and strengthens and purifies, supreme sanity in supreme genius. Anything that is not that is not Adonai.

Hence the refusal of all other Results, however glorious; for they are all relative, partial, impure. Anicca, Dukkha, Anatta: Change, Sorrow, Unsubstantiality; these are their characteristics, however much they may appear to be Atman, Sat, Chit, Ananda, Soul, Being, Knowledge, Bliss.

But the main consideration was one of expediency. Has not John St. John possibly been stuffing himself both with Methods and Results?

Certainly this morning was more like the engorgement of the stomach with too much food than like the headache after a bout of drunkenness.

A less grave fault, by far; it is easy and absurd to get a kind of hysterical ecstasy over religion, love, or wine. A German will take off his hat and dance and jodel to the sunrise — and nothing comes of it! Darwin studies Nature with more reverence and enthusiasm, but without antics — and out comes the Law of Evolution. So it is written "By their fruits ye shall know them." But about this question of spiritual overfeeding — what did Darwin do when he got to the stage (as he did, be sure! many a time) when he wished every pigeon in the world at the devil?

Now this wish has never really arisen in John St. John; however bad he feels, he always feels that Attainment is the only possible way out of it. This is the good Karma of his ten years' constant striving.

Well, in the upshot, he will get back to Work at once, and hope that his few hours in the world may prove a true strategic movement to the rear, and not a euphemism for rout!

5.4. There are further serious considerations to be made concerning Adonai. This title for the Unknown Thought was adopted by O.M. in November, 19—, in Upper Burma, on the occasion of his passing through the ordeal and receiving the grade which should be really attributed to Daath (on account of its nature, the Mastery of the Reason), though it is commonly called 7°=4°.

It appeared to him at that period that so much talk and time were wasted on discussing the nature of the Attainment — a discussion foredoomed to failure, in the absence of all Knowledge, and in view of the Self-Contradictory Nature of the Reasoning Faculty, as applied to Metaphysics — that it would be wiser to drop the whole question, and concentrate on a simple Magical Progress.

The Next Step for humanity in general was then "the Knowledge and Conversation of the Holy Guardian Angel."

One thing at a time.

But here he finds himself discussing and disputing with himself the nature of that Knowledge.

Better far act as hitherto, and aspire simple and directly, as one person to another, careless of the critical objections (quite insuperable, of course) to this or any other conception.

For as this experience transcends reason, it is fruitless to argue about it.

Adonai, I invoke Thee!

Simpler, then, to go back to the Egoistic diction, only remembering always that by "I" is meant John St. John, or O.M., or Adonai according to the context.

5.30. Have read some of THE Books* to induct myself again into the Work.

Therefore will I kindle the holy Incense, and turn myself again to the One Thought.

6.27. All this time in Hanged Man position, and thinking of everything else.

As bad as it was on the very first day!

7.10. More waste time aimlessly watching a poker game. Walked down to Café de Versailles. Dinner. Hors d'Oeuvre, Escargots, Cassoulet de Castelnaudary, Glacé, $1/2$ Evian. Am quite washed-out. I have not even the courage of despair. There is not enough left in me to despair.

I don't care.

7.35. One gleam of light illumines the dark path — I can't

[* See *The Holy Books of Thelema* for Crowley's Class A or inspired writings.]

enjoy my dinner. The snails, as I prong them forth, are such ugly, slimy, greasy black horrors — oh! so like my soul! ... Ugh!

I write a letter to F—r and sign myself with a broken pentagram.

It makes me think of a "busted flush" ...

But through all the sunlight peeps: *e.g.,* These six snails were my six inferior souls; the seventh, the real soul, cannot be eaten by the devourer.

How's that for high?

8.3. Possibly a rousing mantra would fix things up; say the Old Favourite:

Aum Tat Sat Aum

and give the Hindus a chance.
We can but try.
So I begin at once.

9.10. This is past all bearing. Another hour wasted chatting to Nina and H—. The mantra hardly remembered at all. I have gone to bed, and shall take things in hand seriously, if it kills me.

9.53. Since 9.17 have done Pranayama, though allowing myself some irregularities in the way of occasional omission of a Kambhakham.

'Tis very hard to stick to it. I find myself, at the end of above sentence, automatically crawling into bed. No, John!

10.14. Have been trying to extract some sense from that extraordinary treatise on mysticism, *Konx Om Pax.** Another failure, but an excusable one.

I will now beseech Adonai as best I may to give me back my lost powers.

For I am no more even a magician! So lost am I in the illusions that I have made in the Search for Adonai, that I am become the vilest of them all!

[* By Crowley. Facsimile edition available from The Teitan Press.]

10.27. A strange and unpleasant experience. My thought suddenly transmuted itself into a muscular cry, so that my legs gave a violent jerk. This I expect is at bottom the explanation of the Bhuchari-Siddhi. A very bad form of uncontrolled thought. I was on the edge of sleep; it woke me.

The fact is, all is over! I am done! I have tried for the Great Initiation and I have failed; I am swept away into strange hells.

Lord Adonai! let the fires be informing; let them "balance, assain, assoil."

I suppose this rash attempt will end in Locomotor Ataxia or G.P.I.

Let it! I'm going on.

11.47. The first power to return is the power to suffer.

The shame of it! The torture of it!

I slept in patches as a man sleeps that is deadly ill. I am only afraid of failing to wake for the End of the day.

God! what a day!

... I dare not trust my will to keep me awake; so I rise, wash, and will walk about till time to get into my Asana.

Thirst! Oh how I thirst!

I had not thought that there could be such suffering.

THE ELEVENTH DAY

12.19. It seems a poor thing to be proud of, merely to be awake. Yet I was flushed with triumph as a boy that wins his first race.

The powers of Asana and Pranayama return. I did 21 Breathcycles without fatigue.

Energy returns, and Keenness to pursue the Path — all fruits of that one little victory over sleep.

How delicate are these powers, so simple as they seem!

Let me be very humble, now and for ever more!

Surely at least that lesson has been burnt into me.

And how gladly I would give all these powers for the One Power!

12.33. Another smart attack of diarrhea. I take 4 gr. Plumb. c.

Opio and alter my determination to stay out of bed all night, as chill is doubtless the chief cause.

... It is really extraordinary how the smallest success awakes a monstrous horde of egoistic devils, vain, strutting peacocks, preening and screaming!

This is simply damnable. Egoism is the spur of all energy, in a way; and in this particular case it is the one thing that is not Adonai (whatever else may be) and so the antithesis of the Work.

Bricks without straw, indeed! That's nothing to it. This job is like being asked to judge a Band contest and being told that one may do anything but listen. Only worse! One could form some idea of how they were playing through other senses; in this case *every* faculty is the enemy of the Work. At first sight the problem seems insoluble. It may be so, for me. At least, I have not solved it. Yet I have come very near it, many a time, of old; have solved it indeed, though in a less important sense that now I seek. I am not to be content with little or with much; but only with the Ultimate Attainment.

Apparently the method is just this; to store up — no matter how — great treasures of energy and purity, until they begin to do the work themselves (in the way that the Hindus call Sukshma).

Just so the engineer — five feet six in his boots — and his men build the dam. The snows melt on the mountains, the river rises, and the land is irrigated, in a way that is quite independent of the physical strength of that Five foot Six of engineer. The engineer might even be swept away and drowned by the forces he had himself organised. So also the Kingdom of Heaven.

And now (12.57) John St. John will turn himself to sleep, invoking Adonai.

1.17. Can neither sleep nor concentrate.

Instead grotesque "astral" images of a quite base gargoylish type.

I supposed I shall have to pentagram them off like a damned neophyte.

Je m'emmerde!*

[* To hell with me.]

3.8. Praise the Lord, I wake! If that can be called waking which is a mere desperate struggle to keep the eyes open.

3.18. Pranayama all wrong — very difficult. Rose, washed, drank a few drops of water. (N.B. — To-night have drunk several times, a mouthful at a time; other nights, and days, no. All entries into body recorded duly.)

3.30. Have done 10 Breath-Cycles; am quite awake.
It will therefore now be lawful again to sleep.

8.12. Awoke at 7.40, read a letter which arrived, and tried quite vainly to concentrate.

8.52. Have risen, written a letter. Will break my fast — café croissant — and go a walk with the New Mantra, using my recently invented method of doing Pranayama on the march. The weather is again perfect.

9.14. Breakfast — eaten Yogin-wise — at an end. The walk begins.

11.15. The walk over. Kept mantra going well enough. Made also considerations concerning the Nature of the Path
The upshot is that it does not matter. Acquire full power of Concentration; the rest is only leather and prunella.
Don't worry; work!
I shall now make a pantacle to aid the said faculty of concentration.
The Voice of the Nadi (by the way) is resounding well, and the Chittam is a little better under control.

1.5. Have worked well on the Pantacle, thinking of Adonai. Of course we are now reduced to a "low anthropomorphic conception" — but what odds? Once the Right Thought comes it will transcend any and all conceptions. The objection is as silly as the objection to illustrating Geometry by Diagrams, on the ground that printed lines are thick — and so on.
This is the imbecility of the "Protestant" objection to images. What fools these mortals be!

The Greeks, too, after exhausting all their sublimest thoughts of Zeus and Hades and Poseidon, found that they could not find a fitting image of the All, the supreme — so they just carved a goat-man, saying: Let this represent Pan!

Also in the holiest place of the most secret temple there is an empty shrine.

But whoso goes there in the first instance thinks: There is no God.

He who goes there at the End, when he has adored all the other deities, knoweth that No God.

So also I go through all the Ritual, and try all the Means; at the End it may be I shall find No rituals and No means, but an act or a silence so simple that it cannot be told or understood. Lord Adonai, bring me to the End!

1.25. After writing above, and adding a few touches to the Pantacle, am ready to go to lunch.

1.45. Arrived at Panthéon, with mantra.

Rumpsteak aux pommes soufflées, poire, 1/2 Evian, and the three Cs.

Was meditating on asceticism. John Tweed once told me that Swami Vivekananda, towards the end of his life, wrote a most pathetic letter deploring that his sanctity forbade his "going on the bust."

What a farce is such sanctity! How much wiser for the man to behave as a man, the God as a God!

This is my real bed-rock objection to the Eastern systems. They decry all manly virtue as dangerous and wicked; and they look upon Nature as evil. True enough, everything is evil relatively to Adonai; for all stain is impurity. A bee's swarm is evil — inside one's clothes. "Dirt is matter in the wrong place." It is dirt to connect sex with statuary, morals with art.

Only Adonai, who is in a sense the True Meaning of everything, cannot defile any idea. This is a hard saying, though true, for nothing of course is dirtier than to try and use Adonai as a fig-leaf for one's shame.

To seduce women under pretence of religion is unutterable foulness; though both adultery and religion are themselves clean. To mix jam and mustard is a messy mistake.

2.5. It also struck me that this Operation is (among other things) an attempt to prove the proposition:

Reward is the direct and immediate consequence of Work.

Of all the holy illuminated Men of God of my acquaintance, I am the only one that holds this opinion.

But I think that this Record, when I have time to go through it, and stand at some distance, to get the perspective, will be proved a conclusive proof of my thesis. I think that every failure will be certainly traceable to my own damn foolishness; every little success to courage, skill, wit, tenacity.

If I had but a little more of these!

2.22. I further take this opportunity of asserting my Atheism. I believe that all these phenomena are as explicable as the formation of hoar-frost or of glacier tables.

I believe "Attainment" to be a simple supreme sane state of the human brain. I do not believe in miracles; I do not think that God could cause a monkey, clergy-man, or rationalist to attain.

I am taking all this trouble of the Record principally in hope that it will show exactly what mental and physical conditions precede, accompany, and follow "attainment" so that others may reproduce, through those conditions, that Result.

I believe in the Law of Cause and Effect — and I loathe the cant alike of the Superstitionist and the Rationalist.

The Confession of St. Judas McCabbage

I believe in Charles Darwin Almighty, maker of Evolution; and in Ernst Haeckel, his only son our Lord Who for us men and for our salvation came down from Germany: who was conceived of Weissmann, born of Büchner, suffered under du Bois-Raymond, was printed, bound, and shelved: who was raised again into English (of sorts), ascended into Pantheon of the Literary Guide and sitteth on the right hand of Edward Clodd: whence he shall come to judge the thick in the head.

I believe in Charles Watts; the Rationalist Press Association; the annual dinner at the Trocadero Restaurant;

the regularity of subscriptions, the resurrection in a six-penny edition, and the Book-stall everlasting.

AMEN

3.0. Arrived at Brenner's studio, and went on with the *moulage** of my Asana.

4.20. Left the Studio; walk with mantra.

4.55. Mantra-march. Pranayama; quick time. Very bracing and fatiguing, both.

At Dôme to drink a citron pressé.

Reflections have been in my mind upon the grossness of the Theistic conception, as shewn even in such pictures as Raphael's and Fra Angelico's.

How infinitely subtler and nobler is the contemplation of

> the Utmost God
> Hid i' th' middle o' matter,

the inscrutable mystery of the nature of common things. With what awe does the wise man approach a speck of dust!

And it is this Mystery that I approach!

For Thou, Adonai, art the immanent and essential Soul of Things; not separate from them, or from me; but That which is behind the shadow-show, the Cause of all, the Quintessence of All, the Transcender of all.

And Thee I seek insistently; though Thou hid Thyself in the Heaven, there will I seek Thee out; though Thou wrap Thyself in the Flames of the Abyss, even there will I pursue Thee; Though Thou make Thee a secret place in the Heart of the Rose or at the Arms of the Cross that spanneth all-embracing Space; though Thou be in the inmost part of matter, or behind the Veil of mind; Thee will I follow; Thee will I overtake; Thee will I gather into my being.

[* Casting of a sculpture.]

So thus as I chase Thee from fastness to fastness of my brain, as Thou throwest out against me Veil after Magic Veil of glory, or of fear, or of despair, or of desire; it matters nothing; at the End I shall attain to Thee — oh my Lord Adonai!

And even as the Capture is delight, is not the Chase also delight? For we are lovers from the Beginning, though it pleasure Thee to play the Syrinx to my Pan. Is it not the springtide, and are these not the Arcadian groves?

5.31. At home; settling to strictest meditation upon Adonai my Lord; willing His presence, the Perfume and the Vision, even as it is written in the Book of the Sacred Magic of Abramelin the Mage.

8.6. Soon this became a sleep, though the will was eager and concentrated.

The sleep, too, was deep and refreshing. I will go to dinner.

8.22. Arrived, with mantra, at the Café de Versailles.

9.10. $1/2$ doz. Marennes, Râble de Lièvre, citron pressé. I am now able to concentrate OFF the Path for a little. Whether this means that I am simply slipping back into the world, or that I am more balanced on, and master of, the Path, I cannot say.

10.4. Have walked home, drunk a citron pressé at the Dôme, and prepare for the night.

As I crossed the boulevard, I looked to the bright moon, high and stately in the east, for a message. And there came to me this passage from the Book of Abramelin:

"And thou wilt begin to inflame thyself in praying" ...

It is the sentence which goes on to declare the Result. (P.S. — With this rose that curious feeling of confidence, sure premonition of success, that one gets in most physical tasks, but especially when one is going to get down a long putt or a tricky one. Whether it means more than that perception and execution have got into unison [for once] and know it, I cannot say.)

It is well that thus should close this eleventh day of my Retirement, and the thirty-third year of my life.

Thirty and three years was this temple in building. . . .

It has always been my custom on this night to look back over the year, and to ask: What have I done? The answer is invariably "Nothing."

Yet of what men count deeds I have done no small share. I have travelled a bit, written a bit ... I seem to have been hard at it all the time — and to have got nothing finished or successful.

One Tragedy — one little comedy — two essays — a dozen poems or so — two or three short stories — odds and ends of one sort and another: it's a miserable record, though the Tragedy is good enough to last a life. It marks an epoch in literature, though nobody else will guess it for fifty years yet.*

The travel, too, has been rubbish. It's been a pretty, peddling year. The one absolute indication is: on no account live otherwise than alone.

But it is 10.35; these considerations, though in a way pertaining to the Work, are not the Work itself.

Let me *begin to inflame myself in praying!*

THE TWELFTH DAY

12.17. When therefore I had made ready the chamber, so that all was dark, save for the Lamp upon the Altar, I began as recorded above, to inflame myself in praying, calling upon my Lord; and I burned in the Lamp that Pantacle which I had made of Him, renouncing the Images, destroying the Images, that Himself might arise in me.

And the Chamber was filled with that wondrous glow of ultra-violet light self-luminous, without a source, that hath no counterpart in Nature unless it be in that Dawn of the North ...

And there were revealed unto me certain Words of Power ...

And I invoked my Lord and recited the Book Ararita at the Altar ...

This holy inspired book (delivered unto me in the winter of last year) was now at last understanded of me; for it is, though I knew it not, a complete scheme of this Operation.

For this cause I will add this book Ararita at the end of the

[* Probably refers to *The World's Tragedy,* originally published 1910.]

Manuscript. {This has not been permitted. The *Book Ararita* will be issued by the A∴A∴ in due course. — ED.}* I also demanded of mine Angel the Writing upon the Lamen of Silver; a Writing of the veritable Elixir and supernal Dew. And it was granted unto me.

Then subtly, easily, simply, imperceptibly gliding, I passed away into nothing. And I was wrapped in the black brilliance of my Lord, that interpenetrated me in every part, fusing its light with darkness, and leaving there no darkness, but pure light.

Also I beheld my Lord in a figure and I felt the interior trembling kindle itself into a Kiss — and I perceived the true Sacraments — and I beheld in one moment all the mystic visions in one; and the Holy Graal appeared unto me, and many other inexpressible things were known of me.

Also I was given to enjoy the subtle Presence of my Lord interiorly during the whole of this twelfth day.

Then I besought the Lord that He would take me into His presence eternally even now.

But He withdrew Himself, for that I must do that which I was sent hither to do; namely, to rule the earth.

Therefore with sweetness ineffable He parted from me; yet leaving a comfort not to be told, a Peace ... the Peace. And the Light and the Perfume do certainly yet remain with me in the little Chamber, and I know that my Redeemer liveth, and that He shall stand at the latter day upon the earth.

For I am He that liveth, and was dead; and behold! I am alive for evermore, and have the Keys of Hell and of Death. I am Amoun the Sun in His rising; I have passed from darkness into Light. I am Asar Un-nefer the Perfect One. I am the Lord of Life, triumphant over death....

There is no part of me that is not of the Gods....

> The dead man Ankh-af-na-khonsu
>   Saith with his voice of truth and calm:
> Oh Thou that hast a single arm!
>   O Thou that glitterest in the moon!
> I weave Thee in the spinning charm;
>   I lure Thee with the billowy tune.

[* Published in *Equinox* III, 9, *The Holy Books of Thelema*.]

The dead man Ankh-af-na-khonsu
    Hath parted from the darkling crowds,
Hath joined the dwellers of the light,
    Opening Duant, the star-abodes;
        Their keys receiving.
The dead man Ankh-af-na-khonsu
    Hath made his passage into night,
His pleasure on the earth to do
    Among the living.

Amen
Amen without lie
Amen, and Amen of Amen.

12.40. I shall lie down to sleep in my robes, still wearing the Ring of the Masters, and bearing my wand in my hand.

For to me now sleep is the same as waking, and life the same as death.

In Thy L.V.X. are not light and darkness but twin children that chase each other in their play?

7.55. Awoke from long sweet dreamless sleep, like a young eagle that soars to greet the dawn.

9.20. After breakfast, have strolled, on my way to the studio, through the garden of the Luxembourg to my favourite fountain. It is useless to attempt to write of the dew and the flowers in the clear October sunlight.

Yet the light which I behold is still more than sunlight. My eyes too are quite weak from the Vision; I cannot bear the brilliance of things.

The clock of the Senate strikes; and my ears are ravished with its mysterious melody. It is the Infinite interior movement of things, secured by the co-extension of their sum with the all, that transcends the deadly opposites; change which implies decay, stability which spells monotony.

I understand all the Psalms of Benediction; there is spontaneous praise, a fountain in my heart. The authors of the Psalms must have known something of this Illumination when they wrote them.

9.30. It seems, too, that this Operation is transformed. I suppose it must read as a patchwork of most inharmonious colour, a thing without continuity or cohesion. To me, now, it appears from the very start a simple direct progress in one straight line. I can hardly remember that there were checks.

Of course my rational memory picking out details finds otherwise. But I seem to have two memories almost as if belonging to two strata of being. In Qabalastic language, my native consciousness is now Neschamah, not Ruach or Nephesch.*

... I really cannot write more. This writing is a descent into Ruach, and I want to abide where I am.

11.17. At 10.0 arrived at Brenner's studio, and took the pose. At once, automatically, the interior trembling began again, and again the subtle brilliance flowed through me.

The consciousness again died and was reborn as the divine, always without shock or stress.

How easy is magic, once the way is found!

How still is the soul! The turbid spate of emotion has ceased; the heavy particles of thought have sunk to the bottom; how limpid, how lucid is its glimmer. Only from above, from the overshadowing Tree of Life, whose leaves glisten and quiver in the shining wind of the Spirit, drops ever and anon, self-luminous, the Dew of Immortality.

Many and wonderful also were the Visions and powers offered unto me in this hour; but I refused them all; for being in my Lord and He in me, there is no need of these toys.

12.0. The pose over. On this second sitting, practically no thoughts arose at all to cloud the Sun; but a curious feeling that there was something more to come.

Possibly the Proof, that I had demanded, the Writing on the Lamen ...

12.40. Chez Lavenue. Certain practical considerations suggest themselves.

[* The five parts of the soul according to the Qabalah are *Jechidah*, the Self; *Chiah*, the Life Force; *Neschamah*, the Higher Intuition; *Ruach*, the Intellect; and *Nephesh*, the Animal Soul that perceives and feels emotions.]

One would have been much better off with a proper Magical Cabinet, a disciple to look after things, proper magical food ceremonially prepared, a private garden to walk in ... and so on.

But at least it is useful and important to know that things can be done at a pinch in a great city and a small room.

1.14. The lunch is good; the kidneys were well cooked; the tarte aux fraises was excellent; the Burgundy came straight from the Vat of Bacchus. The Coffee and Cognac are beyond all praise; the cigar is the best Cabaña I ever smoked.

I read through this volume of the Record; and I dissolve my being into quintessential laughter.

The entries are some of them so funny! ... Previously, this had escaped me.

1.22. And now the Rapture of it takes me!

1.25. The exquisite beauty of the women in the Restaurant ... what John St. John would have called old hags!

1.27. My soul is singing ... my soul is singing!

1.30. It matters nothing what I do ... everything goes infinitely, incredibly right!

"The Lord Adonai is about me as a Thunderbolt and as a Pylon and as a Serpent and as a Phallus." ...

3.17. Have had a long talk on Art with B——.

"The master considers himself always a student."

So, therefore, whatever one may have attained, in this as in Art, there is always so much more possible that one can never be satisfied.

Much less, then, satiated.

11.15. Having gone back into life of the world — yet a world transfigured! — I did all my little work, my little amusements, all the things that one does, very quietly and beatifically.

About 10.30 the rapture began to carry me away; yet I withstood it and went on with my game of Billiards, for politeness' sake.

And even there in the Café du Dôme was the glory within me,
I therein; so that every time that I failed at a stroke and stood up
and drank in that ambrosial air, I was nigh falling for that intense
sweetness that dissolved away the soul. Even as a lover swoons
with excess of pleasure at the first kiss of the belovéd, even so was
I, oh my Lord Adonai!

Wherefore I am come hither to my chamber to enflame myself
in praying at the Altar that I have set up.

And I am ready, robed, armed, anointed ...

11.35 Ardesco!* ....

The Thirteenth Day.

It is Eight o'clock in the morning.
Being entered into the Silence, let me abide in the Silence!

AMEN

[* I am enflamed.]

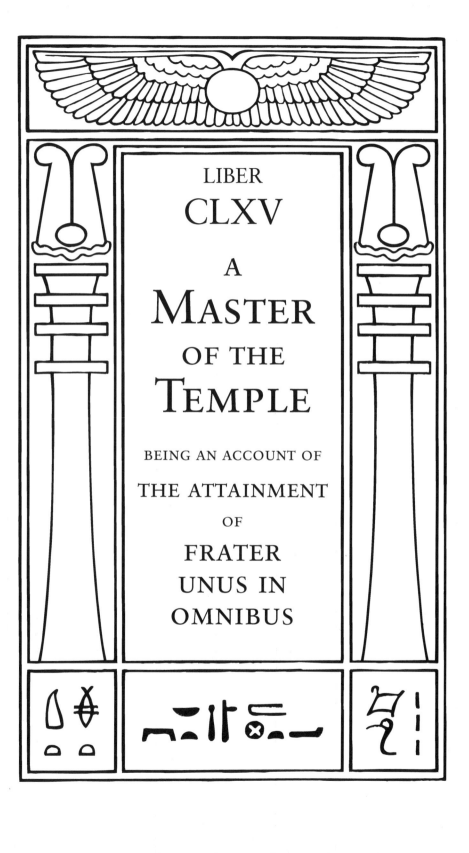

LIBER

CLXV

A

MASTER

OF THE

TEMPLE

BEING AN ACCOUNT OF

THE ATTAINMENT

OF

FRATER

UNUS IN

OMNIBUS

A∴A∴
Publication in Class B.

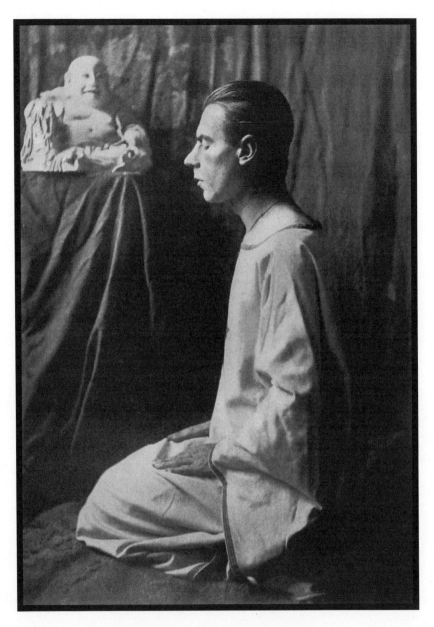

FRATER VNVS IN OMNIBVS
FROM THE PHOTOGRAPH BY HENRY B. CAMP

The MASTER is represented in the Robe of, and described by His name as, a Probationer, as if to assert His Simplicity. He is in His favourite Asana, the Dragon, in profound holy meditation.

Liber CLXV

A Master of the Temple

Section I.
April 2, 1886 to December 24, 1909

CHARLES STANSFELD JONES, whom I usually mention by the motto V.I.O., which he took on becoming a Probationer of the A∴A∴, made his entry into this World by the usual and approved method, on April 2nd, 1886 E.V., having only escaped becoming an April Fool by delaying a day to summon up enough courage to turn out once more into this cold and uninviting World. Having been oiled, smacked and allowed to live, we shall trouble no further about the details of his career until 1906, when, having reached the age of 20 years, he began to turn his attention toward the Mysteries, and to investigate Spiritualism, chiefly with the idea of disproving it. From this year his interest in the Occult seems to date, and it was about this time that he first consciously aspired to find, and get into touch with, a True Occult Order. This aspiration was, as we shall see, fulfilled three years later, when he had an opportunity to become a Probationer of the A∴A∴, and immediately grasped it; but during those three years his researches led him into varied paths: — Spiritualism, Faithism and other Isms on the one hand, and 'The Europe,' 'The Leicester,' and 'The Cosy Corner' on the other: last, but not least, into Marriage, a difficult thing to put on one side and perhaps best left on the other. Having then plunged wholeheartedly into this final experiment, becoming as it were 'Omnia in Uno'* for a time, he emerged in a frame of mind well suited to the study of Scientific Illuminism, of which he was much in need, and, having signed the Probationer's Pledge Form on December 24th, 1909 E.V., he took — after careful thought — the Motto 'Unus in Omnibus'† and has been riding very comfortably ever since.

From this time onward, according to the Rules of the Order, he began keeping a written record of his Work, and this makes our

[* All in One. — JW]
[† One in All. — JW]

task easier; but since he himself became more serious from that moment, we must to a certain extent follow his example and treat what is recorded as the attempt of a struggling soul to obtain Light for himself and others. Whatever his mistakes, however poor his results, or laughable his failures, there is this much to be said for him, that he never turned back.

SECTION II.
DECEMBER 24, 1909, TO MAY 14, 1910

Frater V.I.O. started off bravely enough. As soon as he had read the first number of *The Equinox,* and before he got into touch with any Member of the A∴A∴ he made an attempt at Asana. The earliest record I can find reads as follows:

> Thursday, Nov. 4th, 1909.   11.20 p.m. to 11.41 p.m.
>   Asana. Position 1. The God.*
>   Inclination for back to bend, just above hips, had to straighten up several times.
>   Opened eyes once and moved head, after about five minutes.
>   Breathed fairly regularly after the first few minutes, counting 9 in, holding 4, 9 out, holding 4.
>   Saw various colours in clouds, and uncertain figures, during the latter part of the time.

On December 19th his practice lasted 46 minutes. He hoped to do 60 minutes next time. But he does not appear to have done so, for after signing his Probationer's Oath on December 24th I find no record till January 11th 1910. E.V. the day he received his first written instructions from his Neophyte, Frater P.A.† As those instructions represent the basis upon which he worked for a considerable period, I shall include them here, in spite of the fact that it may have been out of order for him to work on definite instructions at all, since the Probationer is supposed to choose for himself those practices which please him best, and to experiment therewith for himself. Since however he did not know this at the time,

---

[* For terms such as Asana, the God, or the Dragon, mentioned in this diary, please see *Liber E* in appendix 2. — JW]

[† J. F. C. Fuller. — JW]

he cannot be blamed for doing his best along the lines laid down by his Neophyte.[1] In any case he might have done far worse than to strive to carry out these few simple rules which are as follows:

THE RULES

1. Ever be moderate and follow the middle path; rather be the tortoise than the hare; do not rush wildly into anything; but do not abandon what you have taken up, without much forethought.

2. Always keep your body and mind in a healthy and fit condition; and never carry out an exercise, whether mental or physical, when you are fatigued.

3. In an ideal country the hours in which to practice are: at sunrise, sunset, noon and midnight (and always before a meal, never immediately after one).

As this cannot be done with comfort in this country (England), let your chief practice take place an hour or half an hour before your breakfast hour.

4. If possible set apart a room wherein to carry out your exercises; keep it clean, and only keep in it objects which please you; burn a little incense in the room before beginning an exercise; keep the room holy to yourself, and do not allow yourself or another to do anything unbalanced in thought or action in it. In will and deed make this room a temple and a symbol of that greater Temple which is your HIGHER SELF.

THE EXERCISES

The First Exercise.

Rise to time, and without undue haste, wash and dress, robe yourself and enter the room you have set apart; burn a little incense and turning to the East repeat some simple orison

---

[1] It is presumptuous for a Neophyte to lay down rules; for (a) he cannot possibly know what his Probationer needs, having no record to guide him; (b) the Probationer's task is to explore his own nature, not to follow any prescribed course. A third objection is that by putting the Probationer in Corsets, an entirely flabby person may sneak through his year, and become a Neophyte, to the shame of the Order. But this objection is theoretical; for Initiation is overseen from the Third Order, where no Error may endure. O.M.

such as: "May the light of Adonai arise within me, may it guide me through this day and be as a lamp to lighten my darkness." Then make a general confession, as shortly as possible, of your last day's work and enter it in your diary, after which sit down in a comfortable position and do the following.

With your hands upon your knees and your head straight, take in a breath in measured time inwards and concentrate the whole of your thought on that breath as it flows into your lungs, cutting away all other thoughts that may arise at the time; then exhale the breath, still keeping your thought fixed on it. Do this for some ten minutes or a quarter of an hour, and mark down in your diary the number of 'breaks,' or any result. The whole of this practice must be performed rhythmically and harmoniously.

The Second Exercise

As the rush of daily work tends to undo what the morning exercise has done, try your utmost to turn every item of your professional work into a magical exercise. Do all, even the smallest work, in honour and glory of Adonai: excel in your special duties in life, because He is of you, and you of Him; do not think of Him as Adonai, but think of Adonai as the work; and of your daily work create a symbol of the Symbol of "The Great Work which is TO BE."

The Third Exercise

As the rush of your daily work tends to unbalance you, so do the pleasures you indulge in. Cultivate joyfulness in all your amusements; and, when joyful, break out into silent and inward praise of the joy within you. Do not make a prudish exercise of it, work silently and joyously, and do not discuss your results with casual friends. And above all do everything for the honour and glory of Adonai, so that of your daily pleasures you may construct a symbol of that Unchanging Joy that IS.

These instructions were accompanied by a letter from which I quote the following:

"The enclosed exercises perform regularly, say to yourself: 'I will do these for three months; even if I get no benefit from them, yet I am *determined* to do them.' Write to me whenever you like, but don't consider any result that you may get as worth much; for these little exercises are only to produce an equilibrium which is essential before really setting out. If you add any exercise of your own then do it at a definite hour daily and do it continuously; to take up an exercise and then drop it is worse than useless, for it is unbalancing."

Now, as any Probationer knows, as soon as one sets out to do the simplest task regularly and with magical intent, that task becomes not only difficult, but well nigh impossible of performance. This is just what V.I.O. found, and no sooner had his task been set than all kinds of difficulties presented themselves, like the dog-faces demons mentioned by Zoroaster, to prevent its fulfilment. He tried, but at the end of January he writes: "I cannot get on under these conditions. Had plenty of time to do exercises this morning, but was continually interrupted. Did not robe myself as I have no place fit to call a temple." How little did he know at that time how well off he really was in the latter respect! He was living in comfort in a Kensington Flat with every convenience of civilization; a few years later he was glad to do Asana and perform his meditations out in the rain, clad in pyjamas, because his tiny tent in British Columbia was too small to allow of work inside. But we digress. At this point his record breaks off abruptly. He remained in London until May of 1910, when circumstances arose which made it possible for him to visit British Columbia.

Armed then with his instruction paper, THE EQUINOX, and a few Occult books, he sailed for Canada, alone, to start again in new and unploughed fields.

SECTION III.
JULY 25, 1910, TO APRIL 30, 1911

The next entry in his diary is dated July 25th, 1910. It is a general confession of the previous six months. Half of his year of Probation had passed away, and he has not reported to, or received any communication from, the Order. He laments his negligence in this respect, but writes: "Yet know I well that I alone have suffered and shall suffer from this negligence, and I must humbly take any results that may arise out of my failure. Still, even though I may

have neglected the advice given me when I first became a Probationer, I feel that I have progressed, be it never so slightly, along the
Path which from the first I set out to tread. May it not be, O
Adonai, that even now the second six months may be made to balance the first six, and that what is passed may yet be for the best?"

At that time he had not found out that things always turn out
for the best; it took him a long while to realize this, but it is evident
that soon afterwards his efforts produced some result; for we find
an entry on Sunday, August 7th, 1910. "I have found (for a few
moments) the Peace which passeth all understanding. Amen." This
was evidently the foreshadowing of his first really notable result,
the first Dawning of L.V.X. which he experienced on August 29th.
There is an entry on September 2nd, full of joy and gladness and
wonder at his first Illumination; and then, three days later, he had
evidently recognised that this alone was not enough, and this was
evidently the reason for the next somewhat curious entry of September 5th, 7.53 p.m., which I shall quote practically in full:

> I am calm now, as I commence to write what may be the
> last entry in this diary. All that I can remember of my life on this
> planet has, as I look back upon it, been guided by an unseen
> hand. For so short a life (24 years and six months) it has been
> filled with an unusual number of incidents, some painful, some
> joyful and some of a purely spiritual nature. I regret nothing.
> Again three days have passed since I made entry in this book. I
> cannot talk of what has happened during those three days, it
> seems useless to try and do so, in fact it seems useless to make
> this entry at all except that *I know not what is before me,* and I
> feel that had I (or if I) lived longer upon this planet it would
> have been my life work, indeed it must have been, to help oth-
> ers to the Path. Therefore to those who follow after are these
> lines written in the hope that they may be saved one drop of the
> anguish I now suffer. Whatever may have happened in this last
> three days, the results of my thoughts amount to this. I who
> have found the heart of the shining triangle, who have indeed
> become one with the Great White Brotherhood, who have heard
> the Voice of God in all Its sweetness, who have made that mes-
> sage a part (nay all) of my being, who have held my Beloved in
> my arms, who have Become my Beloved and lost myself therein,

who have for ever given up my lower self, who have conquered Death, who have felt the Pain of the whole World, who have found Wisdom, Love and Power, who have given up All to become Nothing, I who have seen the need of the World, have found that books (hitherto my dearest companions) have no longer any word to say to me — have found that knowledge (relative) or what I thought was knowledge, is of no avail to supply the need of all that other part of my Being that my great God-love would give it. I who have conquered Fear and Death, am now confronted with the fact that without Absolute Knowledge all is vain. I am going to ask the One Last Question. WHY? I have written it. An awful stillness falls. I am alone in my lodgings, I have no money, and I cannot use my Will to demand it from others if I can give nothing in return to help them to find what they really seek. I have cried with Christ "Eli, Eli, Lama Sabacthani." I have suffered the Bloody Sweat with Him on the Cross, and now I say with Him, "It is finished." Amen. One last note occurs to me before I wrap up this book and seal it and address it to F. . . in whose hands it will be safe. I looked into the eyes of a little child this evening. Does the answer lie there?

Sep. 5th 12.26 P.M. It is over. I have unsealed the package and once more opened the book. This time it will be but a short entry. Very quietly I knelt; I did not robe or burn incense. I just took with me the memory of the little child who had looked into my eyes as I kissed its forehead. Very quietly I asked my question. I rose and lay upon the bed, and soon the answer came. It came quite silently, and at first I thought I must be mistaken, I had (it seemed) heard it so many times before. No other answer came, so I went out into the streets and along my way. Gradually the fuller meaning has dawned on me, and I have returned to make this entry. I need not add much more. I do not put the answer down. It was given in silence and must remain in Silence. Still there seemed to be just one little ripple of joy in the Great Silent Sea as another soul gently sank to its rest, and the silent voices whispered, "Welcome brother." Then all was calm and Peace as before. The little ripple flowed on to let the whole world know, then, having delivered its message, all was still. Amen.

Whatever the nature of this Illumination, probably a state of Dhyana,* it left a very marked result on the consciousness of Frater V.I.O., and gave him the necessary energy to continue his Work through many a dark and dismal period. He himself could not gauge its value at all at the time. He was alone in Vancouver and out of touch with the Order, having received no further word from his Neophyte since he left England. In fact he heard nothing till January of the following year. He however sent a post-card to say that he had obtained some result.

About this same time I find an entry called "The Philosophy of V.I.O." which seems of interest on account of some similarities to the Law of Thelema, of which he had heard nothing at that time. It reads as follows:

Man is bound by but *One Law*
If he breaks a part of it, he hurts no one but himself.
While he lives in unity with It, he is God.
While he does not live in unity with It he is Man.
While he lives in unity with it he becomes the Law.
To realise the Law and live it is the Great Work.
To break the Law after he has realized it is Sin.
To endeavour to bring all to the knowledge of the Law, is to keep the Law.
Seek ye the Law that ye may be Free.
Wisdom, Love and Power, these three are One. That these should be One is the Law.
By finding the Point from which these three become equal, and there remaining, by this means only, can the Law be Known.
If ye know this, ye know All.
If ye know not this, ye know less than All
Seek ever for the Absolute, and be content with Nothing less.

* * * * *

[* Advanced stage of meditation, a lesser form of Samadhi. Crowley considered Dhyana a result of successful Dharana (the focusing the attention on a single point). The ego is annihilated and conjoined with the object of attention. See *Book IV*, Part I: Mysticism, chapter 6. — JW]

By the end of September the immediate results of this first Illumination seem to have worn off, and we find Frater V.I.O. striving desperately to estimate the value of what had happened to him. He was certainly in a mental muddle, as the following entry shows, yet at the same time his one thought seems to have been to find a means of helping others to find that Light which had so transformed his whole being.

Sep. 24th, 1910.   Driad Hotel. Victoria, B.C.

I sit here with the idea of attempting to classify the results lately obtained. (Since L.V.X. entry.)

I may mention that during the interval I have carefully read and studied Crowley's *Tannhäuser, Sword of Song, Excluded Middle, Time, Berashith, Science and Buddhism, Three Characteristics,* etc.* In the Light of Understanding, all these works have taken on a very different aspect to when I read them previously. Also the Purpose of *Liber LXV* is clear. The result of all this gives me a feeling that I have arrived at the End and also at the Beginning at the same time.

This (by the way) seems the usual experience of the beginner; no sooner does he get a result, any result, than he immediately thinks he is at the end. But V.I.O. is evidently not to be deceived in that way, for he goes on:

Now, had I really arrived at the End, it seems reasonable to suppose I should not be here writing this. My body and mind are at any rate still in existence as a body and mind. But, as these are admittedly impermanent, does it matter much that they continue to exist in this form or no? What has that to do with the Consciousness of the Existence of That which transcends both? Now, had not some part of my present State of Existence *realized* the possibility of another and higher state of Consciousness, should I not still be in that state of uncertainty in which I lived before this realization came? This *realization* having come about has at any rate remained as a glimpse of Being, different from the previous not-being.

[* See Crowley, *Collected Works.* — JW]

The result of his mental analysis appears to amount to this, that he had experienced within himself a state of consciousness full of Peace and Joy, yet which more nearly approximated to Zero than any other term. He can find nothing with which to compare this state, but he recognizes its immense superiority over normal consciousness, and feels an intense desire to make it possible for others to share his experience. Since however he finds it impossible to explain it in words, he recognises that he must obtain the knowledge of some definite System of producing the state scientifically, but since he is not even a Neophyte of the A∴A∴, he wonders if They will recognise him as qualified to demand the right to know and spread Their teachings. He determines in any case to reduce the wants of the Ego as a separate being as far as possible, by forgetting self in his efforts to do all he can for others according to the Light he has obtained.

He found however that the destruction of the Ego was not thus easily accomplished at the first assault. Nevertheless he learned, not from books but from experience, that the Goal was to be found within himself, and that the nearer he could approach to the Consciousness of Nothingness the nearer he got to the Realization of Pure Existence. This reduction of consciousness to Zero then became the fixed aim of his Meditations; and any other experiments he entered upon, were, from that time onward, looked upon as necessary in order that he might fit himself to help others, rather than for his personal development.

On January 7th, 1911, he received No.4 of THE EQUINOX, and on seeing the Frontispiece to *Liber Jvgorvm* he experienced a feeling of decided aversion to cutting his arm in the prescribed manner. But, said he, "Fear is failure and the forerunner of failure"; and it will no doubt be best to undertake a week of this work so as to get used to it, after which I shall probably have no more trouble in this respect. He decided therefore to omit the word AND from his conversation for that period. His record of this experiment is kept in detail[2] and may prove interesting to other Students; so I shall transcribe it in full.

---

[2] The reader is asked to note that only a very few of very many practices are transcribed in this abridged record. This note is especially important, because a casual reader might be lead to suppose that V.I.O. got a great deal for very little. On the contrary, he is the hardest worker of all the Brethren, and well deserved his unprecedented success. O.M.

Saturday, Jan. 7th, 1911.   Vancouver B.C.

4 P.M. Have just received THE EQUINOX and am going to experiment with the Control of Speech by not using the word 'AND' for one week. May My Lord Adonai assist me. Amen.

Sat. 7th., 12 Midnight.

Although continually watchful, have had to chastise myself 15 times since 4 o'c. Will try and make a better record to-morrow. (I am certain that I have not missed cutting arm immediately after using the word.)

Sun. 8th., 11.30 P.M.

Said prohibited word

2. before rising in morning.
1. during conversation.
3. during singing practice.
1. at tea.
1. in evening.
1. Supper.

Total 9

This is certainly better. The three times during singing practice occurred while trying over new music with the choir of which I am a member, and it is very hard to leave out a word when singing. I find this practice makes one speak much less. The word chosen being a conjunction often results in the second part of a sentence remaining unspoken. I never before noticed how unnecessary some of our speech is; in fact I have now no doubt that a great many things are better left unsaid.

Monday, Jan. 9th. Bedtime.

Said word to-day for the first time at Lunch.

1. at 1.20 P.M. Lunch.
1. at 2.25 P.M. at Office.
2. at 4 P.M.   { Was careless enough to repeat a sentence containing it. Gave extra sharp cut.
1. at 5.10 P.M.
1. at 5.30 P.M.

Total 6

I am glad this shows further improvement. I was working and talking at the Office all the evening up to 10 o'c. and then had some conversation at home.

Tuesday, Jan. 10th. 12.35 P.M.

I am annoyed with myself, have been very careless. Had a talk with a man this morning for about 7 minutes, and forgot all about concentration. However, I have more or less formed a habit of speaking in short sentences; so I don't think I said the word more than twice. However am just going to give an extra cut in case, for being careless.

1. before leaving home in morning.
2. during conversation (as above) 12.10 A.M.
1. during Lunch. (This only half sounded, but have recorded it.)
1. at 7.45 P.M. (arms begins to feel sore).
1. at 10.30 P.M. (speaking too quickly to M.). went to bed at 11.10 P.M.

Total 6

Wednesday, Jan. 11. 6.45 P.M.

1. at 9.50 A.M. at Office.

Lunch { 1. while talking to my brother C.
Hour { 1. while talking to my wife.
12–1 o'c. { 1. while talking to my barber.

I consider the above *very bad;* but the explanation is that this particular hour was a great 'rush' as I had to call at my brother's Office, go home for lunch, do some shopping for lunch, and back again to eat same, also get shaved, in one hour. I evidently got flurried and lost control a bit. (Note the time when talking to my brother is doubtful, but have included it.) I think I should here note that on Saturday evening, Sunday and Monday I was quite aware of my task practically *all the time;* even when I made mistakes, they were in almost every case caused through *trying too hard.* Probably, having got over a difficult bit of conversation successfully, I was seduced into the error. Tuesday and to-day have been rather different. I have lapsed a little in vigilance, but attained a certain subconscious wariness. This makes conversation easier, but is not established enough to make me free from errors. In fact I am not sure if I am not getting more careless.

1. at 5.20 P.M. office.
1. at 8.30 P.M. to wife.
1. at 10 P.M. Singing.
1. 10.50. talking to wife.

Total for day, 9

Note. I felt terribly restless all the evening, and had an intense desire to talk freely. Went to a Smoking Concert at 8.45, but left again at 10.5, as I could not stand it any longer. I wanted to sing very much, and in fact did join in one song and made a slip noted above. I find it very difficult to leave out a word throughout a song, even if singing with others.

Thursday, Jan. 12, 7.35 P.M.
Have felt much better to-day and had much more control so far. At 8.58 A.M. I recorded one failure, but this time not spoken audibly; the meaning however was in mind, so I count it. I was repeating the time after being told it by a friend, viz., one *and* a half minutes to nine. Again at 6.35 P.M. once, but also inaudible.

I completed the day successfully with a total of 2 (inaudible).

Friday, Jan. 13, 6.20 P.M.

1. during morning at office.
1. at 2.35 P.M.   all inaudible
1. at 4.30 P.M.
1. at 6.10 P.M. Aloud.

I hardly know whether to count the inaudible ones, but would rather make failure appear worse than to try and deceive myself.

1. at 7.10 P.M. to Mrs. R. *(loud)*
1. at 9.00 P.M. Office.
1. at 10.30 P.M. to wife.
1. at 11.30 P.M. to wife.
---
8 Total for day.

This was a very bad day; and I had so much hoped to get through one clear day without a break! Never mind, better results next experiment.

Saturday, Jan. 14, 6.30 P.M.
Results very poor again.

1. during morning.
1. at 1.45 P.M. to wife.
1. at 3.00 P.M. to wife.

3

Total,	Saturday evening, Jan.7	15
	Sunday	9
	Monday	6
	Tuesday	6
	Wednesday	9
	Thursday	2
	Friday	8
	Sat. till 4 P.M.	3
	Total for week	58

Thus ends first experiment in control of Speech. It has been somewhat disappointing as regards results; but has proved to me how much I needed the exercise. I am very glad I undertook it, and shall try again in the near future.

Note. I have got over the feeling of shrinking at cutting myself. The first cuts were quite short and about half an inch long, afterwards I increased them to as much as 3 inches in length.

From Jan. 21 to 28th, Frater V.I.O. experimented with control of body, by not crossing legs. Same penalty as before. Total breaks for week 24. On Feb. 25th, he records the fact that he had succeeded in performing this practice for a clear week with one doubtful break only during sleep.

The result of these practices on Frater V.I.O. was a marked one. For one thing, the cutting of his arm during the first practice in the control of speech resulted in a subconscious wariness, for during the second — the details of which I have not recorded — he noticed that although the object of the practice was the control of the body by not crossing the legs, yet the attempt of the legs to drop into their old habits often had the effect of making him suddenly more careful in his speech, thus showing that there was an underlying connection in his subconscious mind resulting from his former work. These practices may then be said to have a cumulative effect, which makes them all the more valuable in helping towards the general control of body and mind.

But what is of still greater importance as far as Frater V.I.O. was concerned, they evidently had the effect — heightened perhaps by a letter from his Neophyte — of causing him to make a fresh and more determined effort to perform the Mystical Exercises for a definite period and with regularity, according to his original A∴A∴ instructions. From January 30th, 1911 to April 30th of that year, he kept a scientifically tabulated diary and during the prescribed three months he never missed a day in the performance of his appointed task.

His results, during this period, were perhaps not of a very startling nature, but, as any true Student learns, it is the long and continued "grind," the determined effort to carry out the work in hand or task set, in spite of every obstacle that may arise, that really counts when it comes to lasting results. It is the Will that needs training, and the accomplishment of such work, particularly if uninteresting and tedious in itself, goes far towards that end.

Jany. 30th., 1911. Letter from Frater P.A. his Neophyte. From this letter he learned that many changes had transpired since he left England, and among them that Frater P.A. had severed his connection with the Outer Order, but was willing to continue in charge of him.

Febry. 5th. He wondered if Frater P.A. had only told him this as a test. It must be remembered that all this while he had worked on alone, and had had no news to speak of, and this he attributed to his own failure to carry out his task in detail. In this he was no doubt right to a great extent, for unless any Probationer does what he is instructed, he can expect no further help, which would only mean that the Master concurred in his laziness or weakness.

March 6th., 1911. Up to this time, although he had done the exercises regularly no particular result had occurred, and we find this note: "I do not really look for any results now, or expect any, since control of 'self' is the object of these exercises."

Now it is to be noted that when one really gets to a state when having worked one is content to continue to do so, expecting no results, one often obtains them. (Of course it's no use trying to fool oneself on these things, you can't get a result by just saying you don't care a damn.) Something of the sort seems to have happened in this case, as the following shows.

March 12th. "During Lecture on *Parsifal,* I felt illumination within which permeated my whole being, and I became *conscious once more* of the Truth of *my previous Illumination* which I had lost, as it were."

This entry is interesting. Illumination comes, and at the time there is no doubt about it. IT IS. Then, perhaps, life goes on much as before, except for the ever present remembrance of "Something that happened;" and, having nothing with which to compare it, that Something is difficult to describe or even to formulate. However, immediately one approaches another period one can recognise the symptoms, almost in advance, and the new Illumination is as it were added to the old, and there is fresh wonder and joy in both.

March 15th. I feel as if I were a highly strung musical instrument. My Will runs over the strings, causing complete and harmonious vibrations in my being, which seems to give forth at times an unformulated and therefore most delightful melody.

March 28th. How can I write it, how put into words the

least idea of that which is unformed? Yet I will try while yet a vestige of the thought remains. I have conceived within my womb a child. Or is it that I have for the first time realized that I have a womb? Yet it is so, that "blank" within, into which I have projected my thoughts, and from which they have come forth again 'living' is for a greater purpose. Can I not form therein a child that shall be MYSELF made from the highest ideals, the essence of my pains, refined and purified, freed from dross by the living fire? This life of Service must be lived till I am 'selfless' in all that I knew as myself; but all the time will not my 'child' be growing within me, composed of finer materials? And by complete union therewith ... I cannot formulate any more now.

This entry indicates a recognition of the "formulation of the negative in the ego" which shall eventually destroy it. Is it not written in *Liber LXV* "As an acid eats into steel, and as a cancer utterly corrupts the body, so am I unto the spirit of Man. I shall not rest until I have destroyed it utterly"?

Sunday April 2nd (Fra V.I.O.'s 25th Birthday) During practice I had a distinct consciousness of the 'centre of consciousness' being not 'within' as usual, but above head.

April 3rd. I alternate between a state of 'enjoying any task or position because it is the first that comes to hand and therefore the simplest and best course of action', and 'a feeling of absolute mental torture caused by the necessity of existing at all.' The first appears to give the chance of continually 'enlarging' until one becomes That which I can 'consciously be' for a short period at a time, and the other seems to lead to annihilation. Probably the multiplication of one state by the other is the solution. (Crowley's $0 \times \degree$.)

Sat., April 8th. During the last three days have gradually been nearing another 'climax' which reached, shall I say, its height on Saturday, when I arrived at a state of Illumination which was, as it were 'added to my previous state.' I seized a scrap of paper and wrote "Amid all the complications and perplexity there remains, back of all, the Will. The Will to Be. The

Will to Be Nothing, which is the only state inconceivable to the mind. The old God willed to be something, and the Universe appeared, The New God wills to be Nothing and becomes ? ? ? ? ? ?" After writing the foregoing, there was a state of bliss the reflection of which was caught by the body. So joyful it became that it whirled round in a mad dance, and was filled with music. It was stifled by the confines of the room; but "I" was Free, so it couldn't matter much. (This is the second experience of rhythm filling the body, and causing it to whirl and dance in order to find expression somehow.)

April 9th. Started to read about 8.30 this morning. Sometime during morning lost idea of "ego" to realize All as Self. (Left notes for a couple of hours) I find terrible difficulty in expressing the slightest idea of that which occurred during this state, yet it would seem of importance to do the best I can. That *there is no soul* struck me as a horrible blank. That *I do not, and never have existed as "I"* comes as a wonderful realization while the consciousness of the unreality of the "I" lasts. With the loss of "the ego" comes the consciousness that the whole universe of things and people is but a part of the State then arrived at. That if this little body dies, existence still remains in all the other part of the Universe and therefore the change called Death, occurring in different atoms, all the time, makes no difference. Is there any reason why one should not look upon everything and everybody as parts of Oneself, since one is equally willing to allow any other body to consider you as a part of their imagination only? It would seem that one tiny part — self — has been fondly cherished, while in reality that tiny part is but a reflex of the Whole which is really You, but even this state must in the end give way before the Power of Nothing.

April 16th, 8.30 A.M. Finished reading the Life of Buddha, and then, lying down, composed myself for Meditation. Breathed regularly and deeply for a time, afterwards stopping all entries two or three times. (Shanmukhi Mudra.*) Presently I

[* Closing the Seven Gates. This meditation posture consists of inserting the thumbs into the ears, placing the index fingers against the eyes, middle fingers against nostrils, and ring and little fingers upon the mouth. — JW]

passed into a state which was practically desireless. I could feel the Goal, but the wish to help others made it impossible to Become the State I contemplated. After this, I was surprised, on letting all breath out of the body, to feel a sudden lightness, as if I were about to float. This being unexpected, caused me to turn my thoughts to the body, after which, although I tried, I could not get back to the previous state. I estimate that I remained in the condition mentioned for over an hour, as it was 12 o'c. when I looked at the time. In fact, it may have been nearer two hours.

The above meditation left Frater V.I.O. with a feeling of "Nearly but not Quite." He had, to some extent, gazed at the Goal of Nothingness, but had failed to Become that Goal. The following day there is despondency and dissatisfaction. On April 22nd reason again holds sway, and he tries to use it to discover just where he is, of course without success, since Reason can never explain that which is Beyond Reason. I think at this point he also began to make another grave error; he tried to compare his experiences with those of John St. John, with the result that, later on, when he undertook a Retirement, that of J. St. J. subconsciously influenced him to a great extent, although he would not and could not have admitted it at the time. In these things one must be Oneself, not try to be another. His entry of April 22 is a long one, and I quote it in part.

I wish I could express myself better. On reading J. St. J. again I find that I can comprehend it ever so much better than when I first read it some three months after its publication. Then, it seemed like a dream of the far distant future; now, many parts seem like records of my own experiences, only expressed infinitely better than I have been able to put them. Now, of what value are the experiences I have gained? Why is the state of Oneness with Adonai not lasting, or rather, is it possible to remain always conscious of that State? How is it when reading an account like J. St. John's that I *know* what he is talking about, and can *feel* with him the difficulty of putting these things into words? I could not have *realized* this a year ago, before I entered into certain states of which I cannot gauge the value at all, while in normal consciousness. There is no Doubt

Then. But how may I be Sure always? I will fetch THE EQUINOX, and put down the points as they come to me. Let me quote Page 87 [65 — JW]. "Well, one thing I got (again!) that is that when all is said and done I am that I am, all these thoughts of mine, angels and devils both, are only fleeting moods of me. The one true self of me is Adonai. Simple! Yet I cannot remain in that simplicity." I can realize that state perfectly, but I am not a Magician, I know little or nothing of Ceremonial Magick, except from reading; my results have not been accompanied by visions. What results I have obtained have been in the nature of becoming the thing itself, not seeing it. However, to pass on: Is the idea of coming back to help others (see Sun. Apr. 16) only a form of the Dweller on the Threshold and caused through *fear* of annihilation or madness? Or is it a concession to my own weakness, a pandering to my 'self' because I am really nowhere near ready to hurl myself into the Gulf, instead of which I come back to normal consciousness, and try and make myself believe I have 'given up' what I 'could not get' for the sake of 'others' which do not exist at the time (for me)? This is certainly a difficult one to tackle, I am entering it so as to try and formulate the proposition clearly. Now, the doubt enters my mind, that I have only put it down in order to *appear honest* to Fra. P.A., or anyone who may read this record. NO.... The foregoing thought seems to have a parallel in J. St. J. Again on Page 96 [71 — JW] "I must attain or ... an end to J. St. J." seems similar to the state arrived at on Sept. 5, 1910, when I determined to ask the last WHY? and afterwards entered into Peace. On page 133 [99 — JW] he says "subtly, simply, imperceptibly gliding I passed away into nothing. ... I felt the interior trembling kindle itself into a kiss ... also I was given to enjoy the subtle Presence of my Lord interiorly during the whole of the twelfth day. But he withdrew Himself ... yet leaving a comfort not to be told, a Peace ... The Peace." Yes, with me also the Peace has remained, but sometimes I cannot connect myself with It, or fail to do so, being led away by Maya. Then comes the entry of the Thirteenth Day. "Being entered into the Silence let me abide in the Silence. Amen." And here I am puzzled. Either J. St. J. attained permanently to a State such that he was never again annoyed by the silly mistake of identifying Himself with the body, or he did not.[3] But after all, what has that to do with V.I.O.? It has certainly nothing to do with C.S.J. But how do I stand? This seems to be the position. While in normal consciousness I know that I (or Not I) am ever in the state of which I sometimes catch the reflection when I realize that I am *not* I. There, that is the clearest original thought I have expressed this afternoon, and bad at that. Of course, I am really quite content, it is only when I begin to think and reason about things that I begin to become discontented. It's about time I shut up.

And on April 30th the three months prescribed by his Neophyte came to an end. He writes: "I feel they have been well spent, and that I have gained a more certain control of my body and mind, but realize *how much is* needed before ... 0 x ° . Peace unto all beings. Amen."

SECTION IV.

APRIL 30TH, 1911, TO OCTOBER 13TH, 1912

Frater V.I.O. next experienced a state of "Dryness" such as almost invariably follows a partial success. On Sunday May 7th he writes:

> I have not made an entry in this record for a whole week. I seem to be losing control, and my diary, lying untouched in my drawer, is becoming like a horrible fiend. It worries me when I do not enter it; and yet it requires a great effort even to touch it or take it out, while to enter it daily appears an almost superhuman task. Why is this? I have done exercises this week as usual, but a little earlier than previously, because I have to be at the office by 8.30 A.M. instead of nine o'c. as heretofore. I think Fra. P.A. might write to me. I feel that he is testing me, and have tried to hold to that idea. I know that *really* it does not matter, but I am weak yet, and should so like a little friendly push and a few words of advice. I feel like dropping it all for a time; but

---

[3] He had finished his immediate work, and went back into the world, as per *Liber VII* II, 51–53, bestowing on himself this Benediction as he did so. O.M.

that is perhaps the very thing that is so difficult, in fact, the whole trick! O dear, I am certainly having a spell of 'dryness.' But I will plod on, On, ON, and in, In, IN. O for one kiss, or the echo of a Kiss, My Lord Adonai. I yearn for Thee, I am Parched for Thee. Let me be utterly consumed in Thee! Amen.

Saturday, June 10, 1911. Tonight I must write an entry. I MUST. And it is time. Why have I not done so before? Because I have experienced a 'dryness' for the last month, and have made no definite effort to overcome it, but have just kept a firm hold on the little atom of real Knowledge I have obtained, & setting my face still towards the East, have plodded on with this material existence and the office work I have undertaken. I have experienced an incessant yearning for that "Something" or "Nothing" of which a glimpse had been vouchsafed unto me, and *Waited*. Maybe I should have *Worked* and *waited*, but I did not. I have not heard from Frater P.A. yet, but I wrote again during the month, saying I wanted to do something to help others a little, and asking if he could spare time to advise me on that score. To-day I received THE EQUINOX ordered last April. It had been sent to my brother's Club and had been lying there for a month, and all the while I had been waiting and hoping for its arrival. Then, when hope was about dead, I obtained a trace of it. It came as a drink of sweet nectar to a thirsty pilgrim, and it is wonderful how much better I feel. The note *re* Neophytes and Probationers has set me at rest about the silence of Fra P.A.; and confirms, what all the while I have suspected, that his delay in answering is a test. This confirmation is cheering, however hard the trial may have been, in so far as I had made up my mind to work on, whether he writes or not, and had got quite used to the idea of having to work out my own Path, without outside aid or encouragement.

He was also pleased to find some of his own experiments more or less confirmed in *Liber H.H.H.** of which he writes:

M.M.M. 2, 'mentions the breath playing upon the skin, etc.' I have experienced this, and asked Fra P.A. for instructions

[* See *Equinox* I, 5, also *Book IV*, Part 3, *Magick in Theory and Practice.* — JW]

thereon. Sometimes, after hard breathing, I have been filled with the sensation. I think I understand the 'lightning flash,' but shall experiment. My present knowledge is more as a sheet of summer lightning. The minute point of light has often appeared to me, and I had come to the conclusion that it should be held in the zenith. The radiating cone, I have not experienced. II. A.A.A. The idea of considering one's own death is mentioned. This occurred to me and was carried out before by first Illumination; this serves as a confirmation that I was on the right track. I should have no doubt mentioned these meditations more fully at the time.[4] I have often wondered *how* I got into the state I then experienced, and this copy of THE EQUINOX has revived the memory and gives instruction for obtaining, no doubt, a very much fuller result, only I shall have to work with a big W.

June 12, 1911. On Saturday night, in bed I attempted "thinking backwards" and successfully managed two days, with no breaks in the first day, and practically none for the day before, except a few little incidents during office hours in the morning. When I came to thoughts on waking of Saturday morning and got to the "blank" I experienced some mental visions and 'telephone-cross voices,' but cannot say if they were connected with any dream; then suddenly I found myself lying in bed with the last thoughts of the previous night in mind. Yesterday, I read the article on the subject *(Training of the Mind*)* carefully, also learnt the formula of the four great meditations on Love, Pity, Happiness and Indifference. At night, I again attempted "thinking backwards," but experienced rather more difficulty as conditions were bad. However, once started, I got back through Sunday and very nearly, if not quite as fully, over the two previous days; then, having got into the swing, I roughly attempted a short and incomplete review of my whole life, which although brief, was much fuller than I expected. I remembered things connected with early childhood quite accurately, but of course not with full connections. Then something

---

[4] Observe how the least slackness in writing up the Record avenges itself. The Record is both chart and log to the bold Sea-Captains of The Voyage Marvelous! [* Written by Allen Bennett, published in *The Equinox* I, 5. — JW]

occurred that I really did not expect, and only later trials will prove if it was an illusion or not. Having tried hard to pierce the blank, back of all, I had a sudden clear sensation of lying on a bed with people around, and in particular an elderly man in black velvet and knee breeches, whom I at once felt was my Tutor, leaning over me. The ideas that came with this were that I was quite young, and had some disease like consumption, that the family was wealthy, and the house a Country Residence. These impressions were very real and quite unexpected, but as I used to have a dread of consumption, am still young, and meditation took place lying down, it would seem that very little imagination would make up the rest. However, I mention it, as the experience was different from anything I can previously remember.

July 8th., 1911. About a fortnight ago, I received a letter from Frater P.A.[5] in answer to my previous two. I was pleased to hear from him, but he gave me a good talking to, also some new instructions. He wanted to know, what I meant by making a claim to having attained Samadhi, or something very like it, in August last, and then shortly afterwards started cutting my arm, etc. I have not answered it yet, but this much for reference: (1) I never mentioned Samadhi, nor can I remember claiming to have

[5] Frater P.A. was not a Neophyte, but had been appointed to receive other Probationers for administrative convenience. This was a plain breach of the regulations of the Order, and the result was this comic letter. Frater P.A. was apparently under the impression that as soon as anyone happened along into Samadhi, he was to yawn his "Nunc dimittis." ["Depart in peace," see Luke 2:29 — jw]

This incident should be a warning to all those in charge of authority that they must in no wise vary the strict instructions of the Order, however obvious may appear the advantages of doing so.

The result of Frater P.A.'s presumption in trying to train Frater V.I.O., instead of pressing on to the mark of his own high calling, was that he simply dropped out of the Order altogether, leaving himself as a memorial only this ridiculous episode, in which he appears as a small boy who should have hooked a tarpon when he was fishing for catfish.

Had he adhered to the rules of the Order, attended solely to his own business, and forwarded V.I.O.'s record to his superiors, who were competent to interpret it, we should not have had this excellent example of the results of presumption and folly to guide us for the future, and to enliven our perusal of the record of our conscientious V.I.O. with a touch of timely merriment. O.M.

attained it. (2) I did attain a state of consciousness which has had a lasting effect upon my life and made my viewpoint entirely different from that time. (3) The language I used to describe the state, came perfectly naturally to me, as the most convenient to describe a state foreign to any previous experience. (4) I might have used language of a higher plane than I was on, but I don't see why. (5) I started control of body some months later when I had in some measure lost the complete recollection of the state, or rather when it was little more than a recollection, also, when I first saw picture of man's arm in EQUINOX, I rather dreaded to cut mine, so thought it best to carry out exercise and get over bodily dread of a little pain. I did so and am not sorry.

This letter from Fra P.A. giving new practice, etc., combined with some considerable dissatisfaction on Frater V.I.O.'s part, regarding his present state, caused him to undertake another regular spell of work for 32 days, after which he seems to have recorded very little until March 25 in the following year, viz., 1912. He then experimented with SSS section of *Liber HHH,* from EQUINOX V and obtained automatic rigidity. He writes: "(1) Brain became charged with electric fluid or Prana, in fact whole face and hands became as if connected with an electric battery, also brain seemed luminous but void. (2) Could not awaken spine from 'yoni'; but, after persisting, the part just below small of back became enlivened, then under ribs, then breast and nape of neck. The current became very strong and almost unbearable. Whole body became perfectly and automatically rigid. Hands seemed to feel gnarled and misshapen, contorted by the force in them (I noticed this as a side issue). Feet also became filled with life, etc., etc." He had had some experience with Pranic Currents in his body before, in fact in 1910, but never so fully and completely. He then reported this, and his general progress, to Fra P.A.

In July, he received a letter from Fra P.A., saying that he had now arrived at a stage when he might undertake an Operation for the Invocation of Adonai,[6] which would require Six weeks' work,

[6] No man has the right to make the slightest suggestion to another as to when he should or should not undertake this critical and central Operation. To interfere in any way between a man and his Holy Guardian Angel is the most intolerable presumption. O.M

the last Twelve days of which must be in complete Retirement. At first he could see no possible way to undertake this, owing to, (1) Family Affairs, (2) Office work, (3) Lack of money. He determined however to go ahead in spite of apparent obstacles, and duly made a start at Midnight, August 31. From that time until September 18th he was occupied by the Preparatory work, and from Midnight September 18th to Midnight September 30th by the Purity Section. October 1st to October 12th Proper Retirement, and on October 12th Invocation of Holy Guardian Angel. All this meant a great deal of work and trouble, and much new experience gained, but was on the whole a failure, though a Step on the Path. During this retirement he cut a Wand, as a Symbol not of his will but of the Will of Adonai in him. It would be hardly right to say that this Magical Retirement produced no results, though it may not have produced the One Desired Result. By the time a man has made 671 entries in his Magical Record (as Frater V.I.O. did during those six weeks) and each of those entries has a direct bearing on the matter in hand, he is bound to have produced a state of mind somewhat different from normal consciousness. (It is interesting to note that 671, by a curious coincidence, is the numeration of Adonai, spelt in full, the Central idea of the Invocation.)

We shall not enter into the details of the various practices he performed during this period, but we may mention, for the sake of completeness, a few fragments recorded during the last few days of the Retirement.

> October 9, 9.6 P.M. (This was the 9th day of Section C, and the 39th day of the complete Operation.)
>
> The 'state' is getting more and more difficult to describe, in fact I don't know what to make of it. I might almost say I feel 'normal'; and yet there is a subtle difference. There is (I think) an entire absence of fear, worry, disgust, joy, sorrow, pain, or any of the old states, and this seems to be a condition of *calm observation* without any desire to criticise anything. I suppose, as a matter of fact, it is a state of equilibrium. I think I have it. It is the empty shrine awaiting the in-dwelling of the God.
>
> 10 P.M. I experienced another peculiar state just now, Having closed my eyes for a few moments (concentrating), I thought I would try and think backwards over the last few things I had

been doing, but found, try as I would, I could not think of things done *even a moment before.* All was the "present peculiar experience," and there was no getting away from it. The concentration acted just like a magnet, and became automatic. Again, on trying to look back over this retirement, it appears as a "Single state of consciousness," not as a number of events. I should really have to read my diary if I wanted to know any details in succession just now.

At the end of the 10th day of this Section "C" and the beginning of the 11th Day I think the true climax of the Operation took place, for he writes:

> Oct. 11, 12.30. So did the day start and I knelt at the altar from 12 Midnight until 12.28. During this time did my Lord Adonai begin to manifest within me, so that my being was wrapped away in bliss ineffable. And my body was filled with rapture of His coming until the cry burst from my lips "My Lord and my God." There are no words to describe Thee, my Beloved, though I yet tremble with the joy of Thy presence, yet do I feel that this is but the beginning of the reflection of Thee. O God, wrap me utterly away, beyond even this Bliss. Let me be utterly consumed in Thine Essence. Amen.

However, on The DAY, the 12th of October, when he came actually to use his Invocation (prepared and illuminated during his retirement) expecting the Result might occur, he writes as follows:

> At precisely 6.50. I entered the Temple, lit the incense and robed. All being in order I knelt in prayer and at 7 P.M. I arose and performed the Banishing Ritual of the Pentagram, then, taking the ritual in my left hand and raising the wand in my right, I slowly and clearly read the Oath and the Invocation. Afterwards, I was impressed to make a certain Sign with the wand. And the Word that came to me was ... Kneeling, I felt very calm, and I waited ... afterwards, according to my understanding, I turned off the light, leaving only the lamp of olive Oil, and I lay down upon the place prepared and waited ... and all was very dark and still, with a feeling of absolute calm and control, and I waited ... And nothing happened. Then something

seemed to tell me to get up and to kneel again at the altar, yet I waited, but presently I arose and stood at the altar, and I felt "I am that I am;" but there seemed not much joy in the thought, and yet, I knew that I had done all, even the least thing, to the best of mine understanding and ability ... And it began to dawn upon me that I had failed, but where and how, I know not.

I have been dazzled with no illusionary success, I have overcome the fear of failure, and now, even as a tired warrior, I will go back into the world and — STRIVE.

The Next day. Chaos. Reason is quite inadequate to solve the problem. Here followeth a certain passage from Ezekiel.

"Son of man, behold, I take away from thee the desire of thine eyes with a stroke: yet neither shalt thou mourn nor weep, neither shalt thy tears run down. Forbear to cry, make no mourning for the dead, bind the tire of thine head upon thee, and put on thy shoes upon thy feet, and cover not thy lips, and eat not the bread of men. So I spake unto the people in the morning; and at even my wife died: and I did in the morning as I was commanded. And the people said unto me: Wilt thou not tell us what these things are to us, that thou doest so? Then I answered them. The word of the Lord came unto me saying: Speak unto the house of Israel: Thus saith the Lord God ... Ezekiel is unto you a sign: according to all that he hath done, shall ye do; and when this cometh, ye shall know that I am the Lord. Also, son of man, shall it not be in the day when I take from them their strength, the joy of their glory, the desire of their eyes, and that whereon they set their minds ... In that day shall thy mouth be opened ... and thou shalt speak ... and thou shalt be a sign unto them, and they shall know that I am the Lord." Amen.

A last note: TRUTH must ever be One. Whatever I expected, I found not. But why should I grieve because of having exposed some of my illusions? I have held to the truth, and the Truth remains, for the Truth is ever One, yea, the Truth is Ever One." Amen.

Section V.
January 1st, 1913, to December 31st, 1913

We must now pass on to Fra V.I.O.'s diary for the year 1913 E.V. I can find no written records of the period between October 13th, 1912, when he finished the Retirement, and March 2nd, 1913, when he again began to keep a regular summary of his work. On that date he writes:

> During the last few days some important events have taken place. First however I must mention that I have heard nothing from Frater P.A. since the retirement except a P.C. to say that he had received my record. On ... I received a letter dated in London, Jan. 10th, from the Chancellor of A∴A∴, asking the results of my work since I became a Probationer. Answered same on Jan. 26th, and was surprised and pleased on Feb. 26th, to received a reply passing me to the Grade of Neophyte, followed by the necessary documents. Answered this on Feb. 28th.

This letter from the Chancellor of A∴A∴, passing Frater V.I.O. to the grade of Neophyte, contained the following passage, which is important, in the light of later events:

"We wish our Body to be a Body of Servants of Humanity. A time will come when you will obtain the experience of the 14th Aethyr. You will become a Master of the Temple. That experience must be followed by that of the 13th Aethyr, in which, the Master, wholly casting aside all ideas of personal attainment, busies himself exclusively with the care of others."

The year 1913 was an important one for Frater V.I.O. in many ways. For one thing, it was during this period that he was forced to stand alone, and to rely upon himself and his own judgment of what was the right course of action for the governance of his life and the solution of his family difficulties as well as his occult problems. Hitherto, as before remarked, he had been under the guidance of one upon whom he had looked as his Neophyte, and in whom he had placed the utmost confidence. He now found himself in one of the most trying situations that had up to that time been his lot to cope with, viz.: that he must choose between the continuance of that guidance, and the regular course of training mapped out in the Outer Order of the A∴A∴. He must either resign the grade of Neophyte just conferred upon him, severing his connection with the Outer Order, or cease to work under Frater P.A. altogether. The reasons for this cannot be dealt with fully in this place, nor would they be of the slightest interest to our readers, suffice it to say that Frater V.I.O. had pledged himself to work on certain lines for six months and that these lines had been laid down by Frater P.A. His duty was then fairly clear, so he practically severed himself from obtaining guidance from either his old Neophyte or his newly appointed Zelator, until that period of work, to which he felt bound by his own oath to himself, was over, and at the end of that time, having worked hard and well, Those who were guiding and directing his life made the way clear for him, and he found himself in a position to accept the instruction of the A∴A∴, coming under the direct guidance of Frater O.M. This event must not be supposed to reflect in any way on Frater P.A. for whom he always felt and will feel great love and respect; the circumstances leading up to this change were outside the sphere of influence of Fra V.I.O. and the more difficult to judge owing to his isolation in Canada. With this brief allusion to the change in his occult affairs, we may pass on to a corresponding change in his material surroundings, for although he continued with his usual office work, he lived during the best part of this year under canvas in a small tent by the sea shore, necessitating some miles of walking every day, and throwing him a good deal more in touch with Nature than formerly; also the addition of a 'little stranger' to his family had a marked effect on his home affairs, being as it were the key to the solution of certain problems that had been puzzling him in that direction.

During the period from March 2nd to September 4th, when we might say he was working on alone, his record shows some 340 Meditation practices, mostly in the Asana known as the Dragon, the periods ranging from a few minutes to something over an hour, but most of them comparatively short, the average perhaps being twenty minutes.

After this there is a gap, during which he worked morning and evening most days, but made no further record till November 9, from which date to December 31 over eighty practices are recorded.

Of the details of all this early work it is not necessary to treat very fully, but since, on sending in his record at the end of the year, it was returned by Frater O.M. with various notes and comments of the greatest help and value to Fra V.I.O., I am selecting those passages so commented upon as likely to be of most interest and help to other students.

N.B. The comments of Fra O.M. (in parentheses) follow entries.

March 2, 1913. I have got a zeal for service since the retirement, wanted to take for new Motto "I aspire to serve" but cannot find Latin equivalent. ("Volo servare" would do. But a better idea is "I want to help" rather than "serve." O.M.)

March 22. Feel sorry I missed exercise this morning through slackness.
(When you *detect* slackness, double the exercise, if it kills you. Sure cure! O.M.).

March 25. Dragon Asana. Mantra A.M.P.H. 9.39 to 10.34 P.M. = 55 mins, Breaks 14 to 18, mostly very slight. Interruptions none. Results: Dharana, got feeling on skin and automatic rigidity. Lost all personality most of the time, but only found this out by 'break' which revived it. Brain soon took up Mantra automatically. Illumination in brain after a while. Towards the last saw some visions of sea, &c. (very slight). Space and time annihilated during most of the practice. Good.
(Beginning good — end bad. O.M.)

Mar. 30, 5.15 to 5.46 P.M. = 31 Mins. Counted first seven breaks, then became concentrated and lost count. Interruptions. (1) A safety pin, falling on floor, made me start violently (2) R. called. Results: Breath arose on skin and the 'light' arose. Started to concentrate on spine. Towards the end started a sort of automatic chant of apparently senseless words. Have noticed before that when this occurs, it leads to a kind of ecstasy. Had to leave off, as was called to tea by Ruby.
(Good, but a virtuous woman is above Rubies, and never calls holy men to tea. O.M.)

Apr. 4. Control of Body. While at office kept left elbow at

side for 3 hours. Wished to see if this would be quite easy and found I had no difficulty in remembering. (Good: try something harder. O.M.)

Apr. 6, 9.20–10 P.M. Dragon. This meditation was the best lately. Quickly felt the Prana gripping the body. Conceived the blackness of Understanding becoming penetrated by Wisdom. Brain became luminous. Body rigid. Tension passed and force concentrated at bridge of nose. Concentrated on Ajna. Personality gone. Tried to project consciousness straight up. Was suddenly interrupted by R. who was in bed just by my side. Hardly knew where I was for the moment and had to concentrate on body to regain normal.

(Too big a handicap, having anyone in the room. O.M.)

Apr. 8, 9.25 to 10.11 P.M. = 46 Mins. Dragon. The mind and seer alone remain. Turning back on the seer there seem intervals of blank. This is accompanied with no illumination or joy, and one almost wonders why one had gone so far to obtain this. Probably desire not entirely obliterated. Some disinclination to leave the state. (This sounds better. O.M.)

Apr. 13, 11.21–11.36 P.M. Dragon. A certain bliss arose at the thought that I was but a little child of the Great Father. Joy. Joy. (Yes: too emotional. O.M.)

Apr. 19, 7.07 A.M. to 7.20 A.M. Not anything very definite. There is a certain quality of bliss about these practices which is peculiar to concentration but otherwise indescribable. (This is bad. You do things well, and work hard; but your point of view is all wrong. I feel a sort of sentimentality injuring your scientific attitude. O.M.)

April 20, 2.40–3.10 P.M. Having left home about 2.15 I climbed up towards the mountain till I found a secluded spot; there I knelt down and did breathing exercise. Felt Prana all over body. Invoked Adonai and tried to unite with Him. A brilliant White light filled sphere of consciousness. Arose as Adonai, performed the Ritual of Pentagram, then prayed aloud and fluently, trying to unite consciousness with all Nature. Knelt again in Meditation, and arose much strengthened and with a feeling of the Divine Presence.

(This is excellent for a beginner. But remember — all these divine illuminations are mere Breaks. O.M.)

Note: — I find more and more difficulty in remembering any details of these practices the next day. Concentration was good. In this instance at end of practice could not remember what time I started, although I believe I am correct. I have thought several times lately about this loss of memory. Is it a result, or is it a fault? (It's a good sign, as a rule. O.M.)

May 9, 10.21–10.43 P.M. Dragon. Astral journey of no particular import. Cannot properly identify with image. Seem to see the image while acting in it. (This isn't as bad as it sounds. Don't worry, so long as the Image is quite sure of itself. O.M.) [This, by the way, would have been particularly helpful information, and if Fra. V.I.O. had had it at the time he might have done a good many more Astral journeys. This lack of confidence at first seems to hold back many Students who could otherwise travel on the Astral quite successfully. — ED.]

May 21, 8.45 to 9.34 P.M. = 49 Mins. Thumbs in ears; first 25 mins in Dragon. Then lying flat on back. Cramp in left foot on change of position. After the loud sounds subsided, became concentrated on ringing sound in left ear. Mind became calmer, and I heard the sound of a little silver bell, very clear and sweet, struck a number of times. This still in left ear. Then heard sound of metallic throbbing (if I can use the term) very faintly in right ear. Mind must have been well concentrated as time passed quickly. (Sounds rather good. O.M.)

June 7. *Note.* This afternoon, while reclining in an easy chair, nearly fell asleep; instead, however, I concentrated for some while. On being asked by R. to go and do some little thing for her, I put hands over eyes before rising, and saw a light so peculiar that it is worth mentioning. It had the appearance of being three distinct things at once. Dead black, a beautiful night-sky-blue, but at the same time the very essence of it was *brilliant light.* Quite indescribable in words.

(Seems very good. O.M.)

It may be remarked that Fra. V.I.O. had occupied himself with the contemplation of the Stélé of Revealing, completed therefrom a Pantacle of Nuit, and had obtained a sigil for same, during this day. (This peculiar light is stigmatically characteristic of the Stélé. O.M.)

June 18th, 10.34 to 10.53 P.M. = 19 mins. 14 mins Pranayama 10.20.20. Regular and easy. 5 Mins. Meditation. Mind cleared and became calm. It perhaps appears that little progress is made, and some slackness exists as regards exercises. The truth is, I more and more use the true essence. If a little worry occurs, automatically, I turn to That within which dissolves it at once and restores the balance. It is that NOTHING with which I come into closest contact during meditation, but It is ever present, and I recognize the fact. I believe it to be the true Stone of the Wise which turns everything to gold. I call it Adonai when I give it a name at all. Most often the mind slips into that state without reason or argument.

(Yes: it does appear that more time ought to be given to the Work. But the Progress is not bad for all that. However, I don't quite like the complacent feeling. Nothing replaces hard work. Somebody I know [or don't know] does more actual grind than he ever did. 24 full dress Magick ceremonies in the first 5 weeks of 1914, and about 2 hours every morning writing up the records. And in this please include 2 bad goes of influenza and bronchitis! O.M.)

July 9, 7.20 7.24 A.M. Dragon. Rather bad. Tried to do practice outside in the rain, there being no room in the tent. *Note:* — Man, wife and baby together with all one's earthly belongings in a tent 12' x 10' in wet weather, is certainly a record. (I've been one of 5 big men in a tent 7'6" x 6' in a hurricane blizzard on a glacier. But you win. O.M.)

Aug. 8 *Note.* I begin to feel the fuller life again. These few pages of Edward Carpenter have acted like a draught of living water and revived me a great deal. I feel a secret Joy to-night. The unaccountable inner Joy which transforms everything and frees the soul from its shackles. All seems so good to-night, this day's work, the presence of my two dear ones, and all the dear ones of which I am a part, the presence of Adonai within and without. It is good to have lived for this.

(This is dreadful! You must not mistake 'feeling good' for a mystic state. O.M.)

Aug. 9, 9.59 to 10.26 P.M. During this meditation a certain magical understanding arose whereby it was easy to interpret any common object into a symbol of the Work.

(A bit better. O.M.)

Aug. 18, 11.07 to 11.13 P.M. Even 6 mins is a difficulty now. When will the tide turn again! (The tides are due to the pull of the Sun and Moon. O.M.)

Aug. 19, 7.32 to 7.42 P.M. Slight feeling of Joy. (Bother joy! O.M.)

Aug. 25, 1.33 to 10.55 P.M. Changed my Asana once during practice and found I could move body without affecting the particular part which was in the calm state. (Good. O.M)

Aug. 26. A quiet evening at home, for which I am grateful. It seems as if so little is entered in this diary and so much remains unsaid. How one longs sometimes to *express* things and thoughts and generally ends by some commonplace entry. I think to-night I will try a little more than usual. All this time I have been plodding on, having made up my mind to a course of action in accordance with my aspiration. Day after day I have continued until this round of existence has become almost a fixed habit. My times of meditation and practice have dwindled till they are somewhat short, but for all that, the main idea has never been clouded. I feel far more determined in every way than I did, although less certain of any fixed goal. I know also that I have problems to face, now, or in the future, but have learnt to keep doing what comes to hand, without wavering or despairing. I do not seem to have made much definite progress, yet there are signs which give me to understand that all is as it should be; perhaps I am more in tune and so do not notice such vivid changes. I have found nature very fair and beautiful, this summer. I have got to love Her so much more than formerly.

Then again, I have mastered Her a little more; I have learnt more of swimming, climbing, walking and other exercises through daily practice. I have made new friends, have learnt from them and taught them in return. All this, in spite of the limited existence of living in a tiny tent and often being very hard up. The power to retreat into that part of me which is Peace, free from all strife, remains with me. To be an onlooker at my thoughts and actions and remain the while in perfect rest — very seldom disturbed by outside influences — this is indeed something. Another important thing I would mention. I have an intense longing for more Love, a sort of unsatisfied craving to embrace people, particularly women, and sometimes natural things (this was not meant for sarcasm) such as the earth, the grass, etc. I do not think I expect and ask the love of others so much as I feel the need of entire freedom to love without barrier or restraint; but always there seems a something holding me back, invisible, formless, but a great strength, so that I yearn and open my arms (as it were) but am not satisfied; and so I turn and direct it towards that formless vision of Adonai within. Maybe, some day a spark will fire it and it will break loose; & then? (This sounds very good indeed. O.M.)

Aug. 27. The most perfect peace I have experienced for a long time.

Sep. 1. This is the last day of the six months.

Nov. 9. Nearly two months since I made an entry. Will write down a few of the events that I remember during that time. Have done some slight morning and evening practice almost every day. Have occupied a fair amount of time in giving what instructions I can on occult matters to those who have requested information.

S. and L. have become sufficiently interested to apply for Studentship, and W.* has at last written and asked *re* Probationership.

Have heard finally from Fra P.A. and answered his letter.

[* (S) Wilfred Talbot Smith (founder of Agapé Lodge, (L) Hubert John Lawrence, and (W) Howard Enster White. See Martin Starr, *The Unknown God.* — JW]

Nov. 26, 11.40 to 11.55 P.M. Meditation on Love. Commenced with sending Love to the six directions of space (See "Training of the Mind." EQUINOX vol. 5). Became identified with Love to the exclusion of all other ideas. It is verily a dew which dissolves thought. (Dangerous, though, for a beginner. Often means little more than the maudlin benevolence of one who has dined too well. Fill yourself with Love, and it will flow out of its own accord. O.M.)

Nov. 27. Letter from Chancellor of A∴A∴. Was glad to receive this, as it cleared up a point that had long troubled me. *Note:* This was the point *re* Astral journeys, mentioned before. (This gave Fra. V.I.O. fresh confidence, and we find records of experiments at once. — ED.)

Nov. 27, 11.6 to 11.28 P.M. Astral Journey. Rising on the Planes. Will try and recount this experience in detail as it was somewhat different from any previous experiment. After prayer, formulated astral enclosing body and began to rise. Tried to ascend Middle Pillar. Dark Blue, then more Purple. Presently found my astral body in a sort of open Temple Square with 4 pillars for corners, open sides and a high domed roof. In the centre of the floor was a circular basin of water. Someone said (of the water) "It is Thyself" (or thy mind). Could distinguish nothing for some time. Presently a star appeared in the centre of the pool, evidently reflected through a circular hole in centre of roof. Looking up, could not see this star from where I was standing on the steps at front of Temple. Someone said: "Enter the water." Did so, finding it reached to the neck. Looked up, and could discern the star clearly. Someone said "You must travel up through the roof to the star." Did so, and discovered I was without clothes. Some time elapsed before I could get near the star, but on doing so I was whirled round it three times and alighted. Then became conscious that the body had given place to a flame only. Ascended as a flame into the air. Became dimly conscious that the flame was in the heart of a larger body. Strove still to rise, but came to blackness. Returned and disrobed. Gave thanks and entered diary.

(This is very good indeed, as a start. It should be repeated

with ever-increasing persistence. The time occupied tells me its
faults more than the text. A good 'rising' should take $1^1/2$ to 3
hours. O.M.)

Nov. 28, 11.5 to 11.27 P.M. Astral Journey.

Drew, with wand, in front of me, a circle (three times
round) and formed astral in that. Rose to a great height. Suddenly, as it were, a rope flashed round me and fell, forming a
spiral, ever widening, at the top of which I sat. Stood up on this,
only to fall, down, down, down, not quite vertically into the
water. Rising again, and striking out, I after a short while perceived a boat, something like a gondola, and swam towards it.
It was rowed by a dark-skinned man, old and wrinkled, whom
I at first thought to be an Indian. As I reached the boat and put
my hand on the side, it seemed as if he would strike at me with
his oar, but no, he grinned, and I drew myself into the boat and
sat in the fore part, which was high and covered by a sort of
hood. Presently, it struck me that the man was not living but
dead. Death. We then drifted in a mist, and all became blank for
a while; the memory of boat, man and self, *were all but lost*.
When the mist cleared I realized that the man was no longer
there, and I myself guided the boat. Coming back out of the
mist the waters were blue and no longer black, and I realized
that day was breaking. Gradually I watched the Sunrise, and set
the boat in that direction, rowing so as to keep my face to the
Sun. It seemed like a Portal; but, keeping on, it presently rose,
and by the time it was getting high in the heavens I perceived a
fair City ahead. Domes, Minarets, etc. Arriving there, I for the
first time noticed I was dark skinned and clad in a loin-cloth.
Landing, I was surrounded with men in an Eastern costume,
Arabs or Turks I thought. One old man took me by the hand, I
made the sign of the Pentagram over him, but he smiled and
said "Come along, it's all right," and led me along a street paved
with cobbles, the houses of which overhung, till we reached a
sort of a mosque. Entering this he led me to the altar, which was
supported by brackets from the wall, and above which was a
beautiful stained window. At the sides were thin columns and
sort of boxes, similar to theatre boxes. We knelt at the altar; and
he took my hand and said: "Raise your consciousness." I perceived a star and crescent above me, and a cross dimly formu-

lated in the background. After this, the astral seemed to coincide with the body; but consciousness of the astral surroundings was still clear. Continued to raise consciousness, and to send out thoughts of Love. Perceived around me innumerable streams of thought, interlacing and like a net-work, and when the Love-thought was sent out, the whole net sparkled, as with little specks of gold. Continued in this thought for some minutes, and gradually returned to normal. Gave thanks and entered diary.

(Very nearly in serious trouble, my young and rash friend! It seems that you must go up well outside earth-attraction if you wish to get good astrals. It sounds Sunday-school-talk, and I can give no reason. But I've tried repeatedly going horizontally and downwards, always with the same result. Gross and hostile things are below, pure beings above. The vision is good enough for what it is; it is clear and coherent. But I see no trace of sci-entific method in directing the vision. I explain further in the general comment. O.M.)

About this time Frater V.I.O. appears to have been studying Jnana Yoga. There is a simple entry on November 30th, "THOU ART THAT," without any attempt at comment, and on the fol-lowing day "Ditto, but in a less degree." On December 4 we find this entry:

The reading of 'Jnana Yoga'* revives very clearly the state of Unity produced by the practice of Raja Yoga. There is a clearer conception, and the feeling of being very near the Truth. N.B. During meditation the Light above head was beginning to envelope the mind, but was disturbed by R. calling me to come to bed.

(R. must be told not to call you to come to bed. The feeling that she may possibly do so is enough to prevent concentration. Also, as a general rule, it's very bad to sleep with another person in the room. O.M.)

Dec. 5th. More and More realization of the One Truth. THOU ART THAT. Got some idea that there was only one 'plane' in reality, not many.

[* Probably refers to *Jnana Yoga* by Swami Vivekananda. — JW]

Dec. 6th, 11.22 A.M. Started Neti, Neti[7] again. (Very near, not quite. V.I.O.)

10.45 P.M.

Oh Thou Ever-present, Eternal Silence, wherein all vanishes and emerges clothed in Bliss. I Invoke Thee.

Oh Thou elusive Self of my self, Thou All, wherein all dissolves and becomes Thy Being. I invoke Thee.

Oh Thou Existence of Existences, Thou Knower of Knowledge, wherein knowledge of all else is lost. I Invoke Thee.

Oh Thou Bliss Absolute, Thou One without a second, Thou in Whom Time and Space no longer exist. I invoke Thee.

Oh Thou, who when I think of Thee art God, who when I cease to think of Thee art My self, may I be lost in THEE.

Yet never shall I be lost, for Thou Art, who art not.

Oh Beloved, I come to Thee when I realize that never have I *moved* through all Eternity.

Oh Thou, on Whom man looks through the senses, and sees as the world.

Oh Thou, on Whom man looks through the mind and sees as the world of thought.

Oh Thou on Whom man looks as Thyself and becomes Infinite Bliss, let there be no thought of separateness, for there is none other. Thou Art That.

If I call Thee a Point, Thou laughest, saying "I am the Infinite Circle."

If I worship the Circle, Thou laughest, saying: "I am concealed in the Point."

Only if I claim Thee Wholly, may I define Thee. Then who cares, Aye or Nay?

If I attempt to name Thee, I lose Thee, Oh Thou Nameless unto Eternity, To Whom shall I reveal Thee, who wast never known but to Thyself?

Surely words are vain, O Thou who art beyond the Silence. Aum.

(This is very good. O.M.)

[7] "Not this, not this!" a Hindoo phrase used in the practice of rejecting all thoughts as they arise.

Dec. 11th, 9.52 to 10.37 P.M. Meditation in Asana. Dragon as usual.

Took a few long breaths, filling the body and mind with Love, and then expelling it till it flowed through me. Used mantra: "The Self is Love. That Self am I" first part of the time, afterwards changing to "The Self is THAT, that Self am I."

Eyes half closed, fixed on nose. Shut them about the middle of the meditation and turned them to Ajna. Very few invading thoughts.

Presently all became brilliant light, with which I became identified.

Realization of Oneness. No doubt remained that this was indeed the Union with the Higher Self. Then again arose the question "What about the Others when this state subsides again?" Then it seemed that a voice spoke clearly to the brain, saying: "Truly when united so thou art one with the Holy Guardian Angel that speaks unto thee now. Therefore worry no more about attaining. In future it is thy work to see that not only the part attain, but that other parts, those that are called 'others' in ordinary consciousness, realize the Oneness also." N.B. These are not the words, and do not properly express the meaning. The experience itself was in the nature of *realization* rather than in any language.

(Not at all bad. O.M.)

Dec. 12 To-night, while walking, I thought that some time, when I can find the right person, it would be well to get him to record for me one of these experiences such as that of last night, during its occurrence; (1) providing I could speak without altering the state of consciousness; (2) providing I could find the necessary person.

(No good. O.M.)

Dec. 15th, 11.50 to 12.9 P.M. Astral Journey.

On first trying to project astral it went rapidly off in a N.E. direction (Bad. O.M.) then described a curve to the North and so round twice, and became normal again. Second attempt. Enclosed astral in egg of light, sent it straight up. Egg opened; and I opened my eyes in space. I saw above me a shining object, oblong in shape, and travelling to it, found it almost like a kite.

Leaning upon it, I was carried backwards for some distance, during which time I watched a changing landscape below. Wishing to descend, I dropped towards the Earth, and found body supported by another. When near the ground, skimmed over the earth and eventually came to a dark gateway or tunnel. Walked into this and proceeded, lighted by a silver star on brow, till I arrived at a circular room at the end, lit by one candle placed on a round table at which sat an old white-bearded man writing in a book. I approached him, and said: "Why writest thou, Father?" and he replied "That those who read may live." (I seem to have asked him another question, but cannot remember what.) Then I said: "What writest thou, Father?" And he replied: "Death, always Death." And I said: "Show me thy writing, Father" and looking he wrote the word HARTHA. And I said "This is a mystery to me" so he pointed to it letter by letter and I tried to interpret it Qabalistically, but was not successful. It seemed that the value of the letters was 507. He said I should understand, and with that I left him and returned.

8 P.M., Dec. 16. Have just been working out the meaning of the word obtained last night. I then *thought* the value was 507 "That which causes ferment" or 5 plus 7 = 12 = He longed for, missed, etc. This shows how I went astray. I find however that the word actually adds to 607 = Adam Primus. But 6 plus 7 = 13 Unity, Love, and The Tarot Trump is DEATH, and this is what he said he was writing. (Note Apr. 21, 1917. Ha = The Sun; tha = The Moon, as stated in the *Hatha-Yoga Pradipika.**)

(Well worked out, method good; but not much of a place to have reached. You should have got more of the book, too. O.M.)

Dec 18th. *Note.* There is one thing I had intended to mention before. Instead of sleeping deeply, as was my former habit, I have lately noticed quite a change in this respect. Sometimes, though resting, I retain consciousness most of the night. In this state I appear to think very much along the same lines as I do in ordinary waking consciousness. In the morning I have the abil-

[* Numerous translations available, for example, *The Yoga of Light,* ed. by Hans Ulrich Rieker. — JW]

ity to change from one state to the other quite easily, but on leaving the bed and becoming fully awakened I can seldom remember any particulars of what occurred during sleep.

(This sounds good, as if the Tamo-Guna were breaking up. O.M.)

Dec 19, 11.38. Prayer and Meditation. Felt 'informed' by that Greater Self that Humility, Patience and Selflessness would bring the condition required. Dwelt for awhile in that Boundless Silence of which words can express nothing.

(Humility, like Pride, implies a self. O.M.)

Dec. 26th, 11.3 to 11.20 P.M. Meditation. Gradually separating the Self from the body, mind, life, death, etc., till an entirely impersonal state resulted.

(These things don't mean much, as a rule. They are only what we call 'reverie,' a dulcet meandering of the mind. O.M.)

Dec. 27th, 11.13 to 11.30 P.M. Meditation. After striving to unite consciousness completely with Adonai, the sphere of Consciousness widened out and became one with the Many; so that, when asking of the Self: "What am I? Who am I?" this no longer seemed an individual question, but to be taken up by many units in all parts of space, yet upon a formless plane. I rose higher and tried to unify all these; this resulted in an absolutely impersonal state which continued even after the meditation was over until about 12'clock. While it lasted it was distinctly different from any former experience, especially the earlier part.

(Not very good; seems too much like thinking. O.M.)

Dec. 31, 11.30 to 11.46 P.M. L.B.R. Dragon. Meditation on Love.[8] Afterwards I imagined the dim figure of Nuith overshadowed the Universe. Amen. And now I will go out and wish R. and baby a Happy New Year.

---

[8] (This sort of thing is all wrong. It isn't really meditation at all. You let your mind rove about, instead of pinning it down to a single, simple object. Samadhi never occurs in such conditions. O.M.)

THE PANTACLE OF FRATER V.I.O.

This PANTACLE is a symbolical map of the Universe, as understood by FRATER V.I.O. when a Neophyte of A∴A∴, and offered by him for the Examination of that Grade.

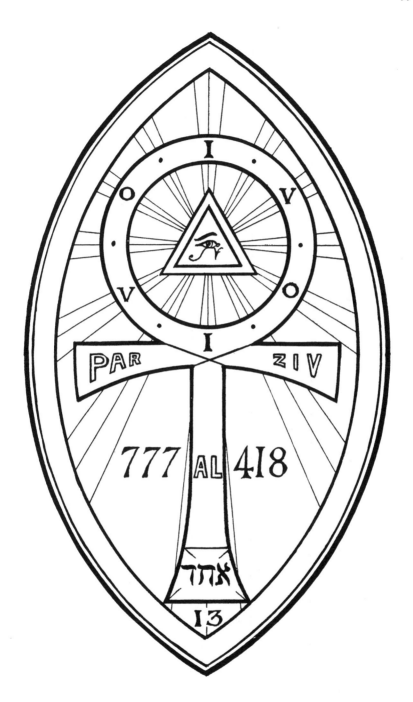

A Summary Comment. By Fra O.M. 7°=4°

I think you are the real man, and will attain. You work hard and regularly, and keep the record well. And you have the Root of the Matter in you. These are your dangers.

(1) You are emotional. This is very bad, and must be got rid of. It's a form of Egoism, and leads to the Left-hand Path. You say: "I object to my wife being run over by a motor-car," and think you are stating an Eternal Truth. Now no elephant in Siam cares whether she is run over or not. Say then: "It is (relatively to V.I.O.) right that he should object, etc., etc." Use this analysis with all emotions. Don't allow yourself to think that your own point of view is the only one. Read *Liber LXV.* Cap I 32–40 and 57–61. This is extremely important: for one thing, if you fail to understand, you will go mad when you come to a certain Gate.

(2) You are inclined to vagueness. This is evidently partly caused by the fog of emotion. Before you can pass to Zelator, you must know and rule the Astral Plane throughout. Astral journeys, however interesting and even splendid and illuminating, don't count unless they are willed. If you want to go to your office, and find yourself at the Town Hall instead, it's no excuse that the Town Hall has fine columns! You should drop all "Meditations on Love." What's the matter with Hate, anyway? From beyond the Abyss, they look as like each other as two new pennies. You really mean "Reflections on Love:" "Jones' Night Thoughts:" "Idle thoughts of an idle fellow." It's a soul-destroying, mind-fuddling practice. If indulged in, it will absolutely ruin all power of concentration.

Now here is your Examination for the Grate of Zelator[9]

(a) Go through a door on which is engraved this figure and explain the figure in detail by means of your visions.

[9] (This Examination is a subtle compliment, amounting almost to Flattery. It is a much harder paper than would be set in most cases. O.M.)

(b) Invoke Mercury and Hod, and travel till you meet the Unicorn mentioned in *Liber LXV* Cap. III verse 2. Report its conversation fully.

(c) Discover by visions the nature of the Alchemical principles, Sulphur, Mercury, and Salt. How do they differ from the 3 Gunas, and the elements Fire, Water, Air?

(d) Give an account of the sign Aquarius in the 4 Worlds, Assiah, Yetzirah, Briah, and Atziluth.

(e) Visit and describe fully the Qliphoth of Aries.

(f) Visit Iophiel and Hismael, and report their appearance, mode of life, and conversation.

Observe. The A∴A∴ work throughout is definite and directed. There is no room for a single loose thought.

(3) You must be perfectly stern and austere about the sanctity of the Work. You wouldn't allow your wife to come to the office and talk: you must make her respect your hour of work at home. Here I foresee trouble: with rarest exceptions a woman objects to a man doing anything of which she is not the centre. His business is only allowable because it provides for her. Herein no compromise is possible. You must be master or slave; and the truest kindness is to be master once and for all, whatever the cost. O.M.

In this defile we must leave our Pilgrim for the present. He is about to confront the denizens of the Astral World, menacing or seducing in turn; and, following the bold Rosicrucian rule, he remains in the current of life, without the safeguard of an absolute external retirement and renunciation, such as is advocated by Eastern teachers. But in the Way of the A∴A∴ externals are of less account than essentials, and V.I.O. was under the guidance and guardianship of an Order whose Omniscience is impeccable, and Its ward sure.

(To be continued)

Appendix

28 THEOREMS OF MAGICK

ALEISTER CROWLEY
FROM *Magick in Theory and Practice*

(1) Every intentional act is a Magical Act.[1]

(2) Every successful act has conformed to the postulate.

(3) Every failure proves that one or more requirements of the postulate have not been fulfilled.

(4) The first requisite for causing any change is thorough qualitative and quantitative understanding of the conditions.

(5) The second requisite of causing any change is the practical ability to set in right motion the necessary forces.

(6) "Every man and every woman is a star."

(7) Every man and every woman has a course, depending partly on the self, and partly on the environment which is natural and necessary for each. Anyone who is forced from his own course, either through not understanding himself, or through external opposition, comes into conflict with the order of the Universe, and suffers accordingly.

(8) A Man whose conscious will is at odds with his True Will is wasting his strength. He cannot hope to influence his environment efficiently.

(9) A man who is doing his True Will has the inertia of the Universe to assist him.

(10) Nature is a continuous phenomenon, though we do not know in all cases how things are connected.

(11) Science enables us to take advantage of the continuity of Nature by the empirical application of certain principles whose interplay involves different orders of idea connected with each other in a way beyond our present comprehension.

(12) Man is ignorant of the nature of his own being and powers. Even his idea of his limitations is based on experience of the past, and every step in his progress extends his

---

[1] By "intentional" I mean "willed." But even unintentional acts so-seeming are not truly so. Thus, breathing is an act of the Will-to-Live.

empire. There is therefore no reason to assign theoretical limits[2] to what he may be, or to what he may do.

(13) Every man is more or less aware that his individuality comprises several orders of exisitence, even when he maintains that his subtler principles are merely symptomatic of the changes in his gross vehicle. A similar order may be assumed to extend throughout nature.

(14) Man is capable of being, and using, anything which he perceives, for everything that he perceives is in a certain sense a part of his being. He may thus subjugate the whole Universe of which he is conscious to his individual Will.

(15) Every force in the Universe is capable of being transformed into any other kind of force by using suitable means. There is thus an inexhaustible supply of any particular kind of force that we may need.

(16) The application of any given force affects all the orders of being which exist in the object to which it is applied, whichever of those orders is directly affected.

(17) A man may learn to use any force so as to serve any purpose, by taking advantage of the above theorems.

(18) He may attract to himself any force of the Universe by making himself a fit receptacle for it, establishing a connection with it, and arranging conditions so that its nature compels it to flow toward him.

(19) Man's sense of himself as separate from, and opposed to, the Universe is a bar to his conducting its currents. It insulates him.

(20) Man can only attract and employ the forces for which he is really fitted.

(21) There is no limit to the extent of the relations of any man with the Universe in essence; for as soon as man makes himself one with any idea the means of measurement cease to exist. But his power to utilize that force is limited by his mental power and capacity, and by the circumstances of his human environment.

---

[2] i.e., except — possibly — in the case of logically absurd questions, such as the Schoolmen discussed in connection with "God."

(22) Every individual is essentially sufficient to himself. But he is unsatisfactory to himself until he has established himself in his right relation with the Universe.

(23) Magick is the Science of understanding oneself and one's conditions. It is the Art of applying that understanding in action.

(24) Every man has an indefeasible right to be what he is.

(25) Every man must do Magick each time that he acts or even thinks, since a thought is an internal act whose influence ultimately affects action, though it may not do so at the time.

(26) Every man has a right, the right of self-preservation, to fulfil himself to the utmost.[3]

(27) Every man should make Magick the keynote of his life. He should learn its laws and live by them.

(28) Every man has a right to fulfil his own will without being afraid that it may interfere with that of others; for if he is in his proper place, it is the fault of others if they interfere with him.

---

[3] Men of "criminal nature" are simply at issue with their true Wills. The murderer has the Will-to-Live; and his will to murder is a false will at variance with his true Will, since he risks death at the hands of Society by obeying his criminal impulse.

LIBER E VEL EXERCITIORUM
SUB FIGURA IX

ALEISTER CROWLEY
FROM *The Equinox*, Vol. I, No. 1

I

1. It is absolutely necessary that all experiments should be recorded in detail during, or immediately after, their performance.

2. It is highly important to note the physical and mental condition of the experimenter or experimenters.

3. The time and place of all experiments must be noted; also the state of the weather, and generally all conditions which might conceivably have any result upon the experiment either as adjuvants to or causes of the result, or as inhibiting it, or as sources of error.

4. The A∴A∴ will not take official notice of any experiments which are not thus properly recorded.

5. It is not necessary at this stage for us to declare fully the ultimate end of our researches; nor indeed would it be understood by those who have not become proficient in these elementary courses.

6. The experimenter is encouraged to use his own intelligence, and not to rely upon any other person or persons, however distinguished, even among ourselves.

7. The written record should be intelligently prepared so that others may benefit from its study.

8. The Book *John St. John* published in the first number of *The Equinox* is an example of this kind of record by a very advanced student. It is not as simply written as we could wish, but will show the method.

9. The more scientific the record is, the better. Yet the emotions should be noted, as being some of the conditions. Let then the record be written with sincerity and care; thus with practice it will be found more and more to approximate to the ideal.

II

Physical clairvoyance.

1. Take a pack of (78) Tarot playing cards. Shuffle; cut. Draw one card. Without looking at it, try to name it. Write down the card you name, and the actual card. Repeat, and tabulate results.

2. This experiment is probably easier with an old genuine pack of Tarot cards, preferably a pack used for divination by some one who really understood the matter.

3. Remember that one should expect to name the right card once in 78 times. Also be careful to exclude all possibilities of obtaining the knowledge through the ordinary senses of sight and touch, or even smell. There was once a man whose finger-tips were so sensitive that he could feel the shape and position of the pips and so judge the card correctly.

4. It is better to try first the easier form of the experiment, by guessing only the suit.

5. Remember that in 78 experiments you should obtain 22 trumps and 14 of each other suit; so that without any clairvoyance at all, you can guess right twice in 7 times (roughly) by calling trumps each time.

6. Note that some cards are harmonious. Thus it would not be a bad error to call the five of Swords ("The Lord of Defeat") instead of the ten of Swords ("The Lord of Ruin"). But to call the Lord of Love (2 Cups) for the Lord of Strife (5 Wands) would show that you were getting nothing right.

Similarly a card ruled by Mars would be harmonious with a 5, a card of Gemini with "The Lovers."

7. These harmonies must be thoroughly learnt, according to the numerous tables given in 777.

8. As you progress you will find that you are able to distinguish the suit correctly three times in four and that very few indeed inharmonious errors occur, while in 78 experiments you are able to name the card aright as many as 15 or 20 times.

9. When you have reached this stage, you may be admitted for examination; and in the event of your passing you will be given more complex and difficult exercises.

III

Asana — Posture.

1. You must learn to sit perfectly still with every muscle tense for long periods.

2. You must wear no garments that interfere with the posture in any of these experiments.

3. The first position: (The God). Sit in a chair; head up, back straight, knees together, hands on knees, eyes closed.

4. The second position: (The Dragon). Kneel; buttocks resting on the heels, toes turned back, back and head straight, hands on thighs.

5. The third position: (The Ibis). Stand, hold left ankle with right hand, free forefinger on lips.

6. The fourth position: (The Thunderbolt). Sit; left heel pressing up anus, right foot poised on its toes, the heel covering the phallus; arms stretched out over the knees; head and back straight.

7. Various things will happen to you while you are practising these positions; they must be carefully analysed and described.

8. Note down the duration of practice; the severity of the pain (if any) which accompanies it, the degree of rigidity attained, and any other pertinent matters.

9. When you have progressed up to the point that a saucer filled to the brim with water and poised upon the head does not spill one drop during a whole hour, and when you can no longer perceive the slightest tremor in any muscle; when, in short, you are perfectly steady and easy, you will be admitted for examination; and, should you pass, you will be instructed in more complex and difficult practices.

IV

Pranayama — Regularisation of the Breathing.

1. At rest in one of your positions, close the right nostril with the thumb of the right hand and breathe out slowly and completely through the left nostril, while your watch marks 20 seconds. Breathe in through the same nostril for 10 seconds. Changing hands, repeat with the other nostril. Let this be continuous for one hour.

2. When this is quite easy to you, increase the periods to 30 and 15 seconds.

3. When this is quite easy to you, but not before, breathe out for 15 seconds, in for 15 seconds, and hold the breath for 15 seconds.

4. When you can do this with perfect ease and comfort for a whole hour, practice breathing out for 40 and in for 20 seconds.

5. This being attained, practice breathing out for 20, in for 10, holding the breath for 30 seconds. When this has become perfectly easy to you, you may be admitted for examination, and should you pass, you will be instructed in more complex and difficult practices.

6. You will find that the presence of food in the stomach, even in small quantities, makes the practices very difficult.

7. Be very careful never to overstrain your powers; especially never get so short of breath that you are compelled to breathe out jerkily or rapidly.

8. Strive after depth, fullness, and regularity of breathing.

9. Various remarkable phenomena will very probably occur during these practices. They must be carefully analysed and recorded.

V

Dharana — Control of Thought.

1. Constrain the mind to concentrate itself upon a single simple object imagined. The five tatwas are useful for this purpose; they are: a black oval; a blue disk; a silver crescent; a yellow square; a red triangle.

2. Proceed to combinations of simple objects; *e.g.*, a black oval within a yellow square, and so on.

3. Proceed to simple moving objects, such as a pendulum swinging, a wheel revolving, etc. Avoid living objects.

4. Proceed to combinations of moving objects, *e.g.*, a piston rising and falling while a pendulum is swinging. The relation between the two movements should be varied in different experiments.
Or even a system of flywheels, eccentrics, and governor.

5. During these practices the mind must be absolutely confined to the object determined upon; no other thought must be allowed to intrude upon the consciousness. The moving systems must be regular and harmonious.

6. Note carefully the duration of the experiments, the number and nature of the intruding thoughts, the tendency of the object itself to depart from the course laid out for it, and any other phenomena which may present themselves. Avoid overstrain; this is very important.

7. Proceed to imagine living objects; as a man, preferably some man known to, and respected by, yourself.

8. In the intervals of these experiments you may try to imagine the objects of the other senses, and to concentrate upon them.
For example, try to imagine the taste of chocolate, the smell of roses, the feeling of velvet, the sound of a waterfall or the ticking of a watch.

9. Endeavour finally to shut out all objects of any of the senses, and prevent all thoughts arising in your mind. When you

feel you have attained some success in these practices, apply for examination, and should you pass, more complex and difficult practices will be prescribed for you.

VI

Physical Limitations.

1. It is desirable that you should discover for yourself your physical limitations.

2. To this end ascertain for how many hours you can subsist without food or drink before your working capacity is seriously interfered with.

3. Ascertain how much alcohol you can take, and what forms of drunkenness assail you.

4. Ascertain how far you can walk without once stopping; likewise with dancing, swimming, running, etc.

5. Ascertain for how many hours you can do without sleep.

6. Test your endurance with various gymnastic exercises, club swinging, and so on.

7. Ascertain for how long you can keep silence.

8. Investigate any other capacities and aptitudes which may occur to you.

9. Let all these things be carefully and conscientiously recorded; for according to your powers will it be demanded of you.

VII

A Course of Reading.

1. The object of most of the foregoing practices will not at first be clear to you; but at least (who will deny it?) they have trained you in determination, accuracy, introspection, and many

other qualities which are valuable to all men in their ordinary avocations, so that in no case will your time have been wasted.

2. That you may gain some insight into the nature of the Great Work which lies beyond these elementary trifles, however, we should mention that an intelligent person may gather more than a hint of its nature from the following books, which are to be taken as serious and learned contributions to the study of Nature, though not necessarily to be implicitly relied upon.

The Yi King (S.B.E. Series, Oxford University Press).

The Tao Teh King (S.B.E. Series).

Tannhäuser, by A. Crowley.

The Upanishads.

The Bhagavad-Gita.

The Voice of the Silence.

Raja Yoga, by Swami Vivekananda.

The Shiva Sanhita.

The Aphorisms of Patanjali.

The Sword of Song.

The Book of the Dead.

Rituel et Dogme de la Haute Magie.

The Book of the Sacred Magic of Abramelin the Mage.

The Goetia.

The Hathayoga Pradipika.

The Spiritual Guide of Molinos.

Erdmann's *History of Philosophy.*

The Star in the West (Captain Fuller).

The Dhammapada (S.B.E. Series, Oxford University Press).

The Questions of King Milinda (S.B.E. Series).

777 vel Prolegomena, etc.

Varieties of Religious Experience (James).

Kabbala Denudata.

Konx Om Pax.

3. Careful study of these books will enable the pupil to speak in the language of his master, and facilitate communications with him.

4. The pupil should endeavour to discover the fundamental harmony of these very varied works; for this purpose he will find it best to study the most extreme divergencies side by side.

5. He may at any time that he wishes apply for examination in this course of reading.

6. During the whole of this elementary study and practice he will do wisely to seek out and attach himself to a master, one competent to correct him and advise him. Nor should he be discouraged by the difficulty of finding such a person.

7. Let him further remember that he must in no wise rely upon, or believe in, that master. He must rely entirely upon himself, and credit nothing whatever but that which lies within his own knowledge and experience.

8. As in the beginning, so at the end, we here insist upon the vital importance of the written record as the only possible check upon error derived from the various qualities of the experimenter.

9. Thus let the work be accomplished duly; yea, let it be accomplished duly.

(If any really important or remarkable results should occur, or if any great difficulty presents itself, the A∴A∴ should be at once informed of the circumstances.)

LIBER O
VEL MANUS ET SAGITTAE
SUB FIGURA VI

ALEISTER CROWLEY
FROM *The Equinox,* Vol. I, No. 2

I

1. This book is very easy to misunderstand; readers are asked to use the most minute critical care in the study of it, even as we have done in its preparation.

2. In this book it is spoken of the Sephiroth and the Paths; of Spirits and Conjurations; of Gods, Spheres, Planes, and many other things which may or may not exist.

It is immaterial whether these exist or not. By doing certain things certain results will follow; students are most earnestly warned against attributing objective reality or philosophic validity to any of them.

3. The advantages to be gained from them are chiefly these:

   (a) A widening of the horizon of the mind.

   (b) An improvement of the control of the mind.

4. The student, if he attains any success in the following practices, will find himself confronted by things (ideas or beings) too glorious or too dreadful to be described. It is essential that he remain the master of all that he beholds, hears or conceives; otherwise he will be the slave of illusion, and the prey of madness.

Before entering upon any of these practices, the student should be in good health, and have attained a fair mastery of Asana, Pranayama and Dharana.

5. There is little danger that any student, however idle or stupid, will fail to get some result; but there is great danger that he will be led astray, obsessed and overwhelmed by his results, even though it be by those which it is necessary that he should attain. Too often, moreover, he mistaketh the first resting-place for the goal, and taketh off his armour as if he were a victor ere the fight is well begun.

It is desirable that the student should never attach to any result the importance which it at first seems to possess.

6. First, then, let us consider the Book 777 and its use; the preparation of the Place; the use of the Magic Ceremonies; and finally the methods which follow in Chapter V "Viator in Regnis Arboris," and in Chapter VI "Sagitta trans Lunam."

(In another book will it be treated of the Expansion and Contraction of Consciousness; progress by slaying the Chakkrâms; progress by slaying the Pairs of Opposites; the methods of Sabhapaty Swami, etc., etc.)

II

1. The student must first obtain a thorough knowledge of Book 777, especially of columns i, ii, iii, v, vi, vii, ix, xi, xii, xiv, xv, xvi, xvii, xviii, xix, xxxiv, xxxv, xxxviii, xxxix, xl, xli, xlii, xlv, liv, lv, lix, lx, lxi, lxiii, lxx, lxxv, lxxvii, lxxviii, lxxix, lxxx, lxxxi, lxxxiii, xcvii, xcviii, xcix, c, ci, cxvii, cxviii, cxxxvii, cxxxviii, cxxxix, clxxv, clxxvi, clxxvii, clxxxii.

When these are committed to memory, he will begin to understand the nature of these correspondences. (*See* illustrations "The Temple of Solomon the King" [*Equinox* I, 2]. Cross references are given.)

2. If we take an example, the use of the table will become clear.

Let us suppose that you wish to obtain knowledge of some obscure science.

In column xlv, line 12, you will find "Knowledge of Sciences."

By now looking up line 12 in the other columns, you will find that the Planet corresponding is Mercury, its number eight, its lineal figures the octagon and octagram. The God who rules that planet Thoth, or in Hebrew symbolism Tetragrammaton Adonai and Elohim Tzabaoth, its Archangel Raphael, its Choir of Angels Beni Elohim, its Intelligence Tiriel, its Spirit Taphtatharath, its colours Orange (for Mercury is the Sphere of the Sephira Hod, 8), Yellow, Purple, Grey, and Indigo rayed with Violet; its Magical Weapon the Wand or Caduceus, its Perfumes

Mastic and others, its sacred plants Vervain and others, its jewel the Opal or Agate; its sacred animal the Snake, etc., etc.

3. You would then prepare your Place of Working accordingly. In an orange circle you would draw an eight-pointed star of yellow, at whose points you would place eight lamps. The Sigil of the Spirit (which is to be found in Cornelius Agrippa and other books) you would draw in the four colours with such other devices as your experience may suggest.

4. And so on. We cannot here enter at length into all the necessary preparations; and the student will find them fully set forth in the proper books, of which the *Goetia* is perhaps the best example.

These rituals need not be slavishly imitated; on the contrary the student should do nothing the object of which he does not understand; also, if he have any capacity whatever, he will find his own crude rituals more effective than the highly polished ones of other people.

The general purpose of all this preparation is as follows:

5. Since the student is a man surrounded by material objects, if it be his wish to master one particular idea, he must make every material object about him directly suggest that idea. Thus in the ritual quoted, if his glance fall upon the lights, their number suggests Mercury; he smells the perfumes, and again Mercury is brought to his mind. In other words, the whole magical apparatus and ritual is a complex system of mnemonics.

(The importance of these lies principally in the fact that particular sets of images that the student may meet in his wanderings correspond to particular lineal figures, divine names, etc. and are controlled by them. As to the possibility of producing results external to the mind of the seer [objective, in the ordinary common sense acceptation of the term] we are here silent.)

6. There are three important practices connected with all forms of ceremonial (and the two Methods which later we shall describe). These are:

(1) Assumption of God-forms.

(2) Vibration of Divine Names.

(3) Rituals of "Banishing" and "Invoking."

These, at least, should be completely mastered before the dangerous Methods of Chapters V and VI are attempted.

III

1. The Magical Images of the Gods of Egypt should be made thoroughly familiar. This can be done by studying them in any public museum, or in such books as may be accessible to the student. They should then be carefully painted by him, both from the model and from memory.

2. The student, seated in the "God" position, or in the characteristic attitude of the God desired, should then imagine His image as coinciding with his own body, or as enveloping it. This must be practised until mastery of the image is attained, and an identity with it and with the God experienced.

It is a matter for very great regret that no simple and certain test of success in this practice exists.

3. The Vibration of God-names. As a further means of identifying the human consciousness with that pure portion of it which man calls by the name of some God, let him act thus:

4. (a) Stand with arms outstretched.[1] (*See* illustration [p. 177].)

(b) Breathe in deeply through the nostrils, imagining the name of the God desired entering with the breath.

(c) Let that name descend slowly from the lungs to the heart, the solar plexus, the navel, the generative organs, and so to the feet.

(d) The moment that it appears to touch the feet, quickly advance the left foot about 12 inches, throw forward the body, and let the hands (drawn back to the side of the eyes) shoot out, so that you are standing in the typical position of the God Horus,[2] and at the same time imagine the Name as rushing up and through the body, while you breathe it out through the nostrils with the air which has been till then retained in the lungs. All this must be done with all the force of which you are capable.

(e) Then withdraw the left foot, and place the right forefinger[3] upon the lips, so that you are in the characteristic position of the God Harpocrates.[4]

---

[1] This injunction does not apply to gods like Phthah or Harpocrates whose natures do not accord with this gesture.

[2] *See* illustration "Blind Force," [p. 3].

[3] Or the thumb, the fingers being closed. The thumb symbolises spirit, the forefinger the element of water.

[4] *See* illustration "Silent Watcher," [p. 158].

5. It is a sign that the student is performing this correctly when a single "Vibration" entirely exhausts his physical strength. It should cause him to grow hot all over, or to perspire violently, and it should so weaken him that he will find it difficult to remain standing.

6. It is a sign of success, though only by the student himself is it perceived, when he hears the name of the God vehemently roared forth, as if by the concourse of ten thousand thunders; and it should appear to him as if that Great Voice proceeded from the Universe, and not from himself.

In both the above practices all consciousness of anything but the God-form and name should be absolutely blotted out; and the longer it takes for normal perception to return, the better.

IV

1. The Rituals of the Pentagram and Hexagram must be committed to memory. They are as follows:

The Lesser Ritual of the Pentagram

(i) Touching the forehead say Ateh (Unto Thee).

(ii) Touching the breast say Malkuth (The Kingdom).

(iii) Touching the right shoulder, say ve-Geburah (and the Power).

(iv) Touching the left shoulder, say ve-Gedulah (and the Glory).

(v) Clasping the hands upon the breast, say le-Olahm, Amen (to the Ages, Amen).

(vi) Turning to the East make a pentagram (that of Earth) with the proper weapon (usually the Wand). Say (i.e., vibrate) I H V H.

(vii) Turning to the South, the same, but say A D N I.

(viii) Turning to the West, the same, but say A H I H.

(ix) Turning to the North, the same, but say A G L A.
Pronounce: Ye-ho-wau, Adónai, Eheieh, Agla.

  (x)   Extending the arms in the form of a Cross say:

  (xi)   Before me Raphael;

  (xii)   Behind me Gabriel;

  (xiii)   On my right hand Michael;

  (xiv)   On my left hand Auriel;

  (xv)   For about me flames the Pentagram,

  (xvi)   And in the Column stands the six-rayed Star.

(xvii-xxi)   Repeat (i) to (v), the Qabalistic Cross.

The Greater Ritual of the Pentagram

The Pentagrams are traced in the air with the sword or other weapon, the name spoken aloud, and the signs used, as illustrated.

THE PENTAGRAMS OF SPIRIT

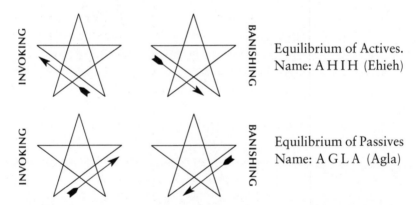

Equilibrium of Actives.
Name: A H I H (Ehieh)

Equilibrium of Passives
Name: A G L A (Agla)

The Signs of the Portal (*see* illustrations): Extend the hands in front of you, palms outwards, separate them as if in the act of rending asunder a veil or curtain (actives), and then bring them together as if closing it up again and let them fall to the side (passives).

(The Grade of the "Portal" is particularly attributed to the element of Spirit; it refers to the Sun; the Paths of ם, ר, and צ, are attributed to this degree. *See* 777 lines 6 and 31 bis).

THE SIGNS OF THE GRADES

1. Earth: the god Set fighting.
2. Air: the god Shu supporting the sky.
3. Water: the goddess Auramoth
4. Fire: the goddess Thoum-aesh-neith
5–6. Spirit: the rending and closing of the veil.

7–10. THE LVX SIGNS.

7. ✠ Osiris slain — the Cross.
8. L Isis mourning — the Svastika
9. V Typhon — the Trident
10. X Osiris risen — the Pentagram

THE PENTAGRAMS OF FIRE

Name: A L H I M
(Elohim)

The signs of 4°=7°: Raise the arms above the head and join the hands, so that the tips of the fingers and of the thumbs meet, formulating a triangle. (*See* illustration.)

(The Grade of 4°=7° is particularly attributed to the element Fire; it refers to the planet Venus; the paths of ק, צ, and פ are attributed to this degree. For other attributions *see 777* lines 7 and 31).

THE PENTAGRAMS OF WATER

Name: A L (El)

The signs of 3°=8°: Raise the arms till the elbows are on a level with the shoulders, bring the hands across the chest, touching the thumbs and tips of fingers so as to form a triangle apex downwards. (*See* illustration.)

(The Grade of 3°=8° is particularly attributed to the element of Water; it refers to the planet Mercury; the paths of ר and ש are attributed to this degree. For other attributions *see 777*, lines 8 and 23).

THE PENTAGRAMS OF AIR

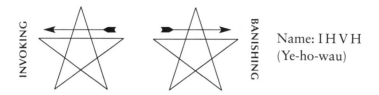

Name: I H V H
(Ye-ho-wau)

The signs of 2°=9°: Stretch both arms upwards and out-wards, the elbows bent at right angles, the hands bent back, the palms upwards as if supporting a weight. (*See* illustration.)

(The Grade of 2°=9° is particularly attributed to the element Air; it refers to the Moon; the path of ה is attributed to this degree. For other attributions *see 777* lines 9 and 11).

THE PENTAGRAMS OF EARTH

Name: A D N I
(Adonai)

The Sign of 1°=10°: Advance the right foot, stretch out the right hand upwards and forwards, the left hand downwards and backwards, the palms open. [*See* illustration.]

(The Grade of 1°=10° is particularly attributed to the element of Earth, *see 777* lines 10 and 32 bis).

The Lesser Ritual of the Hexagram

This ritual is to be performed after the "Lesser Ritual of the Pentagram."

(i)   Stand upright, feet together, left arm at side, right across body, holding the wand or other weapon upright in the median line. Then face East and say:

(ii) I.N.R.I.

Yod. Nun. Resh. Yod.

Virgo, Isis, Mighty Mother.

Scorpio, Apophis, Destroyer.

Sol, Osiris, Slain and Risen.

Isis, Apophis, Osiris, IAO.

(iii) Extend the arms in the form of a cross, and say: "The Sign of Osiris Slain." (*See* illustration).

(iv) Raise the right arm to point upwards, keeping the elbow square, and lower the left arm to point downwards, keeping the elbow square, while turning the head over the left shoulder looking down so that the eyes follow the left forearm, and say, "The Sign of the Mourning of Isis." (*See* illustration).

(v)   Raise the arms at an angle of sixty degrees to each other above the head, which is thrown back, and say, "The Sign of Apophis and Typhon." (*See* illustration).

(vi) Cross the arms on the breast, and bow the head and say, "The Sign of Osiris Risen." (*See* illustration).

(vii) Extend the arms again as in (iii) and cross them again as in (vi) saying: "L.V.X., Lux, the Light of the Cross."

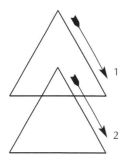

(viii) With the magical weapon trace the Hexagram of Fire in the East, saying, "Ararita" (אראריתא).

This word consists of the initials of a sentence which means "One is His Beginning: One is His Individuality: His Permutation is One."

This hexagram consists of two equilateral triangles, both apices pointed upwards. Begin at the top of the upper triangle and trace it in a dextro-rotary direction. The top of the lower triangle should coincide with the central point of the upper triangle.

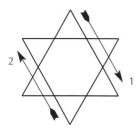

(ix) Trace the Hexagram of Earth in the South, saying "ARARITA." This Hexagram has the apex of the lower triangle pointing downwards, and it should be capable of inscription in a circle.

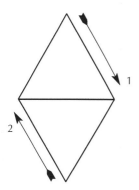

(x) Trace the Hexagram of Air in the West, saying "ARARITA." This Hexagram is like that of Earth; but the bases of the triangles coincide, forming a diamond.

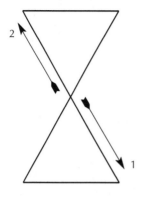

(xi) Trace the hexagram of Water in the North, saying "ARARITA." This hexagram has the lower triangle placed above the upper, so that their apices coincide.

(xii) Repeat (i-vii)

The Banishing Ritual is identical, save that the direction of the Hexagrams must be reversed.

The Greater Ritual of the Hexagram

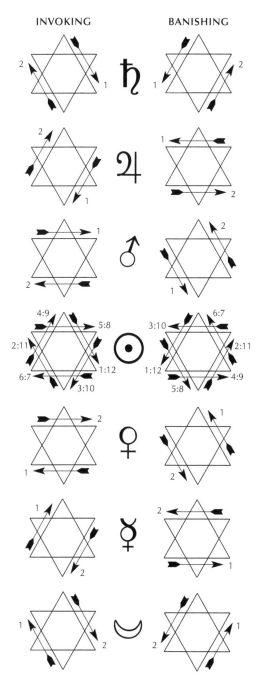

INVOKING   BANISHING

To invoke or banish planets or zodiacal signs.

The Hexagram of Earth alone is used. Draw the hexagram, beginning from the point which is attributed to the planet you are dealing with. (See 777 col. lxxxiii).

Thus to invoke Jupiter begin from the right-hand point of the lower triangle, dextrorotary and complete; then trace the upper triangle from its left hand point and complete.

Trace the astrological sigil of the planet in the centre of your hexagram.

For the Zodiac use the hexagram of the planet which rules the sign you require (777, col. cxxxviii); but draw the astrological sigil of the sign, instead of that of the planet.

For Caput and Cauda Draconis use the lunar hexagram, with the sigil of ☊ or ☋.

To banish, reverse the hexagram.

In all cases use a conjuration first with Ararita, and next with the name of the God corresponding to the planet or sign you are dealing with.

The Hexagrams pertaining to the planets are as in plate on preceding page.

2. These rituals should be practised until the figures drawn appear in flame, in flame so near to physical flame that it would perhaps be visible to the eyes of a bystander, were one present. It is alleged that some persons have attained the power of actually kindling fire by these means. Whether this be so or not, the power is not one to be aimed at.

3. Success in "banishing" is known by a "feeling of cleanliness" in the atmosphere; success in "invoking" by a "feeling of holiness." It is unfortunate that these terms are so vague.

But at least make sure of this: that any imaginary figure or being shall instantly obey the will of the student, when he uses the appropriate figure. In obstinate cases, the form of the appropriate God may be assumed.

4. The banishing rituals should be used at the commencement of any ceremony whatever. Next, the student should use a general invocation, such as the "Preliminary Invocation" in the *Goetia* as well as a special invocation to suit the nature of his working.

5. Success in these verbal invocations is so subtle a matter, and its grades so delicately shaded, that it must be left to the good sense of the student to decide whether or not he should be satisfied with his result.

V

1. Let the student be at rest in one of his prescribed positions, having bathed and robed with the proper decorum. Let the place of working be free from all disturbance, and let the preliminary purifications, banishings and invocations be duly accomplished, and, lastly, let the incense be kindled.

2. Let him imagine his own figure (preferably robed in the proper magical garments and armed with the proper magical weapons) as enveloping his physical body, or standing near to and in front of him.

3. Let him then transfer the seat of his consciousness to that imagined figure; so that it may seem to him that he is seeing with its eyes, and hearing with its ears.

This will usually be the great difficulty of the operation.

4. Let him then cause that imagined figure to rise in the air to a great height above the earth.

5. Let him then stop and look about him. (It is sometimes difficult to open the eyes.)

6. Probably he will see figures approaching him, or become conscious of a landscape.

Let him speak to such figures, and insist upon being answered, using the proper pentagrams and signs, as previously taught.

7. Let him travel about at will, either with or without guidance from such figure or figures.

8. Let him further employ such special invocations as will cause to appear the particular places he may wish to visit.

9. Let him beware of the thousand subtle attacks and deceptions that he will experience, carefully testing the truth of all with whom he speaks.

Thus a hostile being may appear clothed with glory; the appropriate pentagram will in such a case cause him to shrivel or decay.

10. Practice will make the student infinitely wary in these matters.

11. It is usually quite easy to return to the body, but should any difficulty arise, practice (again) will make the imagination fertile. For example, one may create in thought a chariot of fire with white horses, and command the charioteer to drive earthwards.

It might be dangerous to go too far, or to stay too long; for fatigue must be avoided.

The danger spoken of is that of fainting, or of obsession, or of loss of memory or other mental faculty.

12. Finally, let the student cause his imagined body in which he supposes himself to have been travelling to coincide with the physical, tightening his muscles, drawing in his breath, and putting his forefinger to his lips. Then let him "awake" by a well-defined act of will, and soberly and accurately record his experiences.

It may be added that this apparently complicated experiment is perfectly easy to perform. It is best to learn by "travelling" with a person already experienced in the matter. Two or three experiments will suffice to render the student confident and even expert. See also "The Seer," [*The Equinox* I, 2] pp. 295–333.

VI

1. The previous experiment has little value, and leads to few results of importance. But it is susceptible of a development which merges into a form of Dharana — concentration — and as such may lead to the very highest ends. The principal use of the practice in the last chapter is to familiarise the student with every kind of obstacle and every kind of delusion, so that he may be perfect master of every idea that may arise in his brain, to dismiss it, to transmute it, to cause it instantly to obey his will.

2. Let him then begin exactly as before, but with the most intense solemnity and determination.

3. Let him be very careful to cause his imaginary body to rise in a line exactly perpendicular to the earth's tangent at the point where his physical body is situated (or to put it more simply, straight upwards).

4. Instead of stopping, let him continue to rise until fatigue almost overcomes him. If he should find that he has stopped without willing to do so, and that figures appear, let him at all costs rise above them.

Yea, though his very life tremble on his lips, let him force his way upward and onward!

5. Let him continue in this so long as the breath of life is in him. Whatever threatens, whatever allures, though it were

Typhon and all his hosts loosed from the pit and leagued against him, though it were from the very Throne of God Himself that a Voice issues bidding him stay and be content, let him struggle on, ever on.

6. At last there must come a moment when his whole being is swallowed up in fatigue, overwhelmed by its own inertia.[5]

Let him sink (when no longer can he strive, though his tongue by bitten through with the effort and the blood gush from his nostrils) into the blackness of unconsciousness; and then, on coming to himself, let him write down soberly and accurately a record of all that hath occurred, yea a record of all that hath occurred.

EXPLICIT

[5] This in case of failure. The results of success are so many and wonderful that no effort is here made to describe them. They are classified, tentatively, in the "Herb Dangerous," Part II, [*The Equinox* I, 2].

THE BOOK

ALEISTER CROWLEY
FROM *Book IV,* Part 2, *Magick*

The Book of Spells or of Conjurations is the Record of every thought, word, and deed of the Magician; for everything that he has willed is willed to a purpose. It is the same as if he had taken an oath to perform some achievement.

Now this Book must be a holy Book, not a scribbling-book in which you jot down every piece of rubbish that comes into your head. It is written, *Liber VII,* v, 23: "Every breath, every word, every thought, every deed is an act of love with Thee. Be this devotion a potent spell to exorcise the demons of the Five."

This Book must then be thus written. In the first place the Magician must perform the practice laid down in *Liber CMXIII* so that he understands perfectly who he is, and to what his development must necessarily tend. So much for the first page of the Book.

Let him then be careful to write nothing therein that is inharmonious or untrue. Nor can he avoid this writing, for this is a Magick Book. If you abandon even for an hour the one purpose of your life, you will find a number of meaningless scratches and scrawls on the white vellum; and these cannot be erased. In such a case, when you come to conjure a demon by the power of the Book, he will mock you; he will point to all this foolish writing, more like his own than yours. In vain will you continue with the subsequent spells; you have broken by your own foolishness the chain which would have bound him.

Even the calligraphy of the Book must be firm, clear, and beautiful; in the cloud of incense it is hard to read the conjurations. While you peer dimly through the smoke, the demon will vanish, and you will have to write the terrible word "failure."

And yet there is no page of this Book on which this word is not written; but so long as it is immediately followed by a new affirmation, all is not lost; and as in this Book the word "failure" is thus made of little account, so also must the word "success" never be employed, for it is the last word that may be written therein, and it is followed by a full stop.

This full stop may never be written anywhere else; for the writing of the Book goes on eternally; there is no way of closing the record until the goal of all has been attained. Let every page of this Book be filled with song — for it is a Book of incantation!

THE METHOD OF TRAINING

ALEISTER CROWLEY
EXTRACTED FROM *Magick Without Tears*

CARA SOROR,

Do what thou wilt shall be the whole of the Law.

The first and absolutely essential task for the Aspirant is to write his Magical Record.

You know some elementary Mechanics — the Triangle of Forces, and all that. Well, if we have a body acted on by two equal forces, one pulling it East, the other South, it will tend to move in a South-Easterly direction. But if the "south" force is (say) twice as strong, it will move south of South-East.

Now you, sitting in your study reading this letter, got there and were compelled to do that, as the result of the impact upon you of countless quintillions of forces of every kind. I don't expect you to discover all these and calculate and report them; but I want you to set down all the main currents. For so you should be able to get some sort of answer to the question, "Where do we go from here, boys?"

I am not a guesser; and I cannot judge you, or advise you, or help you, unless and until I know the facts as thoroughly as you are able to allow me to do.

The construction of this Record is, incidentally, the first step in the practice called Sammasati, and leads to the acquisition of the Magical Memory — the memory of your previous incarnations. So there is another reason, terrifically cogent, for writing this Magical Record as clearly and as fully as you can.

The best explanation of how to set about the task is given in *Liber Thisharb*.

Some of this sounds rather advanced and technical; but it ought to give you the general idea. You should begin with your parents and the family traditions; the circumstances of your birth and education; your social position; your financial situation; your physique, health, illnesses; your vita sexualis; your hobbies and amusements; what you are good at, what not; how you came to be interested in the Great Work; what (if you have been on false trails, Toshophists, Anthroposophagists, sham Rosicrucians, etc.) has been "your previous condition of servitude"; how you found me, and decided to enlist my aid.

That, by itself, helps you to understand yourself, and me to understand you.

From that point the keeping of the Record is quite easy. All you have to do is to put down what practices you mean to begin, how you get on with them from day to day, and (at intervals) what I have to say about your progress.

Remember always that we have no use for piety, for vague chatter, for guesswork; we are as strictly scientific as biologists or chemists. We ban emotion from the start; we demand perception; and (as you will see later on) even perception is not acceptable until we have made sure of its bases by a study of what we call the `tendencies'.

That is all about the Magical Record; the way is now clear to set forth our Method. This is two-fold. (1) Yoga, introversion, (2) Magick, extroversion. (These are rough but useful connotations.) The two seem, at first glance, to be opposed; but, when you have advanced a little in both, you find that the concentration learnt in Yoga is of immense use in attaining the mental powers necessary in Magick; on the other hand, the discipline of Magick is of the greatest service in Yoga.

. . .

Love is the law, love under will

ON THE MAGICAL DIARY

EXTRACT FROM A LETTER:
ALEISTER CROWLEY TO ROY LEFFINGWELL
OCTOBER 23, 1942

The Magical Diary is the First condition of Advancement. It is your compass, your log, and your sheet-anchor. Begin by a summary of your life, including its origins such as family history, up to the point where you decide to devote yourself to the Great Work. The idea is to map out all the causes which brought you to that Gateway. From this alone you should be able to divine much of *who you are,* whence you have come, and whither you are bound — to have it clear what the Great Work means to you. This should help you to choose a Motto: extremely important, as the motto actually rules you: it is the word of your self-determined Destiny. It helps you furthermore to select the right practices.

You then carry on daily, *not* recording the time you shaved, and the temperature of your bath-water, but all the work you do, and such reflections as pertain to your progress. (The Diary in the "Blue Equinox," Vol. III, No. 1, is a very good model.*) This acts as your conscience and your tutor; also, when you get fits of depression, it is immensely comforting.

Your are supposed to send a copy, neatly typed, double spacing, to your Neophyte for his comments at the end of 11 months. (Double spacing always please! It is one of my manias: but it does make such a difference.)

[* *I.e.,* Jones's diary with Crowley's comments, *A Master of the Temple,* reproduced here.]

Culinary Glossary
of John St. John

Gwynneth Cheers & James Wasserman

½ *Evian* — Specialty water from Evian springs in the French Alps.

½ *Graves* — Another fine Bordeaux wine.

Andouillette aux Pommes — Pork sausage with potatos, wine, olive oil, shallots, and cooked apples.

Bisque d'Ecrevisses — Crayfish soup made with butter, chopped onion, carrots, celery and parsley, with rice, thyme, cognac, white wine, consommé, heavy cream, chives, and tomato paste.

Bouillabaisse — A Provençal soup made with white fish, prawns, olive oil, onion, bayleaf, pepper, Tabasco, parsley, and saffron.

Brioche — A soft, light-textured bun made from eggs, butter, flour, and yeast.

Café crème — Coffee with cream.

Café croissant — A buttery and flakey puff pastry roll with breadlike texture.

Café Noir — Black coffee.

Camembert — Type of cheese named after the French village where it was made.

Cassoulet de Castelnaudary — A traditional Toulouse stew composed of white dry beans, carrots, onion, garlic, tomato, conserve of duck, with mutton and pork.

Cêpes Bordelaise — Mushrooms Bordeaux style, cooked in duck fat, garlic, lemon juice and lemon skins, parsley, salt and pepper.

Citron pressé — A squeezed lemon drink.

Contrefilet rôti — Roast meat.

Coupe Jack — Desert dish of mixed fruit, vanilla ice cream, and whipped cream.

Demi Clos du Roi — Red Burgundy wine.

Demi perdreau a la Gelée — Small young partridges served in cold gelatin.

Entrecôte aux pommes — Rib steak with cooked apples.

Épinards — Spinach.

Escargot — Snails.

Filet de Porc — Slender slice of pork.

Garibaldi biscuits — A classic sweet British biscuit with chopped currants.

Gauffrettes — Small wafers made with flour, brown sugar, milk, and egg yolks.

Glace — Either a frozen ice cup or ice cream.

Glace au Café — Iced coffee.

Glace casserole — Frozen caramel with cream, egg yolks, and cane sugar.

Hors d'Oevres — Appetizers served at the beginning of a meal.

Lait Chaud — Hot milk.

Marennes Verts — Green oysters from the Marennes region in eastern France.

Marrons Glace — Steamed chestnuts, peeled and trimmed, slowly cooked in a sugar syrup for over a week, then drained and glazed.

Merusault — A quality wine produced in the Burgundy region of France.

Nuit Blanche — "Sleepless night": cocktail composed of fresh cream, cognac, amaretto, and coffee liqueur.

Poire — Pear.

Râble de Lièvre poivade puree de marrons — This is the back of a game rabbit cooked in a pepper sauce made with diced carrots, celery, onion, a slice of lean ham, sherry, and vinegar, with mashed chestnuts.

Rognons Brochette — Calf kidneys with bacon and mushrooms served on a buttered small skewer.

Rumpsteak aux pommes soufflées — Roast beef from the hip area of the cow, with light apple pastry.

Tarte aux fraises — Strawberry tart.

Tartes aux Cérises — Cherry tart.

Tournedos Rossini — Filet mignon, with slices of foie gras (duck or goose liver), butter, white bread, olive oil, garlic, and truffles, in a sauce of veal stock, port wine, Madeira, and brandy.

Tripe a la Mode de Caen — Tripe (stomach lining from an ox or other ruminant) made with calf's foot, apple brandy, dry white wine, beef broth, chopped carrots, onions, garlic, shallots, celery, parsley. All these vegetables are grown in Caen in Normandy.

Selected Bibliography

Frater Achad (Charles Stansfeld Jones): *The Anatomy of the Body of God* (Weiser Books)
The Egyptian Revival (Weiser Books)
Liber XXXI (Level Press)
Q.B.L. (Weiser Books)
XXXI Hymns to the Star Goddess (93 Publishing)

Bloom, William: *The Sacred Magician — A Ceremonial Diary* (Gothic Image Publications)

Crowley, Aleister: *Book IV*, Parts 1 and 2, *Mysticism* and *Magick* (Weiser Books)
The Book of the Law (Weiser Books)
The Collected Works of Aleister Crowley, in 3 volumes (Yogi Publication Society)
Commentaries on the Holy Books and Other Papers (Weiser Books)
The Confessions of Aleister Crowley, ed. Symonds and Grant (Hill & Wang)
The Diary of a Drug Fiend (Weiser Books)
The Equinox of the Gods (Thelema Media)
The Equinox, Volume I, Numbers 1–10 (Weiser Books)
The Equinox, Volume 3, Number 1 (Weiser Books)
The Holy Books of Thelema (Weiser Books)
The Goetia, ed. by Crowley, tr. by Mathers (Weiser Books)
Konx Om Pax (The Teitan Press)
Liber Aleph (Weiser Books)
The Magical Record of the Beast 666, ed. Symonds and Grant (Next Step Publishing)
Magick: Book IV, Parts 1–4, ed. by Hymenaeus Beta [This is the definitive publication of *Mysticism, Magick, Magick in Theory and Practice,* and *The Equinox of the Gods.*] (Weiser Books)
Magick in Theory and Practice (Magickal Childe)
Magick Without Tears (Thelema Media)
The Magical Diaries of Aleister Crowley — 1923 Diary, ed. Stephen Skinner (Weiser Books)

The Perfumed Garden of Abdullah the Satirist of Shiraz [Bagh-i-Muattar] (The Teitan Press)

777 (Weiser Books)

The Vision & the Voice with Commentary, and Other Papers, ed. Hymenaues Beta, includes the Paris Working Diary (Weiser Books)

The World's Tragedy (Thelema Media)

Fortune, Dion: *The Mystical Qabalah* (Weiser Books)

Johnston, Charles (ed.): *The Yoga Sutras of Patanjali* (John M. Watkins)

Mathers, S. L. MacGregor (ed.): *The Book of the Sacred Magic of Abramelin the Mage* (DeLaurence)

Reiker, Hans-Ulrich (ed.): *The Yoga of Light, Hatha Yoga Pradipka,* tr. Elsy Becherer (Herder and Herder)

Richmond, Keith (ed.): *The Magical Record of Frater Progradior* [Frank Bennett] (Neptune Press)

Starr, Martin P.: *The Unknown God: W. T. Smith and the Thelemites* (The Teitan Press)

Uprety, Thakur Krishna (tr.): *The Shiva Samhita* (Raja Yoga Kuti) Contains the full text as opposed to more easily available translations. École Satyam de Hatha Yoga 110 Mc Gill #201 • H2Y 2 E5 Montréal, Canada.

Swami Vivekananda: *Jnana Yoga* (Ramakrishna-Vivekananda Center)

Zoroaster: *The Chaldean Oracles,* ed. by Sapere Aude [William Wynn Westcott] (Weiser Books)